THE REFERENCE SHELF (*Continued*)

Volume XVI. $6

No.

1. Representative American Speeches: 1941-1942. A. C. Baird. $1.25.

2. Plans for a Postwar World. J. E. Johnsen. $1.25.

3. Independence for India. J. E. Johnsen. $1.25.

No.

4. Wage Stabilization and Inflation. J. E. Johnsen. $1.25.

5. World Peace Plans. J. E. Johnsen. $1.25.

6. Representative American Speeches: 1942-1943. A. C. Baird. $1.25.

7. Reconstituting the League of Nations. J. E. Johnsen. $1.25.

Volume XV. $4.80

No.

1. Representative American Speeches: 1940-1941. A. C. Baird. $1.25.

2. Universal Military Service. R. E. Summers and H. B. Summers. $1.25.

3. Federal Regulation of Labor Unions. J. V. Garland. $1.25.

4. Federal Price Control. J. E. Johnsen. $1.25.

No.

6. Wages and Prices. R. E. Summers. $1.25.

7. The Closed Shop. J. E. Johnsen. $1.25.

9. Permanent Price Control Policy. J. E. Johnsen. $1.25.

10. A Federal Sales Tax. E. R. Nichols. $1.25.

Volume XIV. $3.60

No.

1. Representative American Speeches: 1939-1940. A. C. Baird. $1.50.

2. Interstate Trade Barriers. J. E. Johnsen. $1.25.

6. Compulsory Military Training. J. E. Johnsen. $1.25.

No.

8. International Federation of Democracies. J. E. Johnsen. $1.25.

9. Debate Index. Supplement. J. E. Johnsen. 75c.

10. Federal Aid for Education. J. E. Johnsen. $1.25.

Volume XIII. $3.00

No.

4. Europe: Versailles to Warsaw. R. S. Kain. $1.25.

5. Public Housing in America. M. B. Schnapper. $1.25.

6. United States Foreign Policy (Supplement) J. E. Johnsen. 75c.

No.

9. The National Labor Relations Act. Should It Be Amended? J. E. Johnsen. $1.25.

10. Trade Unions and the Anti-Trust Laws. J. E. Johnsen. $1.25.

THE REFERENCE SHELF

Vol. 20   No. 3

THE DILEMMA OF
POSTWAR GERMANY

Compiled by
JULIA E. JOHNSEN

THE H. W. WILSON COMPANY
NEW YORK   1948

PREFACE

Postwar Germany has been a major problem to the Allied nations undertaking its occupation since V-E Day. A healthy Germany is essential for the welfare of Europe; but reconstruction policies for Germany and surrounding countries must avoid the disastrous errors made by the Allies after World War I which led to a revived Germany strong enough to challenge the world.

Much in the postwar policies undertaken in Germany has proved to be highly controversial and debatable. The leading problems—zonal divisions, reparations, deindustrialization, decartelization, reestablishment of a stable economy, denazification, reeducation—have been dealt with by authorities of varying points of view. The readings presented here have been chosen out of the mass of discussion to furnish background material for better general understanding of the problem as a whole and for more specialized study of various aspects.

Acknowledgments are gratefully made to all who have so courteously contributed materials and copyright permissions for this publication.

JULIA E. JOHNSEN

June 21, 1948

CONTENTS

POSTWAR PROBLEMS

THE GENESIS OF UNITED STATES
GERMAN POLICY [1]

The policy of the United States toward Germany after the advent of the Nazi regime to power on January 30, 1933, was progressively influenced by the development of Nazi policy, which became more and more menacing to world peace and security. There was a steadily growing popular indignation at those actions of the Nazi Government which violated moral sensibilities, aroused fears for the general security, and threatened Europe with a new Armageddon.

On December 29, 1940, President Roosevelt issued a clear challenge: "The Nazi masters of Germany have made it clear that they intend not only to dominate all life and thought in their own country, but also to enslave the whole of Europe, and then to use the resources of Europe to dominate the rest of the world." In his address on the "Four Freedoms," January 6, 1941, and again in the Atlantic Charter, formulated with Prime Minister Churchill on August 14, 1941, Mr. Roosevelt set forth the acceptable principles of an enduring peace, for the attainment of which the "final destruction of the Nazi tryanny" was prerequisite.

The guiding objectives of the Government with respect to Germany were (1) the total destruction of the Nazi regime, and (2) insurance against the reappearance in the future of a regime or ideology calculated to disturb the general peace and security. More specifically, as the war progressed, the basic purposes of this Government with respect to Germany were, first, to effect the unconditional surrender of Germany and the destruction of its military power, and, secondly, to assure that Germany should

[1] United States. Department of State. *Occupation of Germany: Policy and Progress, 1945-1946.* p. 1-5. Government Printing Office. Washington, D.C. August 1947.

never again become a menace to American security or to the peace of the world.

The outbreak of war between the United States and Germany did little to alter official policy except to center the entire effort of the nation upon the military task of defeating the Nazis and their Axis associates. But there was from the first a keen awareness that the defeat of Germany alone would be insufficient to insure the attainment of our stated objectives. This war, the second against Germany within a generation, made doubly clear the necessity for a program of preventive and remedial measures applicable to a vanquished Reich. There was a general realization that the German question was central to the whole problem of peace in Europe and to world security. The profound interest of the American people in this vital issue was a measure of their awareness of its gravity. The Government, particularly those officials who were entrusted with the formulation of policy, recognized conflicting yet sincere convictions among groups and individuals concerning the treatment of Germany, views ranging from a so-called "soft" to a "hard" peace for Germany. The official consensus, however, was that our German policy must be realistic, and that the best policies were those calculated to achieve most effectively the lasting pacification of Germany and the maintenance of world security.

The making of policy has been a continuing process since Pearl Harbor and will doubtless continue, perhaps for years, until the German problem in its long-term aspects has been fully dealt with. While the basic principles remain fixed, policy has had to adjust itself to current exigencies and unforeseeable situations. It has been necessary to coordinate United States policy with the policies of those governments associated with this nation in the war against Germany and in the occupation and administration of Germany. An effective policy for Germany must be a joint policy, and the necessity for maintaining Allied unity has been considered to be of primary importance.

During the course of the war the guiding principles of American policy toward Germany were set forth in a series of presidential declarations. In his message to Congress September 17, 1943 President Roosevelt asserted: ". . . there is one thing I want to make perfectly clear: When Hitler and the Nazis go out, the Prussian military clique must go with them. The war-breeding gangs of militarists must be rooted out of Germany—and out of Japan—if we are to have any real assurance of future peace. . . . We shall not be able to claim that we have gained total victory in this war if any vestige of Fascism in any of its malignant forms is permitted to survive anywhere in the world." In his address of December 24, 1943, the President reiterated his intention that Germany be "stripped of her military might and be given no opportunity within the foreseeable future to regain that might." The German people must be rid "once and for all of nazism and Prussian militarism and the fantastic and disastrous notion that they constitute the 'master race'." But the United Nations "have no intention to enslave the German people. We wish them to have a normal chance to develop, in peace, as useful and respectable members of the European family."

Elaborating upon these purposes of the Allies in his address to the Foreign Policy Association October 21, 1944, the President declared that the Germans would not be left "a single element of military power—or of potential military power." But, he continued,

I should be false to the very foundations of my religious and political convictions, if I should ever relinquish the hope—and even the faith—that in all peoples, without exception, there live some instinct for truth, some attraction toward justice, and some passion for peace—buried as they may be in the German case under a brutal regime. We bring no charge against the German race, as such, for we cannot believe that God has eternally condemned any race of humanity. . . . There is going to be stern punishment for all those in Germany directly responsible for this agony of mankind. The German people are not going to be enslaved. . . But it will be necessary for them to earn their way back into the fellowship of peace-loving and law-abiding nations.

In his last address touching upon the German problem, given before Congress March 1, 1945, Mr. Roosevelt dealt more specifically with the treatment of the vanquished enemy. Unconditional surrender and the destruction of nazism, its laws and institutions, would be insisted upon. There must be complete disarmament of Germany, involving destruction of all

armed forces and armaments and the eradication of militaristic
influence from public, private, and cultural life. The General
Staff would be dismembered. There must be speedy, severe, yet
just punishment of war criminals. Reparations were to be made
in kind. An economy adequate to sustain the German people
should be retained, but no power to wage aggressive war.

Common policy with respect to Germany was developed in
a number of conferences between the heads of government of
the United States, Great Britain, and the Soviet Union. The
most significant policy decisions were set forth in the Crimea
declaration of February 11, 1945, and the Potsdam declaration
of August 2, 1945. The first of these followed closely the
principles enunciated by President Roosevelt; it also provided
for a reparation commission to exact compensation in kind for
war damage. The second elaborated the political and economic
principles to govern the treatment of Germany in the initial
control period, and included agreements relative to reparation,
disposition of eastern German areas, transfer of German popula-
tions, and punishment of war criminals.

The chief agency for coordinating Allied policy for Germany
prior to surrender was the European Advisory Commission,
created by the Moscow conference of November 1943. It included representatives of the United States, Great Britain, the
Soviet Union, and, in its later stages, France. The Commission
met in London from December 1943 to July 1945. Its principal
achievements were the formulation of terms governing the surrender of Germany and the assumption of supreme authority by
the four chief Allied powers, the determination of zones of
occupation, the creation of control machinery, and the drafting
of additional requirements to be imposed upon Germany after
surrender. It was replaced after July 1945 by the Council of
Foreign Ministers. Since July 1945 the Control Council and its
subordinate agencies at Berlin have been the chief instruments
for the working out of agreed quadripartite policy for Germany
as a whole. In December 1946 the Council of Foreign Ministers
agreed to place the German problem on its agenda for its meeting in Moscow on March 10, 1947.

Within the general framework of broad policy as set forth by the President and in international agreements, the Department of State, together with the War and Navy Departments, the Joint Chiefs of Staff, and other interested governmental agencies, has been active since early in 1942 in formulating policy directives dealing with the problems that have arisen in our treatment of Germany both before and after surrender. These have become the basis for military government in the United States zone. In some instances they have been submitted to the European Advisory Commission and to the Control Council as a basis for negotiation of joint policy.

The controlling directive for United States policy in Germany for the period immediately following Germany's defeat is J.C.S. [Joint Chiefs of Staff] 1067, formulated in definitive form in April 1945. This document includes a statement of general objectives and specific directions concerning the military, political, economic, and financial treatment of Germany. Although superseded in part by later directives and quadripartite agreements, it remains the most comprehensive statement of policy as applied in the areas of Germany under American jurisdiction.

The determination of policy governing so vast and complex a problem as the treatment of defeated Germany has, of necessity, been influenced by the course of events and by the interests and relationships of the controlling powers. Policies flowing from the wartime association of the United Nations and shaped by the major powers have largely been implemented. These relate to the immediate task of liquidating German military power and the sources of its strength, and are of short-term import. At the present time, after more than a year and a half of full quadripartite occupation and control, the long-range aspects of policy are assuming paramount significance. These aspects were dealt with concretely in a statement by Secretary of State James F. Byrnes at Stuttgart, Germany, on September 6, 1946. The task of reconstruction has barely begun and major decisions as to the future of Germany, its status in Europe, and its relationships with the major powers and the United Nations still await agreement at the intergovernmental level.

The difficulties in the problem of dealing with Germany have arisen from the threefold collapse which that nation experienced after defeat. There was a material collapse which saw German economy prostrate as a consequence of the destruction wrought by war and by last-ditch Nazi efforts to stave off defeat. Most of Germany's cities lay in ruins, industrial plants were devastated, and the homes of a large part of the population were reduced to rubble. There was a political collapse which resulted from the complete dissolution of the Nazi governmental system and left Germany a political vacuum. And there was a spiritual collapse which left the German people disillusioned with the ideals of national socialism and groping blindly for a new faith and a valid way of life.

It was into this physical and moral chaos that the occupation armies moved. The degree of success or failure which the occupation has achieved must be reviewed in the light of the magnitude of the difficulties under which it was forced to operate.

UNITED STATES POLICY IN GERMANY [2]

I have come to Germany to learn at first hand the problems involved in the reconstruction of Germany and to discuss with our representatives the views of the United States Government as to some of the problems confronting us.

We in the United States have given considerable time and attention to these problems because upon their proper solution will depend not only the future well-being of Germany but the future well-being of Europe.

We have learned, whether we like it or not, that we live in one world, from which we cannot isolate ourselves. We have learned that peace and well-being are indivisible and that our peace and well-being cannot be purchased at the price of peace or the well-being of any other country.

I hope that the German people will never again make the mistake of believing that, because the American people are peace-

[2] By James F. Byrnes, Secretary of State, July 1945-January 1947. Speech at Stuttgart, September 6, 1946. 6p. mim. U.S. Department of State. Reprinted by permission.

loving, they will sit back hoping for peace if any nation uses force or the threat of force to acquire dominion over other peoples and other governments.

In 1917 the United States was forced into the first World War. After that war we refused to join the League of Nations. We thought we could stay out of Europe's wars and we lost interest in the affairs of Europe. That did not keep us from being forced into a second world war.

We will not again make that mistake. We intend to continue our interest in the affairs of Europe and of the world. We have helped to organize the United Nations. We believe it will stop aggressor nations from starting wars. Because we believe it, we intend to support the United Nations Organization with all the power and resources we possess.

The American people want peace. They have long since ceased talk of a hard or a soft peace for Germany. This never has been the real issue. What we want is a lasting peace. We will oppose soft measures which invite breaking of the peace.

In agreeing at Potsdam that Germany should be disarmed and demilitarized, and in proposing that the four major powers should by treaty jointly undertake to see that Germany is kept disarmed and demilitarized for a generation, the United States is not unmindful of the responsibility resting upon it and its major Allies to maintain and enforce peace under the law.

Freedom from militarism will give the German people the opportunity, if they will but seize it, to apply their great energies and abilities to the works of peace. It will give them the opportunity to show themselves worthy of the respect and friendship of peace-loving nations and, in time, to take an honorable place among members of the United Nations.

It is not in the interest of the German people or in the interest of world peace that Germany should become a pawn or a partner in a military struggle for power between the East and the West.

German militarism and nazism have devastated twice in our generation the lands of German neighbors. It is fair and just that Germany should do her part to repair that devastation. Most of the victims of Nazi aggression were before the war less well off than the Germans. They should not be expected by Germany to bear, unaided, the major costs of Nazi aggression.

The United States, therefore, is prepared to carry out fully the principles outlined in the Potsdam Agreement on demilitarization and reparations. However, there should be changes in the levels of industry agreed to by the Allied Control Commission if Germany is not to be administered as an economic unit as the Potsdam Agreement contemplates and requires.

The basis of the Potsdam Agreement was that, as part of a combined program of demilitarization and reparations, Germany's war potential should be reduced by elimination and removal of her war industries and the reduction and removal of heavy industrial plants. It was contemplated this should be done to the point that Germany would be left with levels of industry capable of maintaining in Germany average European living standards without assistance from other countries.

The plants so to be removed were to be delivered as reparations to the Allies. The plants to be removed from the Soviet zone would go to the Soviet Union and Poland, and the plants to be removed from the western zones would go in part to the Soviet Union, but in the main to the western Allies. Provision was also made for the distribution of Germany's foreign assets among the Allies.

After considerable discussion, the Allies agreed upon levels to which the principal German industries should be reduced to carry out the Potsdam Agreement. These levels were agreed to upon the assumption that the indigenous resources of Germany were to be available for distribution on an equitable basis for all Germans in Germany and that products not necessary for use in Germany would be available for export in order to pay for necessary imports.

In fixing the levels of industry, no allowance was made for reparations from current production. Reparations from current production would be wholly incompatible with the levels of industry now established under the Potsdam Agreement.

Obviously, higher levels of industry would have had to be fixed if reparations from current production were contemplated. The levels of industry fixed are only sufficient to enable the

German people to become self-supporting and to maintain living standards approximating the average European living conditions.

That principle involved serious hardships for the German people, but it only requires them to share the hardships which Nazi aggression imposed on the average European.

The German people were not denied, however, the possibility of improving their lot by hard work over the years.

Industrial growth and progress were not denied them. Being obliged to start again like the people of other devastated countries with a peacetime economy not able to provide them more than the average European standard, the German people were not to be denied the right to use such savings, as they might be able to accumulate by hard work and frugal living, to build up their industries for peaceful purposes.

That was the principle of reparations we agreed to at Potsdam. And the United States will not agree to the taking from Germany of greater reparations than was provided by the Potsdam Agreement.

The carrying out of the Potsdam Agreement has, however, been obstructed by the failure of the Allied Control Council to take the necessary steps to enable the German economy to function as an economic unit. Essential central German administrative departments have not been established, although they are expressly required by the Potsdam Agreement.

The equitable distribution of essential commodities between the several zones, so as to produce a balanced economy throughout Germany and reduce the need for imports, has not been arranged, although that, too, is expressly required by the Potsdam Agreement.

The working out of a balanced economy throughout Germany to provide the necessary means to pay for approved imports has not been accomplished, although that, too, is expressly required by the Potsdam Agreement.

The United States is firmly of the belief that Germany should be administered as an economic unit, and that zonal barriers should be completely obliterated so far as the economic life and activity in Germany are concerned.

The conditions which now exist in Germany make it impossible for industrial production to reach the levels which the occupying powers agreed were essential for a minimum German peacetime economy. Obviously, if the agreed levels of industry are to be reached, we cannot continue to restrict the free exchange of commodities, persons and ideas throughout Germany. The barriers between the four zones of Germany are far more difficult to surmount than those between normal independent states.

The time has come when the zonal boundaries should be regarded as defining only the areas to be occupied for security purposes by the armed forces of the occupying powers, and not as self-contained economic or political units.

That was the course of development envisaged by the Potsdam Agreement, and that is the course of development which the American Government intends to follow to the full limit of its authority. It has formally announced that it is its intention to unify the economy of its own zone with any or all of the other zones willing to participate in the unification.

So far only the British Government has agreed to let its zone participate. We deeply appreciate their cooperation. Of course, this policy of unification is not intended to exclude the governments not now willing to join. The unification will be open to them at any time they wish to join.

We favor the economic unification of Germany. If complete unification cannot be secured, we shall do everything in our power to secure the maximum possible unification.

Important as economic unification is for the recovery of Germany and of Europe, the German people must recognize that the basic cause of their suffering and distress is the war which the Nazi dictatorship brought upon the world.

But just because suffering and distress in Germany is inevitable, the American Government is unwilling to accept responsibility for the needless aggravation of economic distress that is caused by the failure of the Allied Control Council to agree to give the German people a chance to solve some of their most urgent economic problems.

So far as many vital questions are concerned, the Control Council is neither governing Germany nor allowing Germany to govern itself.

A common financial policy is essential for the successful rehabilitation of Germany. Runaway inflation accompanied by economic paralysis is almost certain to develop unless there is a common financial policy directed to the control of inflation. A program of drastic fiscal reform to reduce currency and monetary claims, to revise the debt structure and to place Germany on a sound financial basis is urgently required.

The United States has worked hard to develop such a program, but fully coordinated measures must be accepted and applied uniformly to all zones if ruinous inflation is to be prevented. A central agency of finance is obviously necessary to carry out any such program effectively.

It is also essential that transportation, communications and postal services should be organized throughout Germany without regard to zonal barriers. The nation-wide organization of these public services was contemplated by the Potsdam Agreement. Twelve months have passed and nothing has been done.

Germany needs all the food she can produce. Before the war she could not produce enough food for her population. The area of Germany has been reduced. The population in Silesia, for instance, has been forced back into a restricted Germany. Armies of occupation and displaced persons increase demands while the lack of farm machinery and fertilizer reduces supplies. To secure the greatest possible production of food and the most effective use and distribution of food that can be produced, a central administrative department for agriculture should be set up and allowed to function without delay.

Similarly, there is urgent need for the setting up of a central German administrative agency for industry and foreign trade. While Germany must be prepared to share her coal and steel with the liberated countries of Europe dependent upon these supplies, Germany must be enabled to use her skills and her energies to increase her industrial production and to organize the most effective use of her raw materials.

Germany must be given a chance to export goods in order to import enough to make her economy self-sustaining. Germany is a part of Europe and recovery in Europe, and particularly in the adjoining states, will be slow indeed if Germany, with her great resources of iron and coal, is turned into a poorhouse.

When the ruthless Nazi dictatorship was forced to surrender unconditionally, there was no German government with which the Allies could deal. The Allies had temporarily to take over the responsibilities of the battered German state, which the Nazi dictatorship had cut off from any genuine accountability to the German people. The Allies could not leave the leaders or minions of nazism in key positions, ready to reassert their evil influence at first opportunity. They had to go.

But it never was the intention of the American Government to deny to the German people the right to manage their own internal affairs as soon as they were able to do so in a democratic way, with genuine respect for human rights and fundamental freedoms.

The Potsdam Agreement, concluded only a few months after the surrender, bound the occupying powers to restore local self-government and to introduce elective and representative principles into the regional, provincial and state administration as rapidly as was consistent with military security and the purposes of the military occupation.

The principal purposes of the military occupation were and are to demilitarize and denazify Germany, but not to raise artificial barriers to the efforts of the German people to resume their peacetime economic life.

The Nazi war criminals were to be punished for the suffering they brought to the world. The policy of reparations and industrial disarmament prescribed in the Potsdam Agreement was to be carried out. But the purpose of the occupation did not contemplate a prolonged alien dictatorship of Germany's peacetime economy or a prolonged alien dictatorship of Germany's internal political life. The Potsdam Agreement expressly bound the occupying powers to start building a political democracy from the ground up.

The Potsdam Agreement did not provide that there should never be a central German government. It merely provided that, for the time being, there should be no central German government. Certainly this only meant that no central government should be established until some sort of democracy was rooted in the soul of Germany and some sense of local responsibility developed.

The Potsdam Agreement wisely provided that administration of the affairs of Germany should be directed toward decentralization of the political structure and the development of local responsibility. This was not intended to prevent progress toward a central government with the powers necessary to deal with matters which would be dealt with on a nation-wide basis. But it was intended to prevent establishment of a strong central government dominating the German people instead of being responsible to their democratic will.

It is the view of the American Government that the German people throughout Germany, under proper safeguards, should now be given the primary responsibility for the running of their own affairs. More than a year has passed since hostilities ceased. The millions of German people should not be forced to live in doubt as to their fate. It is the view of the American Government that the Allies should, without delay, make clear to the German people the essential terms of the peace settlement which they expect the German people to accept and observe. It is our view that the German people should now be permitted and helped to make the necessary preparations for setting up of a democratic German government which can accept and observe these terms.

From now on thoughtful people of the world will judge Allied action in Germany not by Allied promises but by Allied performances. The American Government has supported and will continue to support the necessary measures to denazify and demilitarize Germany, but it does not follow that large armies of alien soldiers or alien bureaucrats, however well motivated and disciplined, are, in the long run, the most reliable guardians of another country's democracy.

All that the Allied governments can and should do is to lay down the rules under which Germany can govern itself. The Allied occupation forces should be limited to the number sufficient to see that these rules are obeyed.

But the question for us will be: What force is needed to make certain that Germany does not rearm as it did after the first World War? Our proposal for a treaty with the major powers to enforce for twenty-five or even forty years the demilitarization plan finally agreed upon in the peace settlement would have made possible a smaller army of occupation. For enforcement we could rely more upon a force of trained inspectors and less upon infantry.

For instance, if an automobile factory, in violation of the treaty, converted its machinery to the production of weapons of war, inspectors would report it to the Allied Control Council. They would call upon the German government to stop production and punish the offender. If the German government failed to comply then the Allied nations would take steps to enforce compliance by the German government. Our proposal for the treaty was not agreed to.

Security forces will probably have to remain in Germany for a long period. I want no misunderstanding. We will not shirk our duty. We are not withdrawing. As long as an occupation force is required in Germany the Army of the United States will be a part of that occupation force.

The United States favors the early establishment of a provisional German government for Germany. Progress has been made in the American zone in developing local and state self-government in Germany and the American Government believes similar progress is possible for all zones.

It is the view of the American Government that the provisional government should not be hand-picked by other governments, but should be a German national council composed of democratically responsible minister-presidents or other chief officials of the several states or provinces which have been established in each of the four zones.

Subject to the reserved authority of the Allied Control Council, the German national council should be responsible for the proper functioning of central administrative agencies, which should have adequate power to assure the administration of Germany as an economic unit, as was contemplated by the Potsdam Agreement.

The German national council should also be charged with the preparation of a draft of a federal constitution for Germany which, among other things, should ensure the democratic character of the new Germany and human rights and fundamental freedoms of all its inhabitants.

After approval in principle by the Allied Control Council, the proposed constitution should be submitted to an elected convention for final drafting and then submitted to the German people for ratification.

While we shall insist that Germany observe the principles of peace, good neighborliness and humanity, we do not want Germany to become the satellite of any power or to live under a dictatorship, foreign or domestic. The American people hope to see peaceful, democratic Germans become and remain free and independent.

Austria has already been recognized as a free and independent country. Her temporary forced union with Germany was not a happy event for either country and the United States is convinced that it is in the interest of both countries and the peace of Europe that they should pursue their separate ways.

At Postdam specific areas which were part of Germany were provisionally assigned to the Soviet Union and to Poland, subject to the final decisions of the peace conference. At that time these areas were being held by Soviet and Polish armies. We were told that Germans in large numbers were fleeing from these areas and that it would in fact, because of the feelings aroused by the war, be difficult to reorganize the economic life of these areas if they were not administered as integral parts in the one case of the Soviet Union and in the other of Poland.

The heads of government agreed to support at the peace settlement a proposal of the Soviet Government concerning the ultimate transfer to the Soviet Union of the city of Koenigsberg and areas adjacent to it. Unless the Soviet Government changes its view on the subject we will certainly stand by our agreement.

With regard to Silesia and other eastern German areas, the assignment to Poland by Russia for administrative purposes had taken place before the Potsdam meeting. The heads of government agreed that, pending the final determination of Poland's western frontier, Silesia and other eastern German areas should be under the administration of the Polish state and, for such purposes, should not be considered as a part of the Soviet zone of occupation in Germany. However, as the protocol of the Potsdam conference makes clear, the heads of government did not agree to support at the peace settlement the cession of any particular area.

The Soviets and the Poles suffered greatly at the hands of Hitler's invading armies. As a result of the agreement at Yalta, Poland ceded to the Soviet Union territory east of the Curzon Line. Because of this, Poland asked for revision of her northern and western frontiers. The United States will support revision of these frontiers in Poland's favor. However, the extent of the area to be ceded to Poland must be determined when the final settlement is agreed upon.

The United States does not feel that it can deny to France, which has been invaded three times by Germany in seventy years, its claim to the Saar territory, whose economy has long been closely linked with France. Of course, if the Saar territory is integrated with France she should readjust her reparation claims against Germany.

Except as here indicated, the United States will not support encroachment on territory which is indisputably German or any division of Germany which is not genuinely desired by the people concerned. So far as the United States is aware the people of the Ruhr and Rhineland desire to remain united with the rest of Germany. And the United States will not oppose their desire.

While the people of the Ruhr were the last to succumb to nazism, without the resources of the Ruhr nazism could never have threatened the world. Never again must those resources be used for destructive purposes. They must be used to rebuild a free, peaceful Germany and a free, peaceful Europe.

The United States will favor such control over the whole of Germany, including the Ruhr and the Rhineland, as may be necessary for security purposes. It will help to enforce those controls. But it will not favor any controls that would subject the Ruhr and the Rhineland to the political domination or manipulation of outside powers.

The German people are now feeling the devasting effects of the war which Hitler and his minions brought upon the world. Other people felt those devastating effects long before they were brought home to the German people.

The German people must realize that it was Hitler and his minions who tortured and exterminated innocent men, women and children and sought, with German arms, to dominate and degrade the world. It was the massed, angered forces of humanity which had to fight their way into Germany to give the world the hope of freedom and peace.

The American people who fought for freedom have no desire to enslave the German people. The freedom Americans believe in and fought for is freedom which must be shared with all willing to respect the freedom of others.

The United States has returned to Germany practically all prisoners of war that were in the United States. We are taking prompt steps to return German prisoners of war in our custody in other parts of the world.

The United States cannot relieve Germany from the hardships inflicted upon her which the war leaders started. But the United States has no desire to increase those hardships or to deny the German people an opportunity to work their way out of those hardships so long as they respect human freedom and cling to the paths of peace.

The American people want to return the government of Germany to the German people. The American people want to help the German people to win their way back to an honorable place among the free and peace-loving nations of the world.

THE BEGINNINGS OF SELF-GOVERNMENT IN THE AMERICAN ZONE OF GERMANY [3]

On November 24 and December 1, 1946, a page of German history was turned: The people of Bavaria, Württemberg-Baden,

[3] By Velma Hastings Cassidy, Research Associate in Foreign Policy Studies Branch, Division of Research and Publication, Office of Public Affairs, Department of State. From *Department of State Bulletin.* 16:223-33. February 9, 1947.

and Greater Hesse, the three states of the American zone in Germany, adopted constitutions which the popularly elected assemblies had drawn up and which the American Military Government had approved. Each state was constituted as a parliamentary republic governed by a *Landtag* (legislative assembly, elected by proportional representation), a Minister-President (elected by the *Landtag*), and a Cabinet (appointed by the Minister-President).

The steadily increasing transfer to the German authorities of governmental responsibilities has been an outstanding characteristic of American Military Government since its inception. From the beginning of the occupation of Germany by Allied forces shortly after the capitulation of the Reich on May 8, 1945, detailed controls of Military Government (MG) in the American zone, which in the initial post-defeat period were maintained over every unit of German civil administration, have been progressively withdrawn as the German people showed themselves ready for democratic self-government. German civil machinery has been built from the ground up on the principle that, as stated by the Military Governor (Gen. Joseph T. McNarney), "the way to learn democracy is by applying it."

The constitutions having now been adopted in the three states, MG controls will be relaxed so that, in prinicple, Germans may govern themselves without MG participation. Only the measures concerned with reparations, demilitarization, punishment of war criminals, treatment of displaced persons, and possibly certain aspects of denazification will remain under the direct administration of MG. The activities of MG with regard to civil administration will generally be limited to a supervisory process of review, observation, and advice.

The relaxation of controls to this extent does not in any way mean a relaxation of measures to achieve realization of the principal purpose of the occupation—the assurance that "Germany never again will threaten her neighbors or the peace of the world"—and the corollary negative objectives such as the elimination of nazism and militarism in all their forms, as well as the positive objective "to prepare for the eventual reconstruction of German political life on a democratic basis and for eventual peaceful cooperation in international life by Germany."

MG will retain an over-all jurisdiction, and certain restrictions will continue to be imposed on the German civil governments. In giving the approval of MG to the constitutions, Lt. Gen. Lucius D. Clay, Deputy Military Governor, stated that the operation of the constitutions would be subject to general reservations of MG with regard "to the international agreements to which the United States Government is a party, to quadripartite legislation, and to the powers which Military Government must reserve in order to effectuate the basic policies of the occupation." Specific reservations have been made to assure that American policy will be carried out in matters pertaining to denazification and the Anglo-American bipartite economic program.

Approval of the German civil governments' action is based upon the consonance of these actions with the objectives of American occupation policy and basic democratic principles, and not upon MG's views as to the efficiency of the administration. The efficiency of the civil governments of the three *Länder* (states) is not the responsibility of MG except so far as a lack of efficiency interferes with the execution of the approved American policy.

In conformity with the fundamental principles of American occupation policy, the constitutions of the three independent states provide the basic pattern for a decentralized, democratic Germany and point toward the establishment of a central federal government in that country. According to a statement by General McNarney, government in Germany may be said to be "decentralized" when:

1. Power is granted primarily to the states and only in specifically enumerated and approved instances to a federal government.

2. Powers of basic political implication (e.g. the assessment of taxes and police powers) are reserved to the states, and largely administrative powers (e.g. transportation and communications control) are allocated to the Reich.

3. All residual powers are reserved to the people except as the people may delegate them to the states.

4. A substantial number of functions are delegated by the states to the counties and communities. These should include all such functions as may be effectively determined and administered by the community.

The American attitude toward the development of self-administration in the *Länder* of the United States zones and toward the eventual creation of a central German government has been emphasized by former Secretary Byrnes in recent addresses, [for instance] at Stuttgart, on September 6, 1946:

The Potsdam Agreement did not provide that there should never be a central German government; it merely provided that for the time being there should be no central German government. Certainly this only meant that no central government should be established until some sort of democracy was rooted in the soil of Germany and some sense of local responsibility developed.

The Potsdam Agreement wisely provided that administration of the affairs of Germany should be directed toward decentralization of the political structure and the development of local responsibility. This was not intended to prevent progress toward a central government with the powers necessary to deal with matters which could be dealt with on a nation-wide basis. But it was intended to prevent the establishment of a strong central government dominating the German people instead of being responsible to their democratic will.

It is the view of the American Government that the German people throughout Germany, under proper safeguards, should be given the responsibility of running their own affairs.

At Paris, on October 3, he stated further:

In the American zone, we have placed great emphasis upon the development of a sense of local responsibility and have taken the lead in creating *Länder* or states so that the people will look to the states and not to a central government on all matters that do not basically require national action.

We want to see the federal government of Germany created by the states and not the states created by the central government. If we so proceed we do not think we will find that the responsible representatives of the states will want to give excessive powers to the federal government.

From early in 1942 the Department of State together with the War and Navy Departments, the Joint Chiefs of Staff, and other interested agencies progressively formulated American policy for the occupation and control of Germany. The European Advisory Commission, which was created by the Moscow Conference of November 1943, made chiefly specific recommendations for the terms of Germany's unconditional surrender, for the delimitation of the zones of occupation in Germany, and for the inter-Allied control machinery. This commission was set up for the purpose of advising the governments of the United States, Great Britain, and the Soviet Union on non-military problems relating to enemy territories, questions connected with the termination of hostilities, and other matters referred to it by the participating governments. Coordination of Allied policy for the control of Germany after the Potsdam Conference of July-August 1945 has fallen within the competence of the Allied Control Council at Berlin.

In accordance with previously agreed plans, the boundary lines of the American, British, Soviet, and French zones were determined on a provisional basis shortly after the surrender of Germany on May 8, 1945; the Allied forces were distributed to their ultimate zones; and the governments of the United States, the Union of Soviet Socialist Republics, the United Kingdom, and the Provisional Government of the French Republic began the organizational groundwork for the four-power administration and control of Germany on a zonal basis.

The Allied Control Authority, composed of the Control Council, Coordinating Committee, Control Staff (Directorates), and Allied Secretariat, constitutes the supreme governing machinery for Germany. The Commanders in Chief of occupation forces in Germany of the four Allied nations comprise the Control Council, whose decisions must be unanimous on all questions affecting Germany as a whole. Each Commander in Chief is assisted by a political adviser. Subject to agreed quadripartite policies, the Commanders in Chief exercise supreme legislative, executive, and judicial authority within the respective areas occupied by forces under their command.

Gen. Joseph T. McNarney, the Commander of all American troops in the European Theater of Operations, has been the Military Governor of the United States zone. In the latter capacity he has been the representative of the United States on the Allied Control Council. Military Government responsibilities and activities, separate from the Army Command, are delegated to the Office of Military Government for Germany (U.S.), known as "OMGUS" which has been headed by the Deputy Military Governor Lt. Gen. Lucius D. Clay. To assist him in the development, execution, and implementation of Military Government policies within the portions of Germany under American control (the United States zone, the Bremen enclave, and the United States sector of Berlin), and in the negotiation of quadripartite policy, General Clay has had special advisers on political, legal, naval, economic, financial, labor, and associated problems.

General Clay has also been a member of the Coordinating Committee, which is composed of the Deputy Military Governors of the four zones of occupation acting as the representatives of the four Commanders in Chief. The Control Council refers a majority of its problems to the Coordinating Committee for recommendation of action and refers its decisions to the Committee for implementation. Aiding the Coordinating Committee is the Control Staff, in the form of the following twelve Directorates, with four Allied heads comprising each: Military; Naval; Air; Transport; Political; Economics; Finance; Reparation, Delivery, and Restitution; Internal Affairs and Communications; Legal; Prisoners of War and Displaced Persons; and Manpower.

Decisions and agreements of the Allied Control Council and the Coordinating Committee, in the various forms (laws, proclamations, orders, directives, and instructions), are dispatched for implementation, immediately upon signature, to the appropriate authorities in each zone of occupation and in Berlin to the four national elements of the Allied Secretariat. The Secretariat also prepares the agenda and minutes of meetings of the Control Council and the Coordinating Committee.

The three states, Bavaria, Württemberg-Baden, and Greater Hesse, comprising the United States zone are identical neither with the former, traditional German *Länder* in this region nor with the administrative units set up initially for military government after Germany surrendered.

When the French zone was established in July 1945, the boundary line dividing the American and French zones was drawn across *Land* areas as follows (causing complicated problems of governmental structure and administration) ; the *Länder* of Baden and Württemberg were divided between the two zones so that the northern portions, and the *Land* capital in each case, were included in the American zone; that part of *Land* Hesse west of the Rhine as well as the four western *Landkreise* [rural counties] of *Provinz* Hesse-Nassau became part of the French area, the remainder of *Land* Hesse and *Provinz* Hesse-Nassau becoming part of the American zone; and only one *Kreis* [county] was cut from Bavaria and included in the French zone.

After three months of geographic- and governmental-structure reorganization, the formation of the three *Länder* was completed and proclaimed to the German people by Gen. Dwight D. Eisenhower on September 26, 1945.

The German civil governments of the three states in the American zone are fairly uniform on the *Land* level but vary considerably in the lower echelons, depending upon their special situation. Thus, Bavaria has five *Regierungsbezirke* [administrative districts] and Greater Hesse has three *Regierungsbezirke* which administer a substantial number of functions, while Württemberg-Baden has a *Landesbezirk* [regional district] for the administration of Baden whose departments are identical with those of *Land* Württemberg-Baden itself and which operates under the direction of the same Minister-President. The comparative administrative areas of the three *Länder* are as follows:

Land	Area (sq. km.)	Stadt-kreise	Land-kreise	Total Kreise
Bavaria	75,996	22	141	163
Greater Hesse	22,378	9	39	48
Württemberg-Baden	15,631	7	28	35
	114,005	38	208	246

The Office of Military Government is composed of approximately 6,000 officers and enlisted men. This over-all strength includes the personnel engaged in quadripartite government in Berlin; in the three state capitals of Bavaria, Württemberg-Baden, and Greater Hesse; in the two cities which lie outside these states—Berlin and Bremen; and in the small field detachments, composed of four representatives each, which are stationed in each of the counties in the American zone. General Clay stated at a press conference on December 13, 1946, that during the coming months more and more responsibility will be placed in German hands, and as a result the MG staff, in the next six months, will probably be cut from 6,000 to 4,000.

On assuming control of the United States zone after the military and governmental collapse of Germany, MG was faced with the problem of reorganizing the civil government from the bottom up. Reorganization of government above the local level was particularly important. Since most of the important functions of government under the Nazis were performed from the national level and since, in accordance with the Potsdam declaration, no central German government would be established for the time being, the intermediate, regional governments were required to assume the functions formerly exercised by the central government as well as those traditionally exercised by the regional governments. Trained MG detachments at first controlled, directed, and supervised every unit of German civil administration. The problem of reconstruction was critical and complex, since it was difficult to find capable non-Nazis to operate the governmental machinery.

The administrative responsibility for civil government has been built up carefully from the *Gemeinde* [community], *Landkreis*, *Stadtkreis*, and *Regierungsbezirk* levels and now rests upon the *Land* governments. These regional governments now possess full legislative, executive, and judicial power, subject only to MG authority. In accordance with American policy for decentralization of administrative authority, all those powers and functions previously exercised by the Reich have, so far as they continue in existence, devolved upon the *Länder*. Economic activities, broad social-welfare controls, and the supervision of public finances are outstanding examples of this transfer. The *Länder*, in turn, have delegated powers and functions to lower levels, e. g. *Kreis* control of police administration, formerly performed at *Regierungsbezirk* levels.

The Minister-President of each *Land* is responsible for the general conduct of affairs in his respective regional unit to the Office of Military Government for that *Land*. The Directors commanding the Offices of Military Government for the *Länder* are, in turn, responsible to OMGUS for the supervision of German civil government. . . .

Steps were taken by MG from the first to implement the directive to decentralize the German political structure and at the same time to encourage the development of local democratic responsibilities. By the end of July 1945, modified *Land, Regierungsbezirk*, and local administrations had been established and were beginning to function in all areas of the United States zone. *Land* governments had been established with capitals at Munich (for Bavaria), Stuttgart (for Baden and Württemberg), Darmstadt (for Hesse-Nassau), and Marburg (for Hesse). German Minister-Presidents, their cabinets, and officials of lower functional levels for each *Land* were appointed by MG and given authority for the direction and execution of all functions assigned to them, to be exercised under MG supervision.

During the ensuing few months German government and civil administration progressed along the lines of decentralization, denazification, and stabilization of government. Democratization of government was developed through the elimination of Nazi influences, through the preparation for self-government under a system of free elections based on democratic local-government codes, through the use of civilian advisory committees, and through allowing carefully supervised German civil administrations to assume more internal authority as they showed themselves prepared to function on a democratic basis.

A significant milestone in the accomplishment of the objective of decentralizing the German governmental structure and destroying the overwhelming predominance of Prussia was the consolidation in September 1945 of *Land* Hesse and *Provinz* Hesse-Nassau to form the unit now known as Greater Hesse.

This consolidation was made after careful study and discussions with responsible German officials had determined that the consolidation would not violate the historical integrity and traditions of *Land* Hesse, and would conform to economic, political, and geographical patterns. Unification of these two areas had been attempted several times in the past 80 years but had always met strong Prussian opposition.

Formation of Greater Hesse was found to be desirable because Hesse alone was too small to require or support a complete *Land* government—especially while having to bear the costs of an aggressive war—and because the inclusion of the former Prussian *Provinz* Hesse-Nassau in the American zone made it convenient for it to be handled by a *Land* type of government. With this consolidation a state was established which was strong enough to become a basic unit in a federal system of government, and the present zonal pattern of the three independent *Länder* was defined.

Plans were begun in September 1945 for the gradual shifting of the direct MG control exercised over local administration to the *Land* governments during the nine-month period ending in June 1946. It was expected that in progressive stages MG should withdraw military personnel from the lower governmental units, except as required for liaison and security, and deal with these units only through the *Länder* governments. At the end of this nine-month period liaison and security offices, established in place of the MG detachments, would provide for general supervision and reporting on the operation of local German civil government and for liaison between the occupational troops and civil government. It was planned, however, that OMGUS should retain general policy control and close supervision of the *Länder* governments and insure their compliance with MG directives. In fact, it was considered that controls would be more effectively maintained, since a very few German officials then would be held responsible for carrying out policies.

Accordingly, a plan was approved in September 1945 for placing greater administrative responsibility in the hands of German officials by terminating functional responsibilities of the

Landkreis and *Stadtkreis* MG detachments by November 15, 1945, and the *Regierungsbezirk* detachments by December 15, 1945, but continuing general supervisory functions until after the *Landkreis* elections planned for April 1946.

A schedule of spring elections for the United States zone, the first elections in about 14 years for all the lower levels of German civil government, was established by the September 20, 1945, MG directive. The *Länder* governments were required to prepare local government codes and proposals for election procedures, and MG officials checked the proposed codes to insure that they did not conflict with the Allied policies, and they were returned to the *Länder* governments for use as the basis of local government and elections. This series of elections opened with *Gemeinde* elections in January, continued with *Landkreis* elections in April, and closed with *Stadtkreis* elections in May 1946. The United States zone was the first of the four zones in Germany in which popularly based local governments have been established by free elections. Throughout the election schedule, voter participation was high. In the January elections, for example, more than 85 per cent of the eligible voters in communities of less than 20,000 population went to the polls (a larger percentage than in the same area under the Weimar Republic); more than 10,000 communities elected more than 70,000 local councilors.

As early as January 1946 MG's job had become one of general supervision from the top, not one of issuing day-to-day instructions to each county, town, village, or city official. Instructions to local government, from that time on, were given only through the Minister-Presidents at *Land* level; and these instructions, for the most part, were confined to policy delineation.

The first step toward representative government at the *Land* level was taken during January 1946 with the establishment of advisory assemblies in the three *Länder*. Pending the establishment of representative legislative bodies, these advisory councils were designed to provide an initial contact between MG and the German population.

In addition, the preparation by the *Länder* in the United States zone of their own democratic constitutions began in January with the announcement by MG of its intention to permit the holding of assemblies for the purpose of drafting these constitutions. Each Minister-President was directed to appoint a *Land* constitutional commission to prepare a draft constitution to be submitted to the *Land* Constitutional Assembly at its opening session. On June 30, 1946, delegates to the Constitutional Assemblies were chosen in the fourth series of elections held in the American zone.

MG did not interfere in the framing of these constitutions except to require that they provide for the maintenance of a democratic system of government. General McNarney stated in June 1946 that the following conditions must be met before any future German government will be regarded by American authorities as "democratic":

1. All political power must be recognized as originating with the people and subject to their control.

2. Those who exercise political power are obliged regularly to renew their mandates by frequent references of their programs and leadership to popular elections.

3. Popular elections must be conducted under competitive conditions in which not less than two effectively competing political parties submit their programs and candidates for public review.

4. Political parties must be democratic in character and must be recognized as voluntary associations of citizens clearly distinguished from, rather than identified with, the instrumentalities of government.

5. The basic rights of the individual, including freedom of speech, freedom of religious preference, the right of assembly, and freedom of political association, must be recognized and guaranteed.

6. Control over the instrumentalities of public opinion, such as the radio and press, must be diffused and kept free from governmental domination.

7. The rule of law must be recognized as the individual's greatest single protection against a capricious and wilful expression of governmental power, and against the arbitrary domination of agencies of government control.

Under the new constitutions the structure of each *Land* government is parliamentary in form, comprising the *Landtag* (legislative assembly), the Minister-President, and a Cabinet.

The *Landtag* is elected directly by the people for a four-year term. The Minister-President is elected by the *Landtag*, and he in turn appoints and removes the Ministers of his Cabinet. The Supreme Court of each *Land* also is elected by the Legislature.

The constitutions differ in many respects. For example, the governmental system of Bavaria is composed of two houses, the *Landtag* and the Senate. The Senate is composed of 60 members elected for 6 years by various groups such as labor unions, cooperatives, welfare organizations, and universities; it serves only in an advisory capacity but may introduce bills into the *Landtag*. The constitutions of Württemberg-Baden and Hesse contain special "non-confidence vote" clauses whereby the *Landtag* may recall the Minister-Presidents and their Cabinets; that of Bavaria does not contain such a clause. Also, the *Landtag* in Bavaria and in Württemberg-Baden, but not in Hesse, may be dissolved by a plebiscite before its term is up.

These three constitutions place strong emphasis on the protection of individual human rights. Each constitution includes a bill of rights guaranteeing freedom of speech, assembly, the press, and religion, the right of access to information, and the right of judicial protection and equality before the law.

The constitutions provide that education be both free and compulsory, and, although religious instruction is included in the curricula, the religious denomination of the individual is to be respected. Religious associations which were previously public corporations remain so under the new constitutions and retain their right to levy taxes and receive payments from the state. Provisions are made for a social-insurance system and the protection of such basic social rights as the right of labor to organize and bargain collectively within the limits of the law, and employees have the right to be represented in all matters affecting them.

Unlike those of the other *Länder*, the constitution of Bavaria provides that the basic type of school be denominational in character and that in only those communities with a mixed religious population will secular schools be organized, on parental petition. The new constitution provides for a wide degree of socialization in Bavaria by impowering the state to supervise the production and distribution of goods of vital importance to the community. The creation of private cartels and price combines is prohibited. The ownership of public utilities, for the most part, falls to public law corporations and cooperatives.

After the formation of *Land* governmental machinery had been completed in September 1945, with the establishment of the three states and the appointment of Minister-Presidents and their staffs to govern them—Wilhelm Hoegner in Bavaria, Reinhold Maier in Württemberg-Baden, and Karl Geiler in Greater Hesse—MG could concentrate on administrative and supervisory operations. A plan was approved in the same month for coordinating the activities of the three German *Länder* governments in common administrative matters extending beyond the boundaries of the individual *Länder*, which formerly came under the direct control of the German central government, such as communication, transport, and various other political, economic, and cultural activities requiring uniform administration.

Pending the establishment of central administrative machinery for finance, industry, transport, communications, and foreign trade, as provided in the Potsdam agreement, a German organization known as the *Länderrat*, or Council of States, was planned to serve as a means of coordination within the zone and as a further step toward the restoration of German responsibility and self-government, without setting up a zonal administration.

The organization meeting of the *Länderrat* took place on October 17, 1945, in Stuttgart, under the direction of General Clay and Dr. James K. Pollock, who was then Director of the Regional Government Coordinating Office (described below). The participants included the Minister-Presidents of the three *Länder* and the Mayor of Bremen.

At the second meeting of the Minister-Presidents on November 6 the establishment was formally confirmed and the organization plan for the *Länderrat* was approved. The organization has been expanded and strengthened from time to time in order that the *Länderrat* and its numerous committees and subcommittees may absorb increasingly the new tasks and responsibilities assigned by MG.

The Council of States is composed of the Minister-Presidents of Bavaria, Greater Hesse, and Württemberg-Baden. The Mayor of Bremen takes part in *Länderrat* decisions only when interests of his area are concerned. The organization plan charges this coordinating agency with the task of cooperatively working out the problems which affect more than one state in the American zone, with removing difficulties of communication between the *Länder*, and with securing the desired uniformity in the development of political, social, economic, and cultural life in accordance with the American occupation policy. The *Länderrat* statute adopted by that body with the approval of MG in May 1946 also assigns to the *Länderrat* the function of acting as the control channel for relations with the other zones.

Subject to the approval of OMGUS, the *Länderrat* has final decision on all matters within its jurisdiction. Action in the *Länderrat* is not, however, that of a zonal government, superimposed and managed by military authority, but of three self-governing states. Policies established by the *Länderrat* are executed by the Minister-Presidents in their respective *Länder*, through their civil governments. The Council was given authority in May 1946 to take independent action on certain matters without obtaining the prior approval of MG. Excluded, of course, were major decisions and matters within the province of the Allied Control Authority.

Supervision of the *Länderrat* is maintained through the Regional Government Coordinating Office (RGCO), a separate agency of MG, located at Stuttgart, the seat of the *Länderrat*. RGCO operates under the Deputy Military Governor and consists of a Director (now Col. W. W. Dawson), a Deputy Director, and a small working staff. The policy of RGCO is not to dictate to the German officials but to recommend and advise. As a coordinating agency between MG and the German *Länderrat* and its subordinate committees, directorates, and agencies, RGCO insures that items desired by MG are placed on the agenda for consideration and action by the Council, forwards decisions and proposals of the *Länderrat* to OMGUS for approval, and transmits to the *Länderrat* notice of the action taken on such decisions and proposals.

The Secretariat of the *Länderrat* consists of a Secretary General, the permanent representatives of the Minister-Presidents, and a working staff. It serves as the channel for all matters to be presented to the *Länderrat* or its committees by either MG or German civilian sources; it draws up the agenda for the meetings of the *Länderrat*; it prepares measures for decision and facilitates their execution; and it prepares reports and statistics requested by MG.

Numerous committees of German civilian technical advisers function under the direction of the Secretariat. The committees are appointed by the *Länderrat* subject to the approval of the RGCO. Representatives of the RGCO meet with them and advise them in the consideration of legislative and administrative matters. Practically every significant problem of political and economic life in the American zone is handled by the *Länderrat* committees.

Specific committees deal with such problems as food and agriculture, transportation, communications, finance, economics, industry, and trade. One of the most active groups has been the committee on food and agriculture, which is responsible, among other things, for the development of plans to insure the equitable distribution of food supplies throughout the American zone and for the production and processing of agricultural products. Previously, MG coordinated the activities of the *Länder* in these fields.

The Minister-Presidents, the Secretary General, and representatives of MG attend regular monthly meetings of the *Länderrat*, held at Stuttgart. Special meetings may be held upon the request of MG or of a Minister-President. Each Minister-President may have a deputy to assist him and may also call in the respective *Land* Ministers together with their functional experts under whose jurisdiction the various problems fall. Each Minister-President serves in rotation as chairman of the *Länderrat* for a period of three months.

During the interval between the regular monthly meetings of the Council, a Directorate which is composed of seven members—three special delegates for *Länderrat* affairs from the three *Land* governments, the three permanent representatives of the

Minister-Presidents, and the Secretary General—meets once a week. The Directorate was established in May 1946 with authority to act in the name of the *Länderrat* on routine matters which are not of basic importance but which cannot be postponed. Important matters requiring *ad interim* action by the *Länderrat* are decided upon by the Minister-Presidents. On the establishment of the Directorate, the *Länderrat* was for the first time enabled to concern itself exclusively with important matters of policy.

As a school for German self-government, the *Länderrat* has provided the training ground for the assumption of governmental responsibility within a democratic framework. It has furnished the first opportunity in 15 years for German officials to practice democracy and democratic methods—the assumption of personal responsibility, the interchange of ideas, the reconciliation of conflicting interests and views, and the exercise of compromise and concession.

Since its establishment in October 1945 the *Länderrat* has proved its value in coordinating action by the three *Länder* in accordance with Allied and American policy. Considering the handicaps of establishing such an agency—which is without precedent in German political history—the variety, volume, and character of the actions taken by this body have been impressive. A review of important decisions made by the Council of States and of action taken on them by MG shows that the German officials have made good use of the organization and that they recognize its value.

These decisions cover such matters as the operation within the American zone of all railroads, waterways, highways, and postal and telecommunication services; the production, collection, and distribution of food; the establishment of *Land* Central Banks, which have taken over most of the functions formerly performed by the *Reichsbank*; the formulation and administration of the denazification law; the formulation of a uniform price policy and structure; the care and disposition of refugees and expellees; and the adoption of uniform laws for the establishment of labor courts and for the licensing of newspapers, book and magazine publishers, and theatrical and musical producers.

The *Länderrat* has also served as an instrument of American policy in coordinating interzonal problems. Toward this end the first important steps were taken in January 1946 when German officials in the American and British zones met in the *Länderrat* to discuss mutual problems. Subsequent joint discussions resulted in permanent liaison between the *Länderrat* and various civilian agencies in the British zone. Plans were discussed at the various meetings for closer cooperation and for exchange of information and representatives on such matters as legal developments in the two zones, food and agriculture administration, the standardization of statistical procedures, the evacuee problem, and uniform postal organization.

In other interzonal conferences, officials from the American, British, and French zones considered such questions as how to achieve uniformity of legislation and of administration of justice. Representatives of the *Länderrat* and the German Central Administration of the Soviet zone met for the first time in June 1946 and established six committees to discuss in detail the specific requirements of the American and Soviet zones. Three of these committees (on chemicals, metals, and textiles) held meetings late in July. These negotiations constitute the preliminary steps toward the elimination of barriers between the four zones of occupation.

As a preparatory step aimed toward the economic unification of all four zones, General McNarney stated at the July 20, 1946, meeting of the Control Council that the American Government was prepared to enter into administrative agreements with any or all of the other occupying powers in the fields of finance, transport, communications, industry, and foreign trade, for the purpose of effecting a unified economic policy with the zones which would desire it. Only the United Kingdom has to date accepted the invitation.

The progressive working out of administrative details for securing economic unification of the American and British zones will be entrusted to the *Länderrat*, representing the interests of the American zone. Preliminary agreements, now approved by the American and British Military Governments, provide for the establishment of German Bizonal Executive Committees for Economics, Food and Agriculture, Transport, and Communications and Posts, and a Joint Committee on Finance. Whereas the function of the Joint Committee on Finance will be mainly liaison and coordination of planning, the Executive Committees established in the other fields will make decisions on matters specified in the Anglo-American agreement, which will be valid in the two zones, subject to approval by the two Military Governments. Each of the committees consists of six members: the functional Ministers of the three *Länder* of the United States zone, and three representatives of the British zone nominated by the British Military Government.

Joint Anglo-American staffs will be established to communicate quadripartite policy decisions of the Allied Control Authority and to assist the German committees in carrying out their tasks. Addressing the Bizonal Executive Committee for Economics at its first meeting held recently at Minden, Westphalia, Brig. Gen. William H. Draper (American representative on the Anglo-American Bipartite Board and Director of the Economics Division of OMGUS) said:

> Military Government controls are intended as guarantees of the peaceful reconstruction of your country and not as barriers to your endeavor toward a progressive German regime.

With the establishment of executive agencies at bizonal level, the necessity for performing executive functions at zonal level in the fields specified will be greatly reduced if not entirely eliminated, and it is expected that in these fields the functions of the *Länderrat* will be exercised through its representatives on the bizonal agencies.

The acceptance of democratic constitutions by the separate states in the United States zone may be said to mark the end of the initial chapter of American military occupation of Germany. The American zone, comprising three autonomous German states, has been prepared to join with the British, French, and Soviet zones under an eventual central federal government.

IS OUR OCCUPATION POLICY IN GERMANY A FAILURE? YES! [4]

As one of the leaders in the coalition which defeated the German armies and their civilian government, the United States was forced to consider unprecedented problems. They are specifically:

1. To share (for an indefinite period!) the administration of one of the greatest industrial nations of the world with a heterogeneous group of allies;

2. To conduct at least our part of this job in a manner conducive to persuading the defeated Germans of the superiority of democratic institutions and capitalist economy;

3. To collaborate in disarming and denazifying Germany and to put her economy on a basis where it would be both harmless to the rest of the world and capable of feeding, housing, and clothing the German people.

These were the chief tasks ahead of us on V-J Day. More than two years have elapsed since then. Our approach has resulted in an almost complete failure. A sweeping revision of our occupation policy has just been published, with our avowed aim now being to put Germany back on her feet again. Enthusiastic reports about our past activities in Germany come almost exclusively from our occupation officials (who in many cases are perhaps unconsciously influenced by the luxurious Herrenvolk-manner of living which has been their happy lot and that of their families in the midst of German ruin). On no other controversial topic is public opinion so universally agreed as on our failure in Germany. This, for a believer in democratic processes, should at least be sufficiently significant to warrant real soul-searching.

In a totalitarian state the citizen rightly blames his government for such blunders, albeit under his breath and provided he learns about them at all. In a democracy the citizens are the government and have but to blame themselves. What were the mistakes and to what extent were they American mistakes alone?

[4] By Frederick H. Cramer, Professor of History, Mount Holyoke College. *Forum.* 108:164+. September 1947. Reprinted by permission.

We began to treat the Germans to a well-deserved dose of their own medicine. Nonfraternization was our policy. Any psychologist, biologist, or animal breeder could have told those fine minds responsible for this tom-foolery that young men by the million, or more recently by the hundred-thousand are strangely desirous of the company of women. To treat the folks of their girl-friends rough has never been an American trait. Small wonder therefore that nonfraternization became a howling failure. Step by step it had to be abandoned, until by now plane-loads of *Fraüleins* are being flown into this country.

We followed this up by demobilizing our armed forces ruthlessly. In place of a relatively battle-matured soldiery, more and more helpless teen-age boys took over the occupying of Germany. Many of them had volunteered for military duty only after the war and saw in their German venture but a free lark in Europe with plenty of *schnapps,* easy women and raucous song. Unpleasant stories about the black-market activities began to filter back to the United States where the black-market has not yet achieved the status of a semipermanent economic institution. Rape, robbery, and plain vandalism cases larded with mounting venereal disease figures rounded out an already unsavory picture. In short, we had committed ourselves to a long-range military occupation policy without taking remotely adequate steps for creating a corps of trained and reasonably high-class troops.

Another understandable but regrettable error in judgment was our vain endeavor to galvanize political life into action prematurely in Germany. With the abolition of the Nazi regime, only a small group of violent Nazis was thrown out of power and office. The multitude of the civil service workers, the teachers, judges, tax officials and a host of others remained unmolested. Denazification proceedings would have to last nigh unto doomsday to sift even the more palpable Nazi-chaff from the German wheat. The democratic Weimar Republic died, because it believed that efficient civil service, though staffed by antidemocratic nationalists, was preferable to the trouble and near-chaos bound up with the creation of a new "reliable" civil service. Our own policy bears a fatal resemblance to that of the Weimar Republic. In the holy name of efficiency and order, the technicians, the economic and social leaders of old are left in their posts or restored to them.

The real danger of this American efficiency worship is its short-range workability and its long-range futility. In a totalitarian police state, let us say in the Russian zone, the secret police and ruthless terror are able to keep a firm lid on any potentially boiling cauldron of discontent. In a democratic set-up—and that is what we have been trying to build up in our zone—such strong-arm tactics are taboo. Consequently the very same thing, the employing of engineers, technicians, and others regardless of Nazi or non-Nazi antecedents can safely be practiced in the Russian zone. But it is a dangerous folly for a democratic regime to leave vital bastions in the hands of sworn opponents of democracy. The 47 per cent of the Germans who now openly admit that Hitler erred only by losing the war but that his ideas were, indeed, fine, are giving the horse-laugh to our idea of preferring efficient administration to thorough denazification.

In our splendid lack of adequate historical training, we have blithely restored to circulation in dozens of cases school-books which had the merit of antedating 1933, the year in which Hitler came to power. In one instance, only a few days before a history book was thus slated to be issued (the copies having been printed by the hundred thousands), it was discovered that this book, published prior to 1933, was full of rampant nationalism and gross attacks against ourselves and our allies—England and France. Nobody apparently had thought of the fact that the very Nazis and their followers who helped Hitler into the saddle had been brought up exclusively with those pre-1933 schoolbooks! The history-book, in this case, was never issued, but this was one of the few exceptions when primers and other books were not handed out for the German schools in our zone.

In part this coy closing of our eyes to the often unsavory past of German burgomasters and the like was again due to our utter lack of vision and preparedness. Our regime in Puerto Rico or the Virgin Islands had not trained any sizable group of administrators equipped both intellectually and educationally to supervise the running of even one fourth of Germany. The most grievous handicap for which we have to thank our school system and the educational policies in most of our colleges and homes was the woeful lack of German-speaking personnel.   Refugees who had been naturalized in this country were employed with reluctance.   Partly it was feared they would be too anti-German, partly that in a pinch they would be of not impeccable loyalty.

But even all available personnel of this kind would have been far from enough to staff our administrative echelons adequately. Native Americans had abandoned the formerly popular study of German in droves after World War I; immigration from Germany and Austria had dropped to a trickle after the immigration law went into effect in 1924.   There simply was no chance of obtaining a sufficient number of German-speaking Americans who were remotely able to handle administrative routine.   The Russians, on the other hand, could rely on substantial numbers of devoted German Communists for whatever posts they wanted to fill in their own set-up.   The result of this shortage was heightened by the unwillingness of many qualified Americans to risk their professional future in this country by staying on for years in the occupation area.

The result was not only a rapidly dwindling supply of executive personnel, but also the growing importance of "the interpreter," usually a German with enough English to carry on official business between the two sides.   The least of the troubles of the interpreter system is its tediousness.   Things take twice as long, or even longer, often because a series of questions arises from one party's inability to understand the meaning of a poorly translated argument or case history.   With the best of intentions, interpreter-reliant administrators never obtain the desirable touch with the populace they govern.

As time goes on only people with little to look forward to in this country and a hopelessly small band of idealists are likely to continue the thankless task of running a country which we want to have run itself as soon as it can safely be done.   The folly of creating protected American oases in the German wilderness for the families of our personnel may have as its best defence the preservation of some American homes which otherwise would have broken up under the impact of prolonged *Fraülein*-influence upon lonesome Americans.   But the evacuation of already overcrowded Germans for the benefit of American families who live in what is to the Germans unimaginable luxury, especially with regard to food, heat, and clothing, has persuaded many Germans that "bosses are bosses," with the Nazis being at least German bosses as a point in their favor. A large part of British colonial personnel has been disliked by "the Natives" all over the world for exactly the same psychological reason. A native tyrant was at least "one of the gang"; a foreign absolute ruler,—and we *are* ruling our German subjects "absolutely,"—cannot even claim that doubtful privilege.

Another basic handicap has been that we agreed to take over a largely agricultural zone, but one whose products were far from adequate for even modest self-sufficiency at all times. Into this zone have since crowded millions of voluntary or forcibly displaced newscomers. The same has been true for other zones, and all in all, thanks to its relatively rural character and our ability and willingness to provide a rock-bottom minimum diet, our zone has perhaps fared somewhat better than the British. Yet, we also inherited the most reactionary, hidebound, and backward part of Germany, with the possible exception of Pomerania and East Prussia which fell to the Poles and Russians. To introduce democracy in Bavaria is something which evokes a tender smile from anyone who knows dear old Bavaria. If ever it is done, it will take a long, long time, indeed!

The fundamental error was, of course, our agreeing to a multipartite occupation of Germany. This may have been an inevitable concession to our wartime allies, especially in the case of Russia and France, but one wonders what would have happened under a different scheme. That the present one resulted in utter failure we openly acknowledged by trying to pool our zone with the British zone of occupation. The French and Russians have remained aloof till now. At the moment even a dollar-starved Britain raises a major issue by preferring socialized starvation in its own zone of primarily industrial Germany to our pious suggestion to wait with nationalization till the German people can express their wishes more clearly. We assume hopefully, of course, that they will prefer their dear old Krupps and coal-barons to any government bureaucracy running nationalized mining and steel industries.

The impasse into which we have thus maneuvered ourselves stems from the basic misconception of our wartime German policy. Absurdities like the Morgenthau deindustralization fetish still echo in the corridors of many a capital. Similarly, on the political level, the hope of creating a federalized Germany with a weak central government dies hard. For decades Germany has not been able to feed her population from the products of her overworked and overcrowded soil. Industrial exports were the key to the balance of her economy. The American and the British taxpayers are beginning to learn this fact the hard way. It was available in all books on world trade for many years, had the powers that were but deigned to read them. It was equally clear that the Ruhr area was the chief key to German industrial life and its coal the main fuel supply of continental Europe outside Poland and Russia. Today, on a hypothetical diet of 4000 calories a day, the German miners produce about half their prewar output. Enraged congressmen yell "sabotage." Maybe. Certainly there is a good deal of quiet sabotage going on all the time. But what about the miners' families? Four thousand calories from which the miner deducts as much as possible to bolster the starvation rations of a wife and children do not leave much for himself.

The complete dislocation of German economy has been one of the results of our deindustrialization policy. The cure now proposed, however, may be worse than the disease itself. Already howls come from Paris and other capitals about the danger of a revived industrial Germany. The Marshall Plan tossed off in somewhat slapdash fashion at the Harvard commencement brought about the most recent dilemma: our necessarily anti-Russian foreign policy needs the political support of as many European governments as possible. The economic bait of the Marshall Plan served this purpose. At the same time, Germany's still enormous latent industrial potential—70 per cent of which is unused at the moment—is the chief economic asset of continental Europe outside Russia. Logically, from our point of view, we have therefore scrapped our previous Germany policy of deindustrialization. Unfortunately this means that Germany will get stronger, economically first, politically later. Seventy million Germans, squeezed into an area far smaller than even Weimar Germany was, are seething with resentment and wholly unwilling to accept their reduced circumstances as the result of their past criminal folly. These Germans no doubt will be highly unpleasant neighbors in any case, but more particularly so, if endowed with the financial and political backing of the United States and Britain.

This, too, is what we reap: logic demands a reactivation of German industry for the benefit of our own taxpayer, the European economy, and inevitably, alas, the Germans themselves. Logic also demands our trying for the cooperation of the Western European countries of which, at least, France seems inclined to prefer Communism to German resurrection. It does not do to dismiss these sentiments as European hysteria. Our German policy of the past five years has led us into a dead-end road, where we are now damned if we do and damned if we don't.

From the viewpoint of Germany's neighbors it looks somewhat risky to agree to the economic revival of Germany as a prerequisite for future American assistance. We may lose more politically, therefore, than the hoped for curtailing of the economic drain of a starving Germany. Yet, what can a European premier think of the reliability of a country which like ours changes its most important foreign policies overnight, so to speak. With Congress officially promised relief from the grievous danger of a special fall session, why—it is asked over there—do we insist on a European self-help program at the earliest possible moment, a program to which we contribute (before it's even drafted) our unilateral announcement of the reindustrialization of Germany? At the same time we give, of course, no guarantee whatever of supporting any European scheme for the rehabilitation of Europe.

No sane judge can deny that for the hunger-torn, enfeebled neighbors of Germany these prospects are not altogether alluring. The utter failure of our past German occupation policy on every score but that of holding down our slice of the German population is an established fact. Whether or not we can undo at least part of our sins of omission is doubtful. If we count on the inevitability of World War III we have to court the non-German states of Europe at any price. But even allowing for World War III, we may back the wrong horse in strengthening a Germany which our army in its happily depleted peacetime size could not hold against the Russians for a month and whose revived industrial plants if occupied by the Soviet armies we might have to smash with atom bombs at the very outset of such a war. To align ourselves firmly with whatever non-Fascist and non-Communist country in Europe we can is the first prerequisite to the success of our new German policy. Irrevocably assured of American military assistance against any future German pressure, Germany's neighbors would agree far more readily to German reindustrialization than they do now with their only protection a feeble, veto-hampered United Nations.

As a failure, our first two years of occupation of the German zone will rank with our "Reconstruction Period" in the South after 1865. Our modern carpetbaggers may be less crude and fewer in number, but the long memories of the occupied are likely to be even more bitter than those of our most rabid "Southerners." It should be clear, however, that the failure of our major occupation policies is inherent in themselves, as much as in the additional factors, among which were hurried demobilization, lack of trained personnel, and the general and ineradicable aversion of the American people against long-range commitments which really do commit us. In view of these circumstances beyond their control, our occupation personnel, battling it out in Germany, have done the best they could. That they did not succeed was not so much their own fault, as it was that of the men responsible for the master directives.

No contractor can successfully build from incorrect or non-existing blueprints. The usual habit of blaming our German failure overseas on the local personnel stems from pleasant but loose thinking. In a democracy there are no scapegoats, or better, there should be none. We the people are responsible for what is done in our name.

IS OUR OCCUPATION POLICY IN GERMANY
A FAILURE? NO! [5]

The lives of Americans will be affected for more than a generation by what we accomplish or fail to accomplish in the occupation of Germany. Therefore, any concern of the American public about Military Government policies—even if not always justified—is much preferable to apathy.

Whatever charges may be leveled against Military Government—and they are many—no one with a knowledge of the facts can honestly argue that our government began the bleak struggle to win the peace without preparation, plans and policies, or that it has lacked initiative.

At what time the first preparations for Allied government of Germany were started is unknown. In any event, shortly after my arrival in London early in 1943, I found the British had already begun to feel out the United States on its position on the solution of problems which might arise from a future United States-Soviet Russia-United Kingdom occupation of the Reich. In the United States and United Kingdom quarters, a lot of real thinking and planning went on about hypothetical situations which became realities two or three years later. Unfortunately, many a problem we discussed then is today only partially solved.

But there was an early realization of the difficulties which were later to confront us. So much so that the morale of our less optimistic colleagues declined visibly. Nor did we escape the usual disillusionment of planners whose basic assumptions do not quite materialize. Yet one upshot of it all was increased flexibility. "We have made so many plans based on such different assumptions," one officer recently commented, "that I don't see how any new situation can arise which could not be met by some combination of previous plans."

Before the capitulation of Germany, not only detailed plans for Military Government were in existence but also a compre-

[5] By David Glen White, OMGUS, Control Office, Berlin. (Views expressed are those of Mr. White, not Military Government.) *Forum*. 108:165+. September 1947. Reprinted by permission.

hensive United States policy in the form of the subsequently famous Joint Chiefs of Staff Directive 1067 which was issued to General Eisenhower. The directive instructed the United States Commander in Chief to urge its adoption by the other occupying powers.

Some Europeans are inclined to think of Americans primarily as a source of material aid while they consider it their prerogative to supply the policies. Our policy makers in Washington and our administrators in Berlin have never accepted such a passive role. Extremely able statesmen-soldiers such as Eisenhower, McNarney and Clay have consistently pursued an independent United States policy in the Berlin four-power negotiations and have been second to none in seizing the initiative. In doing so they have received wholehearted support from men in Washington such as Secretaries of State Byrnes and Marshall, and Secretary of War Patterson.

Anyone who cares to review the record of our initiative should begin by comparing the Joint Chiefs of Staff Directive to General Eisenhower with the text of the Potsdam Agreement. He may be surprised to find that the latter document incorporates much of the previous United States directive including verbatim passages.

No occupying power has been more persistent than the United States in trying to make quadripartite machinery work or in striving to reach agreements with other powers, particularly the U.S.S.R. These efforts were made undeterred by skeptics, including some in our own ranks, who freely predicted that a Control Council for Germany would never be set up.

By V-E Day, we had captured 78,000 square miles, or about 42.7 per cent of Germany, and United States troops were as far east as Leipzig in important areas earmarked for the Soviet zone of occupation. This valuable territory was evacuated to the U.S.S.R. in order to facilitate the establishment of the Control Council. Finally, upon arrival in Berlin, we furnished such minor items as the building for the Control Council, took the initiative in working out Allied Control Authority procedures, and accepted the chairmanship for the first month of regular meetings. Much of the drive which has since kept the Control

Council going has come from the Americans. Fashionable though it is to minimize the Allied Control Authority's achievements, if one measures them against the fact that every decision required four-power unanimity, the amount of work accomplished is not to be sneered at.

United States policy, which subsequently found its way into the Potsdam Agreement, enjoins that "the administration of affairs in Germany should be directed toward the decentralization of the political structure and the development of local responsibility." Such a policy could be urged with complete sincerity by the United States which has lived under a decentralized, federal form of government for over a century and a half. One great obstacle to the federalization of Germany was the existence of Prussia, a state which through its preponderance of population and area would have relegated all other states (*Länder*) to the position of junior partners. The United States took the lead in the dissolution of Prussia by utilizing those Prussian provinces located in our zone to constitute the enlarged state of Hessen on September 19, 1945. The other three zones of Germany followed suit and the *de jure* dissolution of Prussia was finally confirmed by the Moscow Conference of Foreign Ministers March 10, 1947.

The Potsdam Agreement called for the restoration of local self-government through elective councils as rapidly as was consistent with military security and the purpose of military occupation. Less than six months after Potsdam, the United States Military government set a precedent by ordering local elections to be held. Other elections followed. In our zone, state constitutional assemblies were elected, and constitutions were drawn up and adopted by popular vote. Our initiative in going ahead with elections created a precedent which Military Government in the other three zones were hardly able to ignore.

One of the hottest issues ever to strike Military Government was denazification. Properly understood, denazification, together with the war crimes trials, represents a tremendous departure from the principle of collective guilt. Originally denazification was administered on a basis of rigid categories without much opportunity for an individual to plead extenuating circumstances.

Although this form of denazification meted approximate justice in the majority of cases, enough cases of injustice occurred to cause Military Government officials with a sense of fair play to press for reform.

The reform took place early in 1946. As now carried out in the United States zone, denazification attempts to assess every German's responsibility for the war and to make him share the burdens of defeat in proportion to his individual guilt. Germans under the age of 18, as a group, are considered innocent. Other Germans are classified preliminarily either as exonerated persons or given some other classification varying from "follower" to "major offender." The most important feature of the law is the right accorded to every individual to appear before a tribunal and show cause why his preliminary classification should be modified. Once a classification is sustained even the penalties imposed have a real meaning. Thus a person, who through his support of nazism helped devastate other countries and bring about his own country's destruction, may be assigned to a labor camp to aid repairing war damages, and most of his property may be confiscated for reparations. It is believed that no other zone in Germany can surpass our record for initiative, thoroughness and fairness in denazification.

The Potsdam Agreement promised the treatment of Germany as a single economic unit. When, after 11 months of patient negotiations, the quadripartite implementation of this part of the Potsdam Agreement was still unattainable, the United States Military Government took the lead in breaking the impasse and proposed a joint economic administration with any or all other zones. The British accepted immediately with the subsequent economic fusion of the two zones and, more recently, the establishment of a Bizonal Economic Council. At the same time, our Military Government still hopes for agreement with the U.S.S.R. and France, and continues full-scale participation in the Allied Control Authority in Berlin.

United States policy, which in slightly modified version was written into the Potsdam Agreement, permitted average living standards in Germany not exceeding those of other European countries (excluding the United Kingdom and the U.S.S.R.).

Some idealists among Military Government officials had hoped that this limitation might at some future time become an incentive for the Germans to assist in raising the general European living standards it now seems that the initiative to raise European living standards will come from the Marshall Plan, which has been proposed at a time when it is desirable to stress that the United States is also deeply concerned with Europe's economic requirements outside of Germany and Austria.

In conclusion, there may be some question as to what constitutes the principal objective of United States occupation policy. It is nothing less than preventing Germany from ever becoming again a threat to the peace of the world. Closely tied up with the peace of the world are also our relations with France, the British Empire, and the U.S.S.R., which are profoundly affected by our occupation policies.

We, who are old enough to have seen the United States involved in war with Germany twice, are willing to consider the occupation a success if Germany does not threaten world peace for merely another generation. The steps in the accomplishment of the principal United States objective are the elimination of nazism and militarism, industrial disarmament, demilitarization, and democratization.

It would be fallacious, however, to suppose that a democratic Germany, even with our brand of democracy, must inevitably be friendly to the United States. On the contrary, it is at least conceivable that once a democratic German government achieves some freedom of action, it will strive to play the occupying powers against each other and seek one concession after another, claiming that these are needed to bolster up a democratic regime. Regardless of ideological allegiance, Germany's geographical position and her tradition of *Realpolitik* predisposes her to such a policy.

The democratization of Germany has just started; many obstacles beset its path, and the final outcome is uncertain. But it is an objective we must pursue despite difficulties. Some impetuous critics think Germany should have been democratized within the last two years. Yet, how many of these critics would claim they are able in the space of two years to shape the future outlook of their own children? The democratization of Germany involves an attempt by voluntary methods to shape the future outlook of an entire nation. Meanwhile, certain safeguards must be maintained, the most important of which is continued occupation.

DEMILITARIZATION AND INDUSTRIAL RECOVERY

GERMANY: ITS PREWAR ECONOMIC IMPORTANCE AND PLANS FOR RECONSTRUCTION [1]

An orderly and prosperous Europe requires the economic contributions of a stable and productive Germany, as well as the necessary restraints to insure that Germany is not allowed to revive its destructive militarism.

This statement from the directive approved by the State, War and Navy Departments on United States military government policies in Germany indicates both the need for economic revival in Germany and the difficulties attending efforts to achieve it.

Geography and geology have made Germany the economic center of Europe. Geography gave Germany its rivers and the railways built in its river valleys which have always been the gateway to Central Europe. Geology gave Germany two of the most important coal fields of Western Europe.

By its technological developments, Germany capitalized on the opportunities offered to it by its geography and geology. Thereby, it became a great exporting nation and an important customer for the products of the other countries of Western Europe.

Before the war, Germany supplied to its neighboring countries essential commodities now needed for their rebuilding. Of these commodities, coal and steel are the most important.

In 1937, Germany produced more than one third of continental Europe's coal and more than one fourth of its steel. In 1946, Germany produced only about half of its prewar output of coal and virtually no steel at all.

Since the war, Germany has been able neither to feed itself nor to support itself otherwise. The delay in its own rehabilita-

[1] From Index. 27, no. 3:47-60. Autumn 1947. Reprinted by permission.

tion has seriously retarded economic revival in its neighboring countries.

The industry required to support its people, however, can also support a war machine. Twice in one generation Germany has forced wars of aggression upon the world, so political considerations dictate that some measure of control be kept over Germany's economy to make it impossible for her revived industries to produce war matériel which would enable her again to wage aggressive war.

Thus, as the directive setting forth United States military government policies in Germany indicates, economic considerations demanding the contributions of a "stable and prosperous Germany" for the peace and well-being of Western Europe, must be balanced against political considerations demanding prevention of its "destructive militarism." This article will deal with the economic considerations that make some measure of industrial restoration for Germany imperative and wherever possible will avoid political considerations.

Between the two world wars, Germany was one of the three leading industrial nations of the world. In 1929, Germany's proportion of world trade amounted to about 9.5 per cent in value and this was exceeded only by the United States with 14 per cent and Great Britain with 13.2 per cent. France followed Germany with 6.3 per cent of foreign trade. No other country reached 4 per cent. . . .

Just before the outbreak of World War II, about 35 per cent of German imports came from Western Europe and more than 45 per cent of German exports were sold to Western Europe.

As one of the steps toward rearmament, the Nazis brought all phases of the German economy under strict state control. Domination over industry by the Nazis was made easier by the trend to cartelization in Germany during the 1920's and early 1930's.

In 1936, Germany adopted a four-year plan intended to reduce its dependence on imported raw materials, chiefly through the synthetic production of rubber, oil, textile fibers and fats. While some success was achieved under this plan, at the out-

break of the war Germany still had to depend on foreign
sources for some 70 per cent of its iron ore, 90 per cent of its
copper ore and all of its manganese, chrome, nickel, tungsten
and many other raw materials.

Synthetic rubber production increased from 5,000 tons in
1938 to an annual rate of 117,000 tons at the beginning of
1944. Synthetic oil production increased from 1,600,000 tons
in 1938 to an annual rate of 6,000,000 tons in early 1944.
During the same period, crude oil output expanded from 600,-
000 tons to 2,000,000 tons.

During the war, England and the United States bombed
with increasing severity those areas in which Germany's industries were concentrated, chiefly in the Ruhr and the Saar basins,
with special attention being given to centers of production of
synthetic gasoline and certain parts required for the manufacture of airplanes, such as ball bearing plants, synthetic rubber
factories, and similar plants.

In 1944, the effects of Allied bombings began to reduce
the output of certain key materials. The attack on the Ruhr
area cut steel production so that the total German steel output
declined from 2,000,000 tons in September to 1,000,000 tons in
December of 1944. Coal deliveries at the end of March 1945,
were only 4 per cent of normal.

Under the continued pounding and other effects of war,
the economy began to disintegrate. Albert Speer, Minister of
Armament Production, wrote in his report of March 15, 1945,
that "the German economy is heading for an inevitable collapse
within four to eight weeks."

The end of the war found Germany's war economy destroyed, its agricultural production greatly reduced, its cities in
ruins, and its transportation facilities in a state of collapse.
The territory annexed during and immediately preceding the
war had to be disgorged and the remaining area of the country,
as of December 31, 1937, was divided into four zones of
occupation.

As to the effects of bomb damage on the German civilian
economy, the United States Strategic Bombing Survey indicates
that industrial production of consumer goods in 1944 was 85.4

per cent of that in 1939. The survey states that the civilian economy was "inevitably caught up in the spreading disruption of the latter part of 1944," being affected by the breakdown in transportation, while many plants were forced to shut down for lack of coal; and production was also reduced by the shortage of food and housing.

The survey says, however, "It must be concluded that bomb damage to the civilian economy was not a proximate cause of the military collapse of Germany. There is no evidence that shortages of civilian goods reached a point where the German authorities were forced to transfer resources from war production in order to prevent disintegration of the home front. The most that can be said is that bombing destroyed a substantial part of the consumer goods cushion, and therefore prevented further conversion to war production during 1944. Furthermore, the general strain imposed on the civilian economy by bombing doubtless intensified the effects of the more decisive attacks on other targets."

Germany is now governed by the Allied Control Authority made up of the United States, Great Britain, France and the Union of Soviet Socialist Republics. The basic policy was laid down by the three-power declaration at Potsdam, dated August 2, 1945, to which the United States, Great Britain and the USSR were parties. The basic policy for occupied Germany is implemented by the Control Council made up of the military governors of the four zones of occupation. At Potsdam it was decided that Germany should be treated as a single economic unit during the period of occupation, and "at the earliest practicable date, the German economy should be decentralized for the purpose of eliminating the present excessive concentration of economic power as exemplified in particular by cartels, syndicates, trusts and other monopolistic arrangements."

It was agreed that in organizing the German economy, primary emphasis should be given to the "development of agriculture and peaceable domestic industries." The practical result of the Potsdam Agreement was to set up the framework for four separate Germanies.

The Soviet zone envelops Eastern Germany west of the Oder-Neisse line with its high industrial potential and rich raw material resources. This zone is the best balanced, economically, of the four, producing more than enough food to feed itself, and having extensive brown coal deposits and a number of important industries. The area of the Russian zone is 46,400 square miles and the population is almost 18 million.

While not recognized as a zone of occupation, Poland occupies the area east of the Oder-Neisse line, including Upper Silesia, with its industries and coal regions. Agreement has not yet been reached upon the eastward or some of the other borders.

The British zone, which includes the Ruhr basin where a large part of the German industry is concentrated, is the most valuable industrially of the four zones. The British zone, however, does not produce enough food to be self-supporting. It has been very expensive for the British taxpayers to maintain, for it is estimated the cost to Britain of foodstuffs for the zone amounts to about $300,000,000 a year. This zone has an area of 36,800 square miles and a population of 22,000,000.

The United States zone, which extends southward from the British zone to Austria and eastward from the French zone to Czechoslovakia, is largely agricultural, but has never been able to feed itself. It must get all its coal from the British or French zones, so that its industries are unable to function at anywhere near capacity production. More than four fifths of its steel requirements must be obtained from the other areas. It contains 17,000,000 people in its 42,500 square miles.

The French zone, which extends westward from the United States zone to the French and Luxemburg borders and southward to Switzerland, contains the Saar industrial district, but is not a complete economic entity. The coal mines in the Saar district have been operating at about 85 per cent of normal capacity. This area is the smallest and least populated of all, containing 16,500 square miles and a population of 6,000,000.

The United States and British zones of occupied Germany contain more than 39,000,000 of the 62,000,000 people in Germany, excluding the population of Berlin, which is also divided into four sectors. The two zones contain roughly about three fifths of the industrial capacity and two fifths of the agricultural resources.

The British zone is largely industrialized and the United States zone largely agricultural. Together, the two zones could at least approach self-sufficiency, although they still would be dependent in some measure on imports from other areas.

The three western zones comprise about 70 per cent of Germany's area, and contained about 67 per cent of the total 1939 population. Because of the flow into these three zones of refugees from the Russian zone, of families deported from areas taken from Germany during the war and from adjoining countries, their population percentage today is higher than it was in 1939.

Although the arable land in the three zones amounts to about three fifths of the total, imports are required to support the population. The three zones produced only three fifths of Germany's bread grains before the war.

The miners of the three zones produce more than three fourths of Germany's coal and ore, and the iron and steel plants can turn out more than nine tenths of the total of such products. The three zones produce about three fifths of Germany's total output of nonferrous metals, about four fifths of German iron and steelware, one half of machinery, three fifths of vehicles, nearly three fifths of nonferrous metal wares, two thirds of the chemicals and three fifths of the textiles.

In light manufactures, the three zones produce about one third of all Germany's electric equipment, one half of the optical and precision instruments and one half of the clothing.

In 1936, the three zones accounted for 85 per cent of Germany's exports of mined products, 88 per cent of exported fuels and lubricants, 94 per cent of the iron and steel exported, 72 per cent of primary nonferrous metals exports, 84 per cent of iron and steel wares exported, and 73 per cent of the exported chemicals.

These three zones, however, have not been producing since the end of hostilities at anywhere near a capacity rate. Coal production has been the chief handicap to revived industrial output. As a result of the lack of coal production, Germany's output of steel, machinery, chemicals, textiles and other goods has drastically declined since hostilities ceased.

Western Germany has suffered from a serious food shortage. German farmers, unable to buy anything with Germany's paper money, have hoarded grain and cattle, or else have made their sales in the black market. Workers in many instances have spent their time hunting for food instead of working in the mines and factories.

Observers say that Germany will need substantial food imports in 1948, and, in addition, the steel plants will need iron ore. Other imports will include mine timbers, aluminum, copper, sulphur, fertilizer, rubber and oil. Germany can supply annually at least 50,000,000 tons of the coal western Europe needs for recovery. In return, some foodstuffs might be obtained but little, if any, dollar exchange could be provided.

Germany's extremely low output since the close of hostilities has handicapped the industrial restoration of Western Europe. Since Germany is unable to feed or support itself, its reduced production has also placed a burden on the taxpayers of the United States and the United Kingdom for the occupation of their zones. Several proposals have been advanced, therefore, for Germany's rehabilitation. . . .

Early this year, former President Herbert Hoover pointed out that taxpayers in the United States and Britain are contributing nearly $600,000,000 a year to prevent starvation in their zones with the likelihood that amounts needed will be greater in the years immediately ahead unless action is taken to forestall this. He said revival of German production will do infinitely more for Europe than American loans and charity.

Former President Hoover described the situation in Germany as follows:

In the bizonal area of Germany, after two years since V-E Day, the agricultural production is about 75 per cent of prewar and the industrial production is only at 33 per cent of 1936, and exports are only 3 per cent. . . .

To understand the situation in the German area, we might visualize what would happen if the present policies were imposed on the United States. Suppose America were divided into four zones with little interchange of economic life or food surpluses; with an obligation to tear down and ship abroad 25 per cent of our peace-production plants, and with a restricted level of industry which would destroy 60 per cent of our possible export trade. Then add to this the failure even to designate the plants that are to be removed, so that all initiative to operate the remaining plants is destroyed by uncertainty as to whom the victims will be. Suppose also we were not allowed to produce oil and were limited in fertilizer production. Without relief from some humanitarian country, millions of our people would die.

. . . There are three alternatives before us in our occupied territories: to wash our hands of the whole business and then let the conquered countries drag the whole world to final chaos; or for humanitarian reasons, merely to carry these people on a food subsistence level, hoping for improvement in the attitudes of other nations; or to act at once to free ourselves from their hindrances as far as possible.

Former President Hoover called for the resumption of productivity in German industry subject to a control commission charged with seeing that no part of a revived industry will be put to militaristic uses. He also advocated a unified federal state in Germany, and complete and absolute disarmament of the Germans, with these requirements safeguarded by international guarantees and effective police service by the nations.

Within the last few months, Secretary of State George C. Marshall has proposed a policy for "the revival of a working economy in the world so as to permit the emergence of political and social conditions in which free institutions can exist. . . .

The State, War and Navy Departments approved the text of a new directive to the Military Government in Germany, issued on July 15, which revised the United States policy toward Germany. The directive instructed the United States Military Government of Germany to take the necessary measures to bring about stable political and economic conditions in Germany so that Germany can make a maximum contribution to the recovery of Europe. The directive said that "the level of industry eventually agreed upon for Germany as the basis for reparation removals, while eliminating excess industrial capacity which has been used by Germany for the purpose of making war, should not permanently limit Germany's industrial capacity."

The Potsdam Agreement stated that:

Allied controls shall be imposed upon the German economy, but only to the extent necessary:

1. To carry out programs of industrial disarmament, demilitariza-tion, of reparations and of approved exports and imports.

2. To assure the production and maintenance of goods and services required to meet the needs of the occupying forces and displaced persons in Germany and essential to maintain in Germany average living stand-ards not exceeding the average of the standards of living of European countries. (European countries means all European countries, excluding the United Kingdom and the U.S.S.R.)

3. To insure in the manner determined by the Control Council the equitable distribution of essential commodities between the several zones so as to produce a balanced economy throughout Germany and reduce the need for imports.

4. To control German industry and all economic and financial inter-national transactions, including exports and imports, with the aim of preventing Germany from developing a war potential and of achieving the other objectives named herein.

Former Secretary of the Treasury Henry Morgenthau, Jr. was the spokesman for a body of opinion which called for pastoralizing Germany.

The plans for reparations and the level of postwar German economy in accordance with the Berlin Protocol called for a steel industry production capacity of 7,500,000 ingot tons to be left in Germany with the figure subject to review for further reduction if that should be necessary. The allowable production of steel in Germany was not to exceed 5,800,000 ingot tons in any year without the specific approval of the Allied Control Council.

Under the plan, 40 per cent of the 1936 production capacity of the basic chemical industries, measured by sales in 1936 values, was to be retained, while coal production was to be maximized as far as mining supplies and transportation would allow, with the minimum production estimated at the hard coal equivalent of 155,000,000 tons with at least 45,000,000 tons for export.

The new directive issued July 15, 1947, calls for "the adop-tion of a production and foreign trade program for Germany as a whole which should be directed toward an increasing standard of living in Germany and the attainment at the earliest practicable date of a self-sustaining German economy."

Representatives of sixteen Western European nations, meeting in Paris in August, agreed to set up a Committee of European Economic Cooperation to compile estimates of the amount of help their countries will need with respect to food and agriculture, power, iron and steel and transportation. Other discussions were held simultaneously in Washington between United States and British officials to decide on the course of action to increase Ruhr coal production, and in London between the United States, British and French officials to determine the levels of Germany industry.

The United States and British Military Governments in Germany, accordingly, released a statement late in August saying that production in the United States and British zones of occupied Germany is to be raised to the 1936 level. The statement observes that by 1952 the population of the two zones will probably be from 8,000,000 to 10,000,000 greater than before the war, and on this basis the per capita production capacity in 1952 would be about 75 per cent of that in 1936. Trade and world price as well as population factors were taken into account, the statement continues, adding that the "overriding requirement has been to provide a level of industry necessary to make the area self-supporting." . . .

Already evidence has accumulated that many difficult problems must be solved before the German economy can be restored. One of these arises from the attitudes of Russia and France. Spokesmen for the Russian people, for example, already have asked whether feeding Germany, an enemy, has a higher priority than feeding Russia, an ally. It is also reported that France fears that under the new policy Germany will be given priority over other European nations in reconstruction.

Secretary Marshall has pointed out that the forty-year pact which former Secretary of State Byrnes offered in his Stuttgart speech is still open to Russia and France.

Russia's demand for one fourth of the coal production in the Ruhr has been rejected by the Council of Foreign Ministers. Secretary Marshall replied that this would be impossible without four-power control of food and other resources centered in the Russian zone.

Russia has demanded that seven steel mills in the western zones be dismantled and given to the Russians. Steel production capacity in the Soviet zone is only about 27,000 tons. Under the plans for reparations, German steel production was to be limited to about 5,800,000 tons a year. The capacity greatly exceeds this amount.

Considerable difficulty is anticipated in reaching the export goals set for the western zones. Coal is to be a major export. Coal output in the Ruhr increased at the beginning of 1947, but declined from about 238,000 tons a day in the third week of March to an average of less than 225,000 tons during April and the first week in May, although it is reported to have increased again recently.

One of the reasons for the decline in the coal output was the shortage of food. Miners doing "very heavy" work receive a basic ration of about 4,000 calories as opposed to the current basic consumer ration of 1,550 calories a day. Because they share their rations with their families, miners are said, in many instances, to suffer from under-nourishment. In addition, the average age of the miners is considerably higher than it was before the war, rising from an average of 35 years in 1939 to 43 in 1946. Moreover, some 40 per cent of the more recently employed are reported to have had little or no experience in mining.

Lack of housing has hindered employment of additional miners, since in some parts of the Ruhr more than 80 per cent of the houses were totally destroyed. Other handicaps hindering production have been shortages of material and defects of equipment. It is hard to get suitable timber for pit props and parts for machinery replacement, as well as the proper quality of rubber for belting. The North German Coal Control estimates that existing equipment is adequate for an output of only 350,000 tons a day. It is also estimated that another 70,000 workers are needed and that productivity of the individual miners must be greatly increased.

The official ration in the American zone for the normal consumer varied between 1,545 and 1,560 calories a day during the first three months of 1947. This ranged upward to 2,860 calories for "very heavy" workers. The ration for the normal consumer consists chiefly of potatoes and its caloric content is only slightly more than half the average in prewar Germany.

Dr. Charles E. Brown, American Military Government Medical Nutritionist, in a report on health conditions in the American zone, said that the food shortage in Germany has resulted in average weight losses ranging from 1.8 pounds to 6.3 pounds among Germans of all age groups in the American zone. In March alone, weight losses in all age groups amounted to from 1 to 1½ pounds per person.

The attitude of hopelessness and indifference on the part of the German people reported by many observers is another grave difficulty that must be overcome if production is to be increased to any great extent. One possible solution for this problem that has been advanced is the use of various types of incentives.

A great majority of workers in Germany and England, as well as other groups have been demanding the immediate socialization of the coal and steel industries. In many quarters, red tape is blamed for the low levels of German trade. It is pointed out that restrictions in all the zones handicap both production and marketing.

The total population of Germany in 1946 was 10.2 per cent greater than in 1939. A considerable part of this increase in population is represented by the so-called "displaced persons," most of them being in the United States and British zones.

It has been made abundantly apparent since the war that there can be no return to a self-sustaining economy in Western Europe without the rehabilitation of Germany, among other factors of reconstruction, even though definite progress has been made in individual countries such as Belgium, Holland, Denmark and Norway.

The stake of the United States in the rehabilitation of Germany and of Western Europe is far greater than relief for the taxpayer and the restoration of foreign trade. Without stability in Europe, there can be no peace. Because Germany is the hub of Western Europe, its reconstruction can be viewed as an investment in peace, provided such reconstruction proceeds hand-in-hand with the demilitarization and denazification of the country.

The policy outlined by Secretary Marshall provides for Germany's participation in the ultimate rehabilitation of Western Europe. When the sixteen Western European nations which formed the Committee of European Economic Cooperation have arrived at realistic estimates of the needs of their countries, it will be possible for the United States Congress to decide whether the policy will be implemented with financial aid from this country.

From the economic point of view, there seems to be little hope for the recovery of a sick Europe until Germany is cured.

REPARATIONS PROBLEMS [2]

In January 1924 an authority on reparations, in commenting on the report of the Expert Committee appointed by the Reparation Commission, popularly known as "The Dawes Plan," said: "The reparations problem in all its aspects is far from settled. A new beginning merely has been made." This was more than six years after the capitulation of the German Army.

The Dawes Committee, as will be remembered, had been set up after Germany had defaulted on her reparations payments, to recommend a method of stabilizing the German currency and balancing the German budget. It pointed out in its report, however, that these were essential to Germany's meeting her treaty payments—a euphemism for reparations. As the Committee said, "We have been concerned with the practical means of recovering this debt."

In the light of the current reparations problem, the Dawes report makes interesting reading. It was an attempt to find a way out of the impasse that had been created by the Conference of London, which in May 1921 (seventeen months after the fighting stopped) fixed German reparations obligations at 136

[2] From article by Isador Lubin, Associate United States Representative on the Allied Commission on Reparations. *Academy of Political Science. Proceedings.* 21:522-6. January 1946. Reprinted by permission.

---

billion gold marks or approximately 44 billion . . . gold
dollars. This reparations bill was merely to cover damage done
to the civilian population of the Allies and their property, including pensions for the civilian population. It was not intended to include tribute or punitive damages.

Reparations, as fixed by the London Conference of 1921,
were to be met by annual payments of two billion gold marks
plus 26 per cent of Germany's total exports. These, in part,
were to cover the interest and sinking fund on two series of 5
per cent bonds to be issued during the year 1921, totaling 50
billion marks. A third series of 82 billion gold marks was to be
delivered to the Reparation Commission for later issue.

To overcome the possibility of future default, the Dawes
Plan recommended, among other things, that Germany float a
foreign loan; that the proceeds of the transport tax imposed on
railroad shippers and passengers be devoted to reparations; that
the German-owned railroads be mortgaged and the mortgage
bonds as well as the proceeds from the sale of certain preferred
railroad stock be turned over to the Reparation Commission;
and that an additional five billion gold marks of first mortgage
industrial bonds be also made available. Incidentally, the Dawes
Committee experts suggested that these securities might "be sold
to the extent to which the financial markets are capable of ab-
sorbing them," which, of course, meant sales in foreign markets.
At that time this meant primarily the United States and Great
Britain.

The current reparations plan had its origin in Yalta in February 1945, when we were still shelling Cologne and the Rhine
was still a hurdle that our military technicians figured might take
months to overcome. Negotiations were started by the Allied
Commission on Reparations in Moscow in June, some six weeks
after the fall of Berlin. The plan was formally agreed to by the
United States, Great Britain and the USSR in August.

The question of reparations details was first raised at Yalta
by the USSR. Their representative proposed:

1. Within two years of the end of the war, plant, equipment, German investments abroad, and other assets, to a value of approximately
ten billion dollars, should be removed from the German national wealth.

The main determinant in making these removals, the USSR recommended, should be the extent to which they furthered the military and economic disarmament of Germany.

2. Recurrent reparations in the form of annual deliveries of goods to the total of ten billion dollars should be paid over a period of ten years.

There was no action taken at Yalta as to the use of German labor as reparations. The USSR recommended that this question be put aside and considered at a later date. She further proposed that reparations be distributed in a manner which gave first consideration to those countries which had carried the greatest burden and had contributed the most toward victory. In conformity with this principle, she suggested that the USSR receive one half of the reparations.

It was agreed that a reparations commission, to consist of the United States, the United Kingdom and the USSR, be set up in Moscow to study and make recommendations to the three governments. No commitment was made either by the United States or by Great Britain on the proposals made by the USSR. They were merely to be used as a basis of discussion by the Commission with the further proviso that an additional criterion to be used in the distribution of reparations should be the losses suffered at the hands of the Nazis. The only agreement made at Yalta was that reparations should be paid in the form of removals from the national wealth of Germany and in annual deliveries in kind; that removals should be primarily for the purpose of disarming Germany both militarily and economically; and that the Commission should look into the USSR suggestion that the total should be twenty billion dollars.

The policy of the United States as reflected in its instructions to its delegation to Moscow provided, among other things, that industrial capacity which might be dangerous to the security of the United States should be eliminated. Plant and equipment should be distributed in a manner which would aid most effectively in rebuilding the damage done by Germany and in hastening the restoration and raising the standard of living of the nonenemy nations of Europe. In order to avoid the fiasco of the World War I reparations plan, as a result of which payments could be made by Germany only through the revival and expansion of her industry by outside capital, the delegation was instructed to approve of no plan which would promote or necessitate the building up of the German economy or require the financing of German reconstruction or reparations with foreign funds. Accordingly, such recurring reparations as might be agreed to should be as small as possible as compared with removals of plant and equipment. They should consist, to the greatest extent possible, of raw materials and natural resources, and of a minimum of manufactured goods.

As to the question of reparations in the form of labor, the policy of the United States was that compulsory labor should be required only from the judicially convicted war criminal class. Among the latter were to be included proved members of public and private European Axis organizations that had been adjudicated to be criminal. Such reparations labor as might be furnished should be used principally for reconstruction and repair of war damage; should be limited to a definite span of years and be subject to humane employment and living standards.

At no time during the discussions at either Moscow or Potsdam was the question of reparations labor formally raised by either Great Britain or the USSR. Indeed, the only official action taken on this matter was the formal filing of the United States official policy, namely, that reparations labor should be limited to war criminals and members of criminal organizations.

In the short time between the inauguration of the discussions in Moscow and the meeting in Postdam—slightly more than three weeks—considerable progress was made toward agreeing on fundamental reparations policies. Owing in part to the fact that the unknown state of German industrial equipment at that moment made it impossible to fix a final reparations bill, the Soviet proposal that reparations be fixed at twenty billion dollars, with one half going to the USSR, did not materialize. Moreover, in order to avoid fixing financial commitments which it might later prove impossible for Germany to meet, there was opposition to any valuation of reparations in terms of dollars. The issue was resolved by providing that, regardless of what the value of the plant, equipment and other assets to be removed, as well as of the recurrent payments in kind, turned out to be, each of the three participating governments would give up proportionately from their respective shares such amounts as might be required to meet the valid claims of all the countries entitled to reparations. In other words, the amount that each of the three powers would receive was to remain undetermined. The size of their shares would ultimately be determined by the amounts that would eventually be assigned to all of the other claimant nations. At Potsdam this arrangement was changed and reparations were put on a zonal basis.

There was virtually no difficulty in reaching an agreement on most of the general principles embodied in the instructions to the American delegation. One stumbling block, however, was the question of paying for such imports as were necessary to maintain a minimum German economy. Throughout the proceedings the United States, as well as Great Britain contended that the payment for imports should take precedence over reparations deliveries from current production and existing inventories. With the knowledge that there was no alternative other than for the United States to ship food and other raw materials into Germany even to maintain a subsistence standard of living, it was evident that unless some such provision were agreed to we would find ourselves in the position of financing the German economy while others were taking out the products of German factories and mines as reparations. The Soviet point of view, on the other hand, was that the peoples of the devastated areas of all of Europe, and particularly her own citizens, should not be put into a position where food and materials for Germans would appear to be given preference over their own drastic requirements, not only for reconstruction but for the restoration of their standard of living. This problem, later resolved at Potsdam, and definitions of war booty and restitution, were the more important of the unresolved issues before the Allied Commission on Reparations when the Big Three assembled.

The reparations agreement arrived at in Potsdam is too well known to require much elaboration. Briefly, it provides that the Soviets are to secure their reparations from the zone they occupy in Germany, together with certain German external assets. They are also to receive 10 per cent of the industrial equipment that may be removed from the western zones, plus an additional 15 per cent for which they are to pay in an equivalent value of food, coal and other products. Since the area occupied by the USSR includes German territory already under Polish control, Poland is to have its claims met from the Soviets' share. The claims of all other countries are to be met from the zones occupied by the United States, the United Kingdom and France.

POSTWAR TREATMENT OF GERMANY [3]

How did our policy towards Germany evolve? It was a matter which President Roosevelt considered of crucial importance and about which he held strong convictions. The keystone of the President's wartime policy was the development and maintenance of solidarity among the Allies both to accomplish the complete defeat of our enemies and for the subsequent winning of the peace. Less than one month after we entered the war, the United Nations was founded. The Joint Declaration by the United Nations, issued at Washington on January 1, 1942, stressed the essentiality of the full use of resources to achieve complete victory, and the signatory governments also pledged themselves to refrain from making any separate armistice or peace with the enemies.

As a further step in strengthening the United Nations solidarity and assuring the complete defeat of our enemies, President Roosevelt devised the now famous formula of unconditional surrender. He secured the British Prime Minister's acceptance of this formula at the Casablanca meeting in January 1943, and the principle was subsequently submitted to and accepted by Marshal Stalin.

At the Teheran Conference in November 1943, President Roosevelt, Marshal Stalin, and Prime Minister Churchill reached an understanding for the military occupation of Germany after unconditional surrender had been achieved. Occupation by the forces of the three powers was to be on a zonal basis, with a

[3] By Henry Morgenthau, Jr., Secretary of the Treasury, 1934-1945. *Annals of the American Academy of Political and Social Science.* 246:125-9. July 1946. Reprinted by permission.

consultative and coordinating body at the top. There was also some preliminary discussion of other questions of policy towards defeated Germany. The Teheran plan for three-power occupation of Germany was revised at Yalta to include France as an occupying power.

This, then, was the general background—unconditional surrender, to be followed by military occupation of Germany along zonal lines. This was the framework into which our plans had to be fitted. The policy issues involved began to be considered and discussed at the Cabinet level in the summer of 1944. During a visit to the European theater at that time, I had an opportunity to look into the plans for occupation of Germany which were then being prepared at SHAEF. This planning was being carried on by British and American officers in the staff division concerned with military government. It seemed to me that these military plans placed too great a share of the responsibility for rehabilitating Germany on the occupying forces rather than on the German people themselves, and that not enough emphasis was being placed on the task of destroying Nazi influence and eliminating Germany's industrial potential for war. In any event, it was clear that these were important issues of national policy which ought not to be decided at a technical military level.

On returning to Washington, I reported these impressions and views to President Roosevelt. I found that he, himself, had already given a great deal of thought to these issues and that his own convictions and views were in close accord with the opinions which I had expressed. Following my report to him, the President directed that the question of policy toward defeated Germany be considered by Mr. Hull, Mr. Stimson, and myself. In the ensuing month, the three of us explored and discussed this problem at considerable length. Failing to reach full agreement, each one submitted his own views to the President who made the final decision. That decision was essentially in accord with the President's earlier conclusions and it did not differ significantly from my own views on the subject.

At the Quebec Conference in September 1944, the President raised with Mr. Churchill this question of treatment of Germany. He invited me to Quebec to join in these conversations. At the conclusion of the discussions on this topic, a memomandum of agreement was dictated by Prime Minister Churchill to his secretary and was then read and initialed by him and by President Roosevelt. Because I feel that it may be helpful for the record, I am going to quote this memorandum.

At a conference between the President and the Prime Minister upon the best measures to prevent renewed rearmament by Germany, it was felt that an essential feature was the future disposition of the Ruhr and the Saar.

The ease with which the metallurgical, chemical, and electric industries in Germany can be converted from peace to war has already been impressed upon us by bitter experience. It must also be remembered that the Germans have devastated a large portion of the industries of Russia and of other neighboring Allies, and it is only in accordance with justice that these injured countries should be entitled to remove the machinery they require in order to repair the losses they have suffered. The industries referred to in the Ruhr and in the Saar would therefore be necessarily put out of action and closed down. It was felt that the two districts should be put under some body under the world organization which would supervise the dismantling of these industries and make sure that they were not started up again by some subterfuge.

This program for eliminating the war-making industries in the Ruhr and in the Saar is looking forward to converting Germany into a country primarily agricultural and pastoral in its character.

The Prime Minister and the President were in agreement upon this program.

September 15, 1944   (Intd.) O. K.
                                                    F. D. R.
                                             (Intd.) W. S. C.

After this agreement was reached, the question whether northwestern Germany, including the Ruhr, should be occupied by American or by British forces was quickly settled in Britain's favor. This question had previously been the subject of much debate over a number of months.

Before going ahead to describe the subsequent stages in the development of Allied policy toward Germany, I should like to digress briefly in order to comment on two features of this Quebec memorandum. The first feature is that this laid special emphasis on the disposition of the Ruhr and the Saar. The Saar will, I presume, be formally transferred in due course to France, but the question of the disposition of the Ruhr is still unsettled. The French proposal for internationalization of this critically important industrial area has not been given a thorough hearing. . . .

Second, the Quebec memorandum sets forth the objective of converting Germany into a primarily agricultural country, through the elimination of war-making industries. I believe in this policy. I wish also to emphasize, however, that the policy is an official policy of governments, not—as is so often alleged —a personal scheme or plot of mine.

What this policy means has also been the subject of much misrepresentation, sometimes deliberately hostile. The policy means a reorientation of German economic life away from heavy industries which cater to the war machine, towards agriculture and other activities directly related to the satisfaction of civilian wants.

In my book, *Germany Is Our Problem*, I have put forward a detailed blueprint for effecting this reorientation. Despite her intense concentration on heavy industry and armaments, Germany before the war employed more workers in agriculture than did the United States, out of a smaller working population than ours. During the war, Germany was nearly self-sufficient in foodstuffs. If Germany's industrial war potential is to be eliminated, a substantial proportion of the workers released must be absorbed in agriculture unless they are to remain unemployed in cities. Agricultural activities must become the largest single field of employment for the German population. Far from being an inhuman program, this is the only humane way of effecting the necessary industrial disarmament of Germany. It is probable that the transfer to Poland of a substantial part of eastern Germany will prevent Germany from reaching full-self-sufficiency in food, even with increased productive effort, but this need not interfere with maximum concentration of effort in agriculture.

So far as I am aware, no one has proposed the elimination of all German industry. Certainly I have not, although if I did not know better, listening to my critics would long ago have convinced me that I had. As is clearly set forth on pages 70 and 71 of my book for anyone who wishes to find out, my proposed blueprint, based on Germany's 1937 frontiers, calls for the retention of 6,600,000 workers in industry and an additional 5,000,000 to 6,000,000 in transportation, utilities, and trade. Because of the loss of eastern territory to Poland, a somewhat larger proportion of German workers will have to be employed in light manufacturing to provide the exports to pay for needed food imports. This necessitates some modifications in the detailed blueprint, but does not call for any alteration in the essential substance of the policy. So much for that.

After Quebec, the next forward step in Allied planning for Germany was taken at Yalta in February 1945. The communique issued at the end of this Big Three Conference contained a comprehensive, general agreement on policy toward Germany. Here are the key sentences:

It is our inflexible purpose to destroy German militarism and nazism and to ensure that Germany will never again be able to disturb the peace of the world. We are determined to disarm and disband all German armed forces; break up for all time the German General Staff that has repeatedly contrived the resurgence of German militarism; remove or destroy all German military equipment; eliminate or control all German industry that could be used for military production; bring all war criminals to just and swift punishment and exact reparation in kind for the destruction wrought by the Germans; wipe out the Nazi party, Nazi laws, organizations and institutions, remove all Nazi and militarist influences from public office and from the cultural and economic life of the German people; and take in harmony such other measures in Germany as may be necessary to the future peace and safety of the world. It is not our purpose to destroy the people of Germany, but only when nazism and militarism have been extirpated will there be hope for a decent life for Germans and a place for them in the comity of nations.

The final step in the process of reaching Allied agreement on Germany was taken at Postdam. The accomplishment at Potsdam was to translate into more specific terms the general principles agreed upon at Yalta.

The Potsdam communique contains specific agreements on "the political and economic prinicples to govern the treatment of Germany in the initial control period" and on German reparations. I shall quote only a few significant sentences from the Potsdam Agreement:

In order to eliminate Germany's war potential, the production of arms, ammunition, and implements of war as well as all types of aircraft and sea-going ships shall be prohibited and prevented. Production of metals, chemicals, machinery, and other items that are directly necessary to a war economy shall be rigidly controlled and restricted to Germany's approved post-war peacetime needs. . . . Productive capacity not needed for permitted production shall be removed in accordance with the reparations plan recommended by the Allied Commission on reparations and approved by the governments concerned, or if not removed shall be destroyed. In organizing the German economy, primary emphasis shall be given to the development of agriculture and peaceful domestic industries. The amount of equipment to be removed from the western zones on account of reparations must be determined within six months from now at the latest. Removals of industrial capital equipment shall begin as soon as possible and shall be completed within two years from the determination specified [in the preceding paragraphs].

This completes the story, so far as my knowledge goes, of the main steps in the formulation of Allied policy toward Germany. The process of evolving this policy extended over a period of two and a half years—through Casablanca, Teheran, Quebec, Yalta, and finally Potsdam. President Roosevelt's masterful and wise influence is evident throughout—even at Potsdam when he was no longer alive. I shall always be proud of the part which the President gave me the opportunity to play in assisting in the formulation of a plan for Germany which would contribute towards world peace.

What is our policy toward Germany today? Officially, it presumably still remains the policy contained in the Potsdam protocol and in our published general directive, to the Commander of the United States occupying forces, on the military government of Germany, known as J.C.S. 1067. In any event, no statement has been made to indicate that these documents do not stand as our policy today.

How is the policy being applied? The consensus of almost all observers is that the whole program to make Germany incapable of future aggression is being applied hesitantly and half-heartedly. This is true with respect to denazification, removal of industrial plants, seizure of German external assets and de-cartelization.

Why has the program not been vigorously carried out? It would be easy to blame the men on the spot, to say that the contractor hasn't followed the architect's blueprint. I don't believe that this is the whole story. I think that the men on the spot

haven't received from London, Moscow, Paris, and Washington
the continuing guidance, clarification and support which they
need to do the job and I'm afraid that occasionally the men on
the spot may have received the impression that their governments
don't want the blueprints to be followed very closely anyway.

Why have Britain and the United States been so reluctant to
carry out in Germany the broad policies on which they have professed agreement with each other and with the Soviet Union?
The usual excuse is that humanitarian considerations have made
it necessary to concentrate on rehabilitation, that destruction of
Germany's war potential can come later. But this excuse is
specious. As I have already indicated, the removal of Germany's
war potential goes hand in hand with the reorientation of economic life towards agriculture and light manufacturing to meet
consumer needs.

I cannot escape the feeling that the main reason for reluctance to carry out the program is of a quite different sort. It
is that some of the people concerned really don't want a weak
Germany. Despite the experience of two World Wars, they
still prefer a strong Germany.

Basic conflicts and disagreements among Great Britain,
France, Russia, and the United States made possible the come-
back of German militarism after the defeat of 1918 and led inexorably to World War II. Will disputes among the victors
lead them again into competition for the allegiance of a resurgent
Germany, and from this into World War III? The danger of
the kind of split which would give Germany another chance has
already become serious. Many Germans, even today, are hoping
and working for precisely this objective.

In my judgment, the failure of the occupying powers to carry
out a clearcut, cohesive policy to remove the threat of future
German aggression lies at the heart of present United Nations
difficulties. If we can reach real agreement on the treatment of
Germany, even at this late date, the other elements in the European settlement will fall into place. If we fail in Germany, the
effort to agree on such matters as peace terms for Italy, Rumania
and the rest will be abortive, and the old pattern of European
power politics will become solidly entrenched. The foundation

for renewed German aggression and future war will have been laid.

I call on the signatories of the Potsdam Agreement—the United States, British, and Soviet Governments—to carry out in Germany the spirit and letter of this agreement. Many valuable months have been lost. Even so, it may not be too late if the signatories of the Potsdam Agreement begin now to confirm by action their faith in this agreement and their confidence in each other, so that we may look forward to peace in Europe.

EUROPE AND THE RUHR [4]

Discussion among the Allied powers on the level of industrial output to be permitted to Germany, and the amount of reparations to be exacted, have inevitably focussed attention upon the Ruhr, which is the principal center of German heavy industry. From this angle its future, both political and economic, is of greater importance than that of any other single piece of ex-enemy territory. Britain, as temporary trustee for that part of Germany which includes the Ruhr, is responsible for carrying out any Allied agreements affecting it, and has therefore the most direct interest in seeing that the terms of such agreements are workable. But every country on the continent of Europe is more or less intimately concerned with developments in an area which has been for many decades its main industrial concentration. The fact that it has also been the chief source of Germany's military power in modern times ought not to obscure the part the Ruhr has played, and to a considerable degree must continue to play, in raising and maintaining the level of the European economy. Having been led by Germany into a major war on two occasions within a generation, the world is entitled to take all necessary steps to ensure that there is no third occasion. But security measures which involve economic breakdown and the impoverishment of Europe in the long run only make for greater insecurity. . . .

[4] From *Planning* [organ of Political and Economic Planning, London]. No. 256:1-19. October 4, 1946. Reprinted by permission of New Republic, New York.

In restricting the output of the Ruhr the powers took no account of the needs of those countries which before the war depended on German exports of coal, iron and steel, chemicals and machinery. In the case of coal, the Ruhr is bound to be even more important to the rest of Europe than it was before the war, owing to the disappearance of exports from Britain. The future of the Ruhr must be discussed in relation to the economies of France, Holland, Belgium and Luxembourg, each of which controls a part of the main center of European heavy industry—comprising the Ruhr, Saar, Lorraine, Southern Belgium and Luxembourg—or the ports which serve it. . . .

The characteristics of Ruhr industries were their scale, integration and efficiency; by-products were recovered and used, power conserved, and costs kept low by excellent transport and other facilities. Moreover, the reserve of human skills concentrated in the Ruhr will largely be lost if its industries are destroyed or dispersed to other countries. In view of the manpower situation in many of these countries, it is unlikely that this loss could be made good.

Discussions on the future of the Ruhr have tended to be concerned with the political aspect of the problem. Alternative schemes—of which the French plan for complete separation of the area from the rest of Germany is but one example—have been put forward, but few of them are based on an examination of the economic situation. It is true that any decisions which may be taken about the Ruhr, whether they relate to forms of control or levels of industry, are in essence political decisions. Nevertheless, they must be based squarely on a knowledge of the facts and on the best available estimate of the effect they will have on Germany and the rest of Europe. . . .

The Ruhr is a convenient but loose description of the area . . . which . . . includes not only the land which lies along the valley of the Ruhr River above the hard coal field, but also the brown coal fields west of the Rhine, as well as towns and factories which, although outside the Ruhr valley, are closely linked with it.

This was before the war the greatest coal field and the greatest and most concentrated industrial area in Western Europe.

It was unique in Europe in that it combined the advantages of inland location and direct communication with the sea. Lying almost a hundred miles up the Rhine, it could nevertheless receive ocean-going ships, and its ports handled as much tonnage as Swansea and Cardiff combined. It was linked to the rest of Germany and Europe by canals and a complex of railways and roads. . . .

Some idea of the close knitting of Ruhr industry can be obtained from a study of the great combines which dominated the mining and heavy industries. Twelve firms accounted for 74 per cent of the coal output and 85 per cent of the coke output; of these six were the main iron and steel concerns. Nearly half of the coal output (i.e. about one sixth of the total output of continental Europe, excluding Russia) and a large percentage of the coke ovens were controlled by these six steel firms; the financial integration of the heavy industries was reflected in the physical location of their plant. . . .

Today the Ruhr is in the paradoxical situation of having an increased population and reduced industrial activity, and at the same time a shortage of able-bodied men in almost all categories from unskilled manual labor through the skilled trades to the executive levels. This is the result of the war and postwar conditions. In addition to the casualties suffered, prisoners of war are still retained by many countries, including France, Belgium, Russia and Britain. There is difficulty in recruiting young miners, while the interzonal barriers prevent new labor coming from Eastern Germany to meet the demand. At present the only intake is composed of refugees, chiefly old men, women and children. Thus, while the present population is above the prewar level the available able-bodied manpower is much below.

In the past, owing to its dependence on heavy industry, the Ruhr has been more subject to unemployment than the rest of Germany. The danger of a policy of drastic restriction is that unemployment will again fall heavily on this area. . . .

The direct importance of the Ruhr as a market and as a supplier of coal has been underlined by recent events, which have emphasized its food deficiency and its importance as a source of coal exports. It is impossible to estimate exactly what proportions of Germany's imports of food from Holland and Denmark went to the Ruhr, but they were probably considerable and would be likely to be severely reduced by depression in the Ruhr. Its importance as a market for iron ore has already been indicated, and the extent of transit trade through Holland has been mentioned. Holland before the war had a negative balance of trade with Germany, and paid for part of its essential imports of fertilizers, machinery and iron and steel by the shipping earnings from the Rhine traffic to the Ruhr. Commercial services, such as insurance, were also connected with Ruhr trade and added to Dutch and Belgian exchange resources. The disappearance of Great Britain as a coal exporter has made all these countries look to the Ruhr for a larger part of their supplies, though the present exports are less than a million tons per month. . . .

In the near future, the limiting factors on Ruhr output are the physical effects of war: complete destruction of some plants, unrepaired damage to many others, the effects of food shortage, and the losses of able-bodied labor. These are aggravated by some of the political consequences of the war: the division into zones hampering movements of trade and manpower, and the removal of German directorates and key technicians. But in spite of the desperate position at the moment it should not be thought that the Ruhr, if left unrestricted, is so badly damaged that it could never recover its prewar importance. The steel potential has been reduced by perhaps 2 million tons by the complete destruction of plant, and coal production may be reduced 10 per cent by the loss of collieries which have been so badly damaged as to be virtually irreparable. These, however, are comparatively small reductions in relation to the potential capacity of the surviving plant.

It should be emphasized that, apart from the question of manpower, the potential capacity of the Ruhr is considerably higher than the levels imposed under the reparations plan. The chief factor which will determine the actual capacity of the Ruhr, say five years hence, is the level of output permitted and achieved in the meantime—above all the level of the steel output which is required to make good war damage and maintenance repairs in the mines, the gas grid, the electricity system, the industrial plants, and other buildings in the Ruhr towns. It must also be determined by the priority which such repairs in the Ruhr are given against competing demands for reconstruction elsewhere.

At present the industrial output of the Ruhr is limited by coal supplies, themselves limited by manpower shortages, the effects of the food situation and the policy of maximizing coal exports. But steel supplies for the mines would become the bottleneck if these problems were eased. The level of steel output fixed in the reparations plan is therefore of vital importance.

Under the plan, German steel capacity is to be reduced to 7.5 million tons, and the level of output has been provisionally fixed at 5.8 million tons. This may be compared with a German output of 5.6 million tons in the worst year of the 'thirties, and an output from Belgium and Luxembourg in 1937 of 6.4 million tons. The figure agreed on is the result of a compromise between the powers, and is nearer to the original Russian minimum proposal than to the British figure at the other end of the scale. The Russian proposal was based on the principle of allowing Germany only the European average of steel per head of the population; this average is heavily weighted by the agricultural countries which use little steel. Germany must support a greater density of population and relatively more town dwellers than most countries in Europe, and for this reason alone requires more steel for constructional purposes. Reliable statistics for the prewar consumption of steel in Germany are difficult to obtain, but it is generally thought that an output of 8 to 9 million tons will be found to be the minimum necessary to cover all essential requirements. . . .

The economic facts all point one way. The Ruhr was the most important economic area in Europe so far as coal and steel were concerned. There is no immediate prospect of making good any large cuts in Ruhr output from other sources. The need for Ruhr production is great both in Germany and Europe, yet its production at present is pitifully low. The economic conclusion is therefore that, so far from being restricted, Ruhr production for peace time industries should be stimulated to the utmost.

Having said this, however, one is brought up against the political problem. Europe will not tolerate a third German war. The Allies may prefer to accept a decrease in the rate of their own recovery and to pay for essential imports into Germany (both of which will be inevitable if Germany is left without an exportable surplus) rather than to run the smallest risk of allowing Germany to regain a dominant position in Europe. But if this is to be avoided it will be necessary to devise some form of control which would allow production for peaceful purposes and for the benefit of Europe as a whole to be maximized. Although it will require a measure of agreement and cooperation between the Allied powers which has not so far been forthcoming, it should not be impossible to combine international control of the Ruhr with maximum production. . . . What is clear is that a policy of deindustrialisation is a policy of despair. It says in effect: "Since we cannot tame the animal we must destroy it." Unfortunately, the issue is not so simple, for the destruction of the Ruhr involves the loss of its potentialities for good as well as for evil. Once the industries of the Ruhr have been smashed or transplanted and its workers demoralized, the opportunity to carry out a constructive policy will have been lost.

AMERICAN POLICY CONCERNING GERMAN MONOPOLIES [5]

On February 12, 1947, laws entitled "Prohibition of Excessive Concentration of German Economic Power" were simultaneously promulgated by the military governments in the United States and British zones of Germany. Although it is premature to attempt an appraisal of the actual effect of these "decartelization" laws on the structure of German industry, their enactment signifies the culmination of about a year and a half of effort at statutory implementation of the Potsdam provision that—

At the earliest practicable date, the German economy shall be decentralized for the purpose of eliminating the present excessive concentration

[5] By Isaiah Frank, Chief of the Special Areas Section, Industry Branch, International Resources Division, Office of International Trade Policy, Department of State. *Department of State Bulletin*. 16:913-18. May 11, 1947.

of economic power as exemplified in particular by cartels, syndicates, trusts and other monopolistic arrangements.

An analysis of the economic and political basis for American policy concerning German cartels and combines would lie beyond the scope of the present article. Three considerations, however, may be mentioned as of paramount importance.

1. It is recognized that the emergence in Germany of a liberal democratic government would be prejudiced if the economic power concentrated in the hands of German monopolists could be used in the political sphere to pursue their traditional anti-democratic aims.

2. Our conception of a postwar world free from restrictions on production and trade imposed by international cartels and combines could scarcely be realized if steps were not taken now to prevent the future resumption of German industry's role as organizer and leader of restrictive organizations. Internal combination and cartelization of German industry served as the essential basis for her sponsorship of such organizations in the international field.

3. Allied security interests require the elimination of German monopoly. In combination with other important elements in German society such as "Junkerdom" and a militaristic tradition, the monopolistic organization of German industry has served indirectly as a cause of aggression. Monopoly leads to high prices, reduced output, and excess capacity with resultant pressures to engage in dumping or to enlarge the protected market through territorial conquest. In addition a monopolistic industrial structure tends to increase the rate of profit and therefore of savings while at the same time reducing opportunities for independent investment. Under normal conditions of private capitalism this situation typically aggravates the problem of unemployment and maldistribution of income and makes for political instability and extremism.

This article presents briefly a statement of the position which monopolies occupied in Germany both before and during the Nazi regime and an account of attempts by the United States to deal with the problem since the end of the war.

Concentration of German industry had progressed rapidly before the Nazis came to power. In terms of organization it was achieved principally through the establishment of combines and cartels. Though both forms of organization have assumed numerous variations, the combine may be described essentially as an enterprise uniting under common ownership or management competitors (horizontal combine) or producers at several stages in the production process (vertical combine). Cartels, on the other hand, are contractual arrangements among legally independent enterprises for the purpose of avoiding or reducing competition. Though the controls bearing on any particular market situation were likely to consist of elements of both types of arrangements, the cartel was in a sense a secondary manifestation of the condition in which a relatively few firms controlled a large part of German capital and production. In fields where powerful combines existed the pressure was strong upon all firms in an industry to conform to their policies through participating in a cartel.

The prototypes of the combines were those within so-called "heavy industry." Single *Konzerne* controlled extensive mining properties, coking plants, iron and steel works, heavy engineering works, and in a number of cases inland navigation companies. They dominated the Rhine-Ruhr region, the middle German industrial region, and Upper Silesia. The merger and growth of large firms both vertically and horizontally spread from iron and steel and its closely allied industries to chemicals, the electro-technical field, light metals, and later the great synthetic industries, including textiles.

Many reasons have been advanced for this growth of monopoly in Germany on a scale which has few parallels in industrially developed countries. Considerable emphasis is placed by some economic historians on the relatively late but rapid industrialization of Germany, accounted for in part by the lack of political unification during most of the nineteenth century. In other western countries technical knowledge and organizational forms developed slowly and were accompanied by the establishment of a strong and independent middle class with a tradition of economic liberalism and political democracy appropriate to such a social structure. In Germany, however, the compression of industrial development within a relatively short space of time meant the superimposition of large-scale industry upon a frame-work of institutions essentially preindustrial or "feudal" in char-acter.

Concentration was further encouraged before and during World War I by the allocation of government armament orders which constituted the largest single outlet for the productive capacity of heavy industry. After the war the inflation wiped out substantial elements of small and medium-sized business and left the combines in a position to acquire additional properties at bargain rates. The merger process was abetted by the use for such purposes of indemnities received by heavy industry for the loss of properties in Lorraine and Silesia. In this connection it should be noted that, although the process of trustification relied for its political support upon the conservative elements in the community, it was never vigorously opposed by the Left, which regarded industrial concentration as a process that would facili-tate the tasks of socialization.

The effectiveness of cartel controls in Germany was in good measure a consequence of the dominant role played by the big combines. Though small and inefficient enterprises were some-times kept alive under the protection of cartel agreements, basic policies were set by the larger firms. Voting power within the cartel was commonly based on a member's production quota, a circumstance which encouraged the merger process since the quota went along with the rest of the firm's assets. Cartelization also stimulated vertical combination as a device to avoid the necessity of purchasing materials in high-price, cartelized mar-kets.

Membership in the pre-Nazi cartels was, at least nominally, voluntary except for a few cases such as coal and potash in which compulsory organizations were set up by special parliamentary enactment. The freedom not to join and also to withdraw from cartels made possible in certain fields periodic outbursts of com-petition often induced by struggles surrounding the bargaining for higher quotas.

Private market regulation of the cartel variety was a socially sanctioned and legally accepted way of doing business in Ger-many. Many court decisions reflected the view that price and quota agreements were a more civilized method of ordering the market than the "anarchy" of free competition. At times of national economic crisis, however, public sentiment became aroused against monopolies to the point where the government was forced to take formal steps. The most sweeping of the Weimar decrees for the regulation of cartels in the public interest came in 1923 when the inflation had brought about the impoverishment of substantial sectors of the middle class while at the same time strengthening the position of big business. The 1923 decree vested broad powers in the government to void existing agreements and to enjoin cartels from engaging in practices which were prejudicial to the economic welfare of the community. These powers were strengthened in another decree issued in 1930 in response to pressures that rose during the business collapse.

Despite the considerable grants of statutory power to prevent and remedy the worst abuses of cartels, the Weimar Government seldom took action. The laws remained on the statute books practically as dead letters while the cartels consolidated their position domestically and extended their power beyond Germany's borders to become the dominant factors in the network of international cartels that blanketed European industry.

Though the concentration of German industry progressed rapidly under the Weimar Government, the process was greatly accelerated after the Nazis came to power. One indication of the point reached in this process is furnished by the advance of integration in Germany's coal mines, which, along with potash, represent her only significant indigenous resource of raw materials and the basis for her vast iron and steel, chemical, and synthetic industries. In 1913 the independent coal mines controlled over 50 per cent of the coal fields, whereas in 1940 all but 10 per cent of the coal fields passed into captive hands. This figure was further reduced during the war by the incorporation of some of the remaining mines into the Ruhr steel combines.

The Nazi Government pursued a positive policy of encouragaging the amalgamation of small and especially medium-sized firms into the larger combines. Joint concerns were compulsorily established in certain fields, such as synthetics, where rapid

expansion was desired. Rationalization of industry with a view
to increasing the efficiency of the industrial machine for military
purposes became, in effect, a device for eliminating or combing
out the inefficient, i.e. smaller, concerns. Aryanization of Jewish
property provided an opportunity to acquire the property of
former competitors, a factor which was especially important in
the consumer-goods industries. The Germanization of property
in occupied Europe meant the accretion to existing combines of
substantial blocks of foreign industrial assets, in many cases at
nominal prices. Perhaps of paramount importance in shaping
the attitude of the Nazi Government toward the extension of the
dominion of existing combines was the conviction that such
concentration, by reducing the number of units with which
government would have to deal, would simplify the task of
mobilizing the economy for war and would facilitate administration during active hostilities.

Whereas the Weimar Government merely refrained from
interfering with cartels, the Nazis adopted a conscious policy of
strengthening cartels with a view to using them to further
national objectives.

The movement to consolidate individual business enterprises
had its analogue in the "rationalization" of associations of business. By the latter stages of the war the 2,500 cartels, which
it is estimated had formerly existed, were merged into approximately 500 cartels, mostly of a national character. Much of
this consolidation was accomplished at the direction of the government which, shortly after coming into power, issued a compulsory cartelization decree vesting in the Minister of Economics
the power to create new cartels with compulsory membership
and to order any firm to join an existing cartel.

As industrial capacity in Germany became fully utilized in
response to military demands, the traditional functions of the
cartels as market-regulating bodies disappeared. Price-fixing was
adopted by the government as an anti-inflationary measure,
restrictionism in production gave away to efforts to maximize
output, orders and raw materials became centrally allocated, and
research and technology were compulsorily pooled. In this
economic environment the cartels and super-cartels established

by the authorities (*Gruppen, Ringe, Reichsvereinigungen*) became the self-governing organizations of business, carrying out
under general directives the various regulatory functions involved
in state-planned production and distribution. Needless to say,
the power which the cartels and cartel-like organizations exercised over their members became vastly enhanced by the fact
that they became the officially established points of contact between the central German Government and the individual firms
in an industry.

As the Allied military occupation of Germany progressed,
official recognition was given to the necessity for uprooting
monopolistic organizations from the entrenched positions which
they had established in German economic and political life. In
April 1945 the directive to the Commander in Chief of United
States Forces of Occupation (JCS 1067) included the following:

> You will prohibit all cartels or other private business arrangements
> and cartel-like organizations, including those of a public or quasi-public
> character such as the *Wirtschaftsgruppen* providing for the regulation of
> marketing conditions, including production, prices, exclusive exchange of
> technical information and processes, and allocation of sales territories.
> Such necessary functions as have been discharged by these organizations
> shall be absorbed as rapidly as possible by approved public agencies.
> . . . It is the policy of your government to effect a dispersion of
> the ownership and control of German industry. . . .

This was followed shortly after the formal surrender of Germany by a directive from USFET to the commanding generals
of the military districts outlawing cartels. Then in August of
the same year was signed the Potsdam declaration, reiterating
our commitment to eliminate excessive concentrations of economic power in the form of both combines and cartels.

Implementation of official United States policy in this field
has not been as rapid or vigorous as many had hoped. As with
all occupation policies, the necessity for dealing with certain
pressing short-run problems of economic revival, such as coal,
food, and the foreign-trade deficit, tended to push into the
background long-run objectives having to do with the basic
shape of the German economy. Perhaps even overshadowing
such conflicts of priority, the program has also suffered from
varying interpretations on the part of the occupying powers as

to the ultimate objectives of the deconcentration program and as to the manner in which it ought to be carried out. These differences—though highly revealing in themselves as reflecting some of the basic divergencies in over-all policy with respect to Germany—lie beyond the scope of this article and are mentioned merely in explanation of the difficulties faced by those responsible for implementing the program.

Much of the energies of the Decartelization Branch of the Office of Military Government, United States (OMGUS) has in the past year and a half been taken up with negotiations with the other occupying powers on a law to serve as the basis for a comprehensive program for eliminating German combines and cartels. Simultaneously, extensive investigations and research have been carried forward in preparation for the complex task of corporate reorganization which is to constitute the principal phase of the anti-monopoly program. In addition, a number of *ad hoc* measures have been taken in limited spheres, the general lines of which can be indicated by a few examples.

I. G. Farben's spectacular role in organizing and dominating international chemical cartels and in supporting the German war effort caused it at an early date to be singled out for special attention. I. G. was established in 1925 out of a merger of six of the leading chemical firms in Germany. By 1937 it had a net worth of nearly six billion Reichsmarks and held participations in hundreds of industrial organizations both within and outside Germany. Together with its subsidiaries it had more than 200,000 employees before the war and increased this number to 400,000 during the war.

The Allied Control Authority in November 1945 issued Law No. 9 "providing for the seizure of property owned by I. G. Farbenindustrie and the control thereof." To carry out the law there was created a control committee consisting of one officer appointed by each of the zone commanders. Policies agreed upon by the committee were to be implemented in each zone by the zone commander acting through his control officer. Among the objectives to be accomplished by the committee were the termination of cartel relationships and the dispersion of the ownership of those plants and assets remaining after the destruction of specialized war facilities and the removal of other assets on reparations account. To date, substantial progress has been made in decentralizing the management of the plants and enterprises of I. G. Farben, liquidating central selling agencies, and prohibiting the carrying out of obligations under cartel agreements. The dispersion of ownership of I. G. plants has thus far, however, not progressed beyond the planning stage, and action along these lines awaits quadripartite agreement.

Little coal is mined in the United States zone of Germany and coal distribution in the past was carried on almost exclusively by two cartels—the bituminous coal organization known as Kohlenkontor Weyhenmeyer and Company of Mannheim and the brown coal group, the Rheinische Braunkohle Syndikat. Besides controlling the terms of sale and delivery for practically all coal coming into southern Germany, these two cartels limited wholesalers to particular marketing regions and engaged in a wide variety of other restrictive practices. Trustees have now been appointed over these organizations by OMGUS and their most undesirable activities have been eliminated.

In administering Germany's foreign-trade program, OMGUS has adopted the policy of screening contracts with a view to discouraging business relationships which would tend ultimately to lead to restraints of trade. Sales contracts with foreign buyers are in general not approved if they fix prices or terms of resale, allocate markets or fields, or otherwise restrict the sales or production of a consignee. Contracts are also rejected which create exclusive outlets in any country for German products where the consignee owns or controls facilities for the manufacture of the same or closely similar products.

Quadripartite agreement on the terms of a law which would lay down standards and procedures for dissolving German combines and for eliminating cartels and other practices in restraint of trade had not yet been reached at the time the economic merger of the British and American zones was announced. On February 12, 1947, therefore, parallel laws were simultaneously promulgated in the United States and United Kingdom zones to remain in effect until such time as a quadripartite formula can be worked out. The United States and United Kingdom laws are identical except for two provisions as will be indicated in the following description.

Article 1 constitutes the basic provision and may be regarded as consisting substantively of two parts, one relating to restrictive practices including cartels, and the other to combines. The section on restrictive practices outlaws "cartels, combines, syndicates, trusts, associations or any other form of understanding or concerted undertaking between persons, which have the purpose or effect of restraining, or of fostering monopolistic control of, domestic or international trade or other economic activity, or of restricting access to domestic or international markets." Among the practices which this expression is defined to include are agreements which fix prices, terms, or conditions in the purchase or sale of any product; exclude any person (natural or juristic) from any territorial market or field of business activity, allocate customers, or fix sales or purchase quotas; allocate distributors or products among customers; boycott or discriminate against enterprises for the purpose of reducing competition; limit production or fix production quotas; suppress technology, whether patented or unpatented; extend the use of rights under patents, trademarks, or copyrights to matters not contained in the authorized grant. It will be noted that this recital of practices parallels almost exactly the restrictive practices listed in chapter VI of the present draft charter of the International Trade Organization.

The section of article 1 dealing with combines provides that all economic enterprises having their headquarters in the United States zone (the British zone in the United Kingdom law) and employing in Germany on the effective date of the law or thereafter "more than 10,000 persons shall be examined as *prima facie* constituting excessive concentrations of economic power." A principal object of the investigation would presumably be to determine whether the existing degree of integration is justified on grounds of technological efficiency. If military government or its designated agency makes a finding that the enterprise does in fact constitute an excessive concentration of economic power, the enterprise is to be dissolved in accordance with the relevant provisions of the act. On this point the United States zonal law has a proviso, not paralleled in the United Kingdom version, providing that when an enterprise with more than 10,000 employees is located entirely within the United States zone it shall be dissolved unless military government takes affirmative action in the case in question to exempt the enterprise. Though the inclusion of this clause only in the United States zonal ordinance reflects a divergence of view from the British position that the size of a firm is not in itself crucial in determining excessive concentration, it is doubtful whether the clause will in fact be applicable to more than a few enterprises since most firms which exceed the 10,000-employee standard probably have at least a sales agency outside the United States zone.

Article 1 also provides that firms may be dealt with as excessive concentrations of economic power even when they do not exceed the 10,000-employee standard. In making a determination as to whether such a firm is an excessive concentration, military government is required to consider the following factors: the percentage of total production in the industry controlled by the enterprise; the asset value of the enterprise and its annual volume of business; the number of persons employed; the character of the product or other activity of the enterprise; and the nature and extent of participation by the enterprise in any restrictive agreement or practice.

Article 2 prohibits German participation in international cartels directly or indirectly. Article 3 provides for exemptions from the terms of the law when in the opinion of military government the activities of the enterprise under review are not repugnant to the purposes of the deconcentration law or are required to further the declared objectives of military government.

Article 4 confers broad powers upon the agency designated by military government to enforce the law, including the power to eliminate corporate entities; redistribute and remove property, investments, and other assets; and cancel cartel obligations. The enforcing agency may also delegate any of its powers to appropriate German governmental agencies.

The statute lays down penalties up to 10 years' imprisonment or fines of not more than 200,000 Reichsmarks or both and leaves it to the discretion of military government to decide whether judicial proceedings shall be taken before German courts or military-government courts. Although the law became effective on date of promulgation, violators of the anticombine provisions are not to be subject to criminal prosecution for a period of six months thereafter.

Appended to the ordinance as outlined is an annex entitled "Regulation Number 1." This annex defines the procedure to be adopted by enterprises affected by the law, the procedure governing applications for exemptions, and the rights of subject enterprises to appeal.

This section on exemptions under Regulation No. 1 includes the most important difference between the United States and United Kingdom versions. Both exempt the Reichsbahn, the Reichspost, public utilities, and enterprises taken into control by military government. In the latter connection, however, the annex to the United States law specifies only I. G. Farben as included among enterprises exempt, whereas the British version also includes the Krupp works, the coal industry, and the iron and steel industry.

Detailed provisions are laid down for the submission of reports and other information on the basis of which enterprises will be notified whether they come within the scope of the law. Subject enterprises receiving orders to decentralize or otherwise comply with the law are required within three months of the issuance of such orders to prepare and submit a plan for complying with the law. After approval or amendment of the plan by military government they are to proceed to carry it out within a designated time limit. Enterprises subject to the anticombine provisions of the law are forbidden to dispose of any of their assets without the written approval of military government.

Elimination of excessive concentrations of economic power is a key element in American policy for the democratization of Germany's economic and political structure. The success of the program will depend in good measure on the machinery set up to enforce the relevant statutes and on the perception and vigor displayed by the enforcement personnel. In particular, it will be necessary to integrate closely the administration of the program in the United States and British zones even though a substantial portion of Germany's industrial assets in the United Kingdom zone is not subject to the decartelization law. German agencies or personnel to whom responsibilities are delegated will have to be carefully screened and supervised in view of their inexperience and historical indifference to antitrust objectives. Even in the United States, where the antimonopoly tradition is strong and deeply rooted, the legal and administrative problems connected with enforcement have been vexing and arduous. Although noteworthy results have been achieved in eliminating and preventing restrictive business practices, experience under the antitrust laws and the Public Utility Holding Company Act attests to the difficulties surrounding the accomplishment of effective corporate dissolutions. Since corporate divestitures will constitute the central feature of the German deconcentration program, the task that lies ahead will tax the best efforts of the occupation authorities.

IS THERE A GERMAN POLICY? [6]

First aim of the German policy is to keep Germany at peace —for the good reason that there is still a German danger. Germany is the most populous country in western Europe and, even after allowing for bomb damage, has the largest and most modern industrial plant. Its scientists are still among the best on the Continent. A new generation of Germans would be needed for an old-fashioned war of armies, but even the present generation would be dangerous in the appalling event that it got loose with atomic weapons. However, Germany is not likely very soon to start an independent adventure in the tradition of Bismarck, Wilhelm II, or Hitler. The danger in Germany's surviving strength is that it could make her a useful ally, an effective junior partner, of some other power. A Russo-German partnership would clearly dominate all Europe. However sincerely Englishmen or Americans might believe that a strong

[6] From article by John Kenneth Galbraith, member of the Board of Editors, Fortune; formerly with the State Department. Fortune. 35:126-7+. January 1947. Copyright Time Inc. Reprinted by permission.

affiliation between their countries and Germany would be harmless or merely a matter of self-protection, there is no chance that Russia would agree. The occupying powers, East and West, are already suspecting one another of plans to use or misuse Germany for their own ends. It would be easy for that suspicion to degenerate into a competition for Germany's surviving military strength, and there are many, many Germans who would welcome and abet the contest. Germany could thus become the instrument for destroying whatever chance there may be for agreement between Russia and the West.

The alternatives to this competition are either to declare Germany out of bounds to such rivalry or to destroy the German state forthwith. It is American policy to try the first—that is to neutralize Germany as a military and, so far as possible, as a political force in Europe.

If Germany is not to be "a pawn or a partner in a military struggle for power between the East and the West," the phrase used by Mr. Byrnes at Stuttgart last September, it must have no military power worth competing for, and all countries that fear Germany or its misuse must be able at all times to satisfy themselves that it has none. The American formula to achieve these ends was unveiled for public inspection at the Council of Foreign Ministers meeting in Paris last April and unhappily called a "disarmament" treaty. It excited comparatively little interest, partly because the State Department made no effort to explain the ends it had in view. Although the proposed treaty has met Russian opposition, it is still a cornerstone of United States German policy. By its terms, the occupation armies would eventually be replaced by a comparatively small force of security inspectors who would have access to all of Germany and who would stay for a long time—Mr. Byrnes suggested twenty-five years and told Mr. Molotov he would be happy to raise it to forty. This force would have authority to prevent military training, production of any arms or munitions, or construction of armament plant. It would also supervise any technology that might be put to evil use. Since the inspection would be a joint enterprise, it would eliminate any basis for suspicion that Germany was being groomed as a military ally by another power. The United States, in effect, classed Germany with atomic energy, as a tempting and dangerous instrument, and proposed essentially the same system of control.

The proposed disarmament treaty is also designed to help wind up the unfinished business of the Potsdam conference. Potsdam too, in a primitive fashion, sought to neutralize Germany. The principal formula was economic disarmament, an American invention that the Russians adopted with enthusiasm. To the wholly unimpeachable idea that Germany should repair some of the damage it had done in Europe, Potsdam linked the more questionable notion that, if factories, machinery, and other industrial equipment were removed as reparations, Germany could be made completely and permanently innocuous.

During the autumn and winter of 1945-46 several hundred technicians, economists, soldiers, and negotiators from all four occupying powers set about determining what industry was needed by Germany for a minimum standard of living and what, therefore, could be removed as reparations or, if not removed, should be destroyed. The resulting level-of-industry agreement of last March proposed leaving Germany 7.5 million of some 22 million (metric) tons of steel capacity, from which an annual production of 5.8 million tons was to be allowed. Apart from the much-needed building and building-materials industries, the agreement would have reduced the total capacity of German industry to between 50 and 55 per cent of 1938 capacity. The surviving industry, by common estimate, would have provided the Germans with a standard of living somewhat below what they averaged in 1932, their worst year of depression. The dismantling of munitions and aircraft plants had already been decreed at Potsdam. Ball-bearing plants and the huge synthetic oil, rubber, and nitrogen plants were also abolished, although for the synthetic plants a stay of execution was arranged until gasoline, rubber, and nitrogen could be imported. The agreement, though not so ruthless as popularly alleged, was no halfway measure; were it possible to neutralize Germany by removing or destroying plants and industrial equipment, the plan should have been tough enough to do the job.

Because it was American policy to neutralize but not destroy Germany, the American delegation at Potsdam insisted that during the occupation Germany be treated "as a single economic unit." An agreement was obtained that the now-famous central agencies would be established to provide a unified economic administration of all four zones. What happened to the central agencies is history. The French, although it had been agreed at Yalta that they would share in the German occupation, were not invited to Potsdam. For reasons that have never been explained, when they were later taken in as full partners in Berlin they were not required to subscribe to the Potsdam Agreement. They have vetoed any and all proposals to establish central agencies because they have been unwilling to concede, even to a shadow German Government, any jurisdiction over the Rhineland, Ruhr, or Saar. Behind the French veto there has always been the further question: Would the Russians allow central agencies any freedom for administrative action in the Eastern zone? Is it Russian policy to have a single Germany?

Were Germany to be Balkanized into three or four minor states there would not be much need, as a safety measure, to remove their industry. And the American zone, in particular, would need what industry it now has to survive. There was danger that the plants would be removed and then it would be found that the French or Russians were still blocking unification. Accordingly it had been American policy to link the plant removals to unification. At a meeting of the Coordinating Committee of the Allied Control Council last May, the French repeated their objections to central agencies, and the Russians objected to a compromise proposal that would provide a single administration of exports and imports for all four zones. General Clay thereupon stopped dismantling and shipping plants from the American zone until there should be some progress toward economic unification. The British had not started dismantling plants, and never did. With the minor exception of a few plants that had been listed for delivery in advance of general agreement, and machine tools and other equipment from war plants, the industries of the western zones are still in place. Since most of Germany's heavy industry is in these zones and some 80 per cent of it survived the war, neutralization of Germany so far as it was to be accomplished by removal of industry had come to a full halt.

The disarmament treaty is the chance for a new start—and in a better direction. Although the old idea of economic disarmament has not been formally disavowed by the United States, the original enthusiasm has cooled to the freezing point. One reason is that not only Germany but Europe as a whole would suffer from removal and destruction of German plants on the scale contemplated last spring. But too much has been made of this objection. Germany would have 7.5 million tons of steel capacity, or nearly as much as Japan had during the war. Most of her light manufactures were left intact and free to expand. The United States was not, as popularly supposed, a party to any agreement to turn German industry into goat pasture.

A more serious objection to economic disarmament is that it offers little security. The dismantling or destruction of Germany's industry was aimed at the weapons of World War II. It is hardly likely that Germany would start any new adventure with the old tools. But even for an old-fashioned war, the security promised by economic disarmament was a chimera. If Germany could once be rid of the occupation armies and any form of inspection, it would soon replace the lost factories. Given manpower and technical knowledge, capital plant is easily reproduced—the speed with which the United States built its own war plant was not proof of a superior genius but merely a new demonstration of an old truth. The Germans might, of course, have been prevented forever from rebuilding their industry, but such a permanent limitation was rejected by the State Department in December 1945, and by Molotov last summer. The disarmament treaty is therefore necessary if there is to be any long-run control.

The United States is still committed to the bargain it made at Potsdam: to use surplus German plant as reparations. While the level-of-industry agreement was being negotiated in Berlin, the Western allies, plus Czechoslovakia and Yugoslavia, were meeting in Paris in one of the least publicized conferences in history to agree on their shares in the reparations from the western zones of Germany. The conference reached an agreement on each country's share in the surplus German plant— for the eighteen participating countries the shares ranged from

27.8 per cent for Great Britain down to 0.1 per cent for South Africa. The United States, which along with Canada and South Africa waived part of its claim, received 11.8 per cent. An international agency was then established in Brussels (the Inter-Allied Reparation Agency) to allocate the actual plant and equipment as it became available. So far it hasn't had much business, for it had hardly been established when General Clay stopped dismantling plants.

Were Russia and France to agree to the unification of Germany, then the United States and the United Kingdom would be morally bound to start tearing down and shipping plants again. At Stuttgart Mr. Byrnes made it clear that the old bargain on reparations still stood. Germany does have a lot of surplus capital equipment: in 1943, by reliable estimate, it had more machine tools than the United States; for the near future it has a great surplus of steel plant, and not over half of its 22-million-ton capacity was *ever* used for peaceful purposes; much the same is probably true of engineering, heavy chemical, and other heavy industries.

However it is no longer very likely that German industry will be removed or destroyed down to the level-of-industry agreement. For one reason, it isn't necessary if the neutralization of Germany is obtained through a security force. For another, the Russians, who last spring were the most ardent advocates of a tight ceiling on German industry, have reversed themselves and are now willing to consider an upward revision of the level-of-industry agreement. The Russians appear to have had trouble using the secondhand plants. They would much prefer new steel, machinery, and consumers' goods. The western countries feel the same way.

So a new deal on reparations, which would leave the plants in Germany (always excluding the war plants) and take their products instead, is about to become an issue. . . . Countries that receive reparations in current production will have to supply raw materials, and it will take arduous negotiation to keep the total demands, especially those of Russia, within reason. But there would be many advantages in the change. Countries would get as reparations what they need for recovery. Reparations from current production do not require the large transfers from German into Allied currency that cursed the settlement after World War I. And there would be no further experiment in the dubious economics of moving plants all over Europe.

INSIDE RUSSIAN OCCUPIED GERMANY [7]

The two most drastic policies which the Red Army has carried out in its zone have been the exacting of reparations in kind, and the establishing of the so-called "agrarian reform."

Disregarding the Potsdam Agreements, the Soviets decided unilaterally to satisfy their own demand for reparations in kind, as well as to secure the share Poland is to receive, by stripping the German railroads, public utility installations, and industries, regardless of what such a loss of productive plant capacity would do to the German economy. This process began before Potsdam, and has been carried on ever since.

The Russians ripped up the second tracks of all the double-track railroad lines, including the one between Berlin and Harpko on which the American military train to Frankfurt is operated. The Russians took the good engines and the rolling stock. While I was in Berlin they dismantled the whole central electric railway system, which included all installations and 200 electric engines.

While the American and British armies have demilitarized industries chiefly by blasting to pieces the condemned war plants, I have not found that the Russians have *demolished* any war plants; on the contrary, they ship them out of the country. The pattern of shipping out industrial plants is always the same: Russian engineers call on German managers and crews to restore the plant in question to full capacity. Russian experts help them. When the plant is really in operation once more, other Russians appear on the scene, close down the plant, and begin dismantling operations with Russian crews and soldiers. Only walls and concrete floors are left when this stripping process is completed. Doorknobs, pipes, faucets, wiring—everything—goes.

    [7] From article by Karl Brandt, Economist, Food Research Institute, Stanford University. *Commercial and Financial Chronicle.* 164:478+. July 25, 1946. Reprinted by permisssion.

The Russians set a deadline for these operations, and for speed, work up a competitive spirit among the stripping crews, giving awards to those who complete their job ahead of the others. The result is that the work goes ahead with amazing speed, but there is also a stupendous amount of destruction of values which, by more efficient methods, could have been avoided. What Russia is therefore collecting as reparations is a gigantic pile of junk. Vast amounts of machinery and equipment are rusting on uncounted miles of sidings in Germany and in Poland, corroded by snow, rain, and frost. Yet, in an economy still so hungry for capital, even equipment in such poor condition is welcome in Russia.

Stripping has struck the coal mines, the power plants, the two largest German shoe factories, the largest stocking and sock factory, the sugar mills, farm machinery and fertilizer plants, the largest cornstarch and dextrose plant, automotive and bicycle factories, and many others.

Yet not every factory is dismantled. Some are working to fill Russian orders, and to some extent are even using Russian raw materials. These factories have a delivery quota to meet, and have been promised permission to supply German markets with whatever remains after the quota is met. The big Zeiss optical works at Jena operates overtime with 6,000 laborers, manufacturing equipment for Russia's army, air force, and navy. All goods manufactured for Russian orders are paid for by the German city administrations out of tax revenues.

According to Potsdam, the Russians are entitled to 25 per cent of the industrial reparations to be taken from the three Western zones, and we and the British are willing to transfer such a quota provided the Russians agree to a central administration of all four zones. The Russians foresaw our attempt to use this pressure, have taken all they want from their own zone, ignoring that argument for treating Germany as a unit.

You may say that this ruthless stripping of industries must incite revolt among the Germans against Russian rule. This would be to jump to conclusions too quickly. The stripping of industries satisfies not only the demand of Russia's planners for further rapid industrialization in the USSR, but at the same time it accomplishes a complete social revolution in Germany, which is a most necessary achievement if the Soviet aims are to be realized. The Germans in the Russian zone have already become prostrate proletarians who can do nothing except call on the government for help. They have not only been stripped of everything they owned or earned, but are made incapable of working at jobs, or the jobs they once held have simply been wiped out—which of course crushes any hope of regaining by means of employment some of the things which they lost. Their economic distress plays into the hands of the German Communists, and rule by the German Communists dovetails with Russia's foreign policy.

The agrarian reform is the other barrel of this gun. The large estates have been abolished. Their owners and managing personnel, except those who fled or committed suicide, have with few exceptions been shot or deported. The livestock, including all the draft animals, the tractors, and all machinery of value, were shipped off to Russia. Many of the buildings and farm yards of the large estates are being used as barracks for Red troops. On paper the land has been distributed among farm laborers—refugee peasants and others—in lots of 12 acres each. Most of the fields are untilled because there is no draft-power or equipment with which to cultivate them. Since these large estates were a primary source of food for the cities, food shortages have struck throughout the zone. Horses, cattle, and pigs have been requisitioned from the well-to-do family farmers. Today the Russian zone has less than one third the prewar number of draft horses on farms, and next to none of the 60,000 tractors it used to have.

Farmers are assigned delivery quotas for all products. Deliveries are paid for in prices which are still fixed at the same level as in earlier years. Beyond the quota, farmers may sell in the "free market" at any price. For the time being, quotas are so high that few farmers have anything to sell. Items that can be sold are swapped for second-hand consumer goods, not for the fantastic blackmarket prices.

Farmers are organized in a uniform system of so-called cooperative associations. Upon close inspection, these coops turn out to be corporations of public law with a monopoly to supply farmers with things they need. Any politically undesirable elements may be excluded. If a farmer is excluded, that means the end of farming for him, because there is nowhere else he can obtain supplies of any sort. Because the coops have taken the place of the dealers, no dealer could receive supplies for distribution. These so-called cooperative associations are politically controlled by top German administrators who happen to be trusted Communists.

Agriculture, along with all other branches of the economic system, is under the rule of a Russian-controlled central administration located in the Russian sector of Berlin. Its chief figures are Communists. Its plans and operations are under the surveillance of the NKVD, and get approval from General Sokolovski's headquarters, which in turn receive instructions from Moscow. During the past twelve months, the Red Army has evicted 9,000,-000 Germans from the areas which are, in theory, provisionally transferred to Polish administration, but in practice annexed by the Polish satellite state. Simultaneously, these areas were stripped clean of any movable assets. This procedure has laid waste one fourth of Germany's food production in a time of starvation, and it has dumped additional prostrate millions into the zones of occupation. This serves to multiply economic and social strife in those zones.

Contrary to the practices of the other three armies the Red Army has fostered monetary inflation in its zone as a means of accomplishing the social revolution. When it entered Germany, the Red army received two years' back pay in German occupation marks. A portion of the banknotes was supplied by our government as Russia's share in occupation marks, promised to each of the powers. The Russians printed an additional, probably much larger volume, on plates which our government gave them at their request. On top of this load came vast sums of regular German banknotes seized in the Reichsbank, in all its branches, and in all the other banks. So long as people were still parting with goods for money, this avalanche of marks served the purpose of prying loose additional goods from German civilians. This sort of inflation eats the marrow out of the bones of any society.   All those who own anything get stripped of it. . . .

The German newspapers are being revived, but in the Russian zone they are strictly controlled and strongly flavored accordingly.   Soviet Russia has always exercised special state patronage over the arts and science.   The Red Army, too, pays court to the arts.   Theatres and concert halls in the Russian zone are given priorities for supplies and reconstruction.   Of course, half the plays and films put on are pro-Soviet or German Communist propaganda.   Scientists are treated with great courtesy, and assisted either in their work in Germany, or are invited, and if need be, furnished transportation to Moscow.   The Russians treat their German administrators and experts with respect as equals, supply them with good rations and that very important item, cigarettes.   Their homes are protected against requisitioning by the Red Army.

Society has been reduced to a proletarian status and the only people enjoying better conditions are the civil servants.   Politically, the one-party system is solidly established.

Thus the whole area is so well under Soviet remote control that Russia could even offer soon to withdraw all her troops to the Oder River.   After having carried out her stripping policy, she can even champion the reindustrialization of Germany.

In summary, it is my impression that the Russian zone has become substantially sovietized in one single year of occupation, and has thus passed into the initial stage of "democracy" as understood in Russia—namely, the dictatorship of the proletariat.

In appraising the amazing success of the Russians, we must remember that they have some substantial assets.   They never did bomb German cities, while we did.   They actively supported the German underground and even accepted the aristocratic leaders of the Free German Movement, and pay its general officers, such as von Paulus and Count Eisensiedel, the high compliment of employing them as instructors in their military academy in Moscow, while we have rejected any cooperation whatever with the German underground, even when they were preparing to overthrow the Hitler regime.

An asset in another direction is the fact that the German economy in the Russian zone is now probably in as bad condition as it will ever be, and from now on can only improve. But the deterioration of the German economy in the Western zones will continue, just as long as the area remains separated into compartments. The contrast will not go unnoticed on either side of the dividing line by the civilians ruled under the respective systems.

One of the greatest assets the Russians have is the location of Berlin deep inside the Russian zone. True, Berlin is a four-power city, but at the same time it is the seat of Russia's central administration for her zone, and it is an island in the midst of her zone. For this reason, neither the British nor the French have found it advisable to set up military government headquarters for their zones in Berlin. America, on the other hand, has taken her zone command from Frankfurt to Berlin, and has combined it with the Control Council group. We have the use of one Russian-controlled highway which is neatly studded every few miles with ornate signposts carrying quotations from Stalin's speeches in Russian, and is patrolled from Berlin to Helmstedt, at the American border, by Russian sentries. We are allowed to fly planes through a narrow strip over this highway. We are also permitted to send two Russian-inspected trains a day—one each way—over Russian-controlled tracks. Our telephone and telegraph lines are known to be tapped by the Russians. The German secret police working for the Russians snatch Germans right out of the American, British, or French sectors of Berlin any time they so desire, and the other powers cannot do a thing about it. We are even unable to protect the life and liberty of German Social Democrats, who opposed the merger with the Communist Party, in our own sector. All we can do is to fly them into the American zone.

All of this illustrates merely that when, at the desire of Stalin, the Big Three settled the future occupation of Germany at Teheran, and later at Yalta, the Western powers were not on the alert. . . .

My conclusion from looking behind the iron-curtain into the Russian zone is identical with General Smuts' warning to the British Government. If America is not to be defeated in her foreign policy in Europe, she must revise and reverse her Potsdam course and the level of industry decisions now—before it is too late. You cannot build German democracy in a slum in the midst of 10,000,000 unemployed, and starving women and children.

In sizing up the Russians, let me say this: As individuals, the Russians have all the traits that other people have. We have no quarrel with them. Many of them are most amiable, gifted, civilized people. As a nation, they have become World Problem No. 1 because of their totalitarian, and as such, reactionary regime of state capitalism which ignores the welfare of the individual and surges for power and world domination.

HOW MUCH IN PLANT SHALL GERMANY PAY? [8]

The distribution . . . among the Western Allies [of Germany's surplus industrial plant in the British, American and French occupation zones] is going forward under the much misunderstood title of reparations. Already German machinery under Allied control is making a significant contribution to European reconstruction. But if the nations of Western Europe are to surmount the crisis facing them, they must have more plant and machinery from the idle reserves of industrialized Germany.

This need is a primary factor behind the recent listing by the British and American Military Governments in Germany of many additional plants to be dismantled and shipped out of their zones. The new listings bring the total of such factories— some of which have already been removed—to 682. In addition, 176 plants will be forthcoming from the French zone. The establishments range from steel and chemical works to factories capable of supplying a variety of light consumer goods. The total estimated value is about one billion dollars.

These figures, while not inconsiderable, represent approximately 1 per cent of the number of plants in Western Germany. The present reparations yardstick is the new level of industry plan that provides for an industrial capacity in the western zones

[8] From article by Albert Z. Carr, American member of the Inter-Allied Reparation Agency. *New York Times Magazine.* p. 14+. December 7, 1947. Reprinted by permission.

equal to that of 1936, which is sufficient to support the present German population. It reflects the estimate of what Germany can contribute to European reconstruction without remaining an economic liability for the Allied powers.

It has been officially estimated that under the present level-of-industry and reparations plan, the people of Western Germany in 1951 will have a standard of living approximating 80 per cent of their 1936 standard. This prospect is considerably brighter than that faced by some of the Allied European countries.

The German industrial economy is still by all odds potentially the mightiest in Europe. In 1938 Germany had a steel production capacity of 24,000,000 tons a year. Russia holds that this capacity had been increased by the end of the war to nearly 27,000,000 tons, of which 24,500,000 tons were in the western zones. In 1947 Britain and America decided to permit their zones to retain 10,700,000 tons capacity a year. Even if the Russian figures are exaggerated, there is still a huge surplus of steel and other industrial capacity in Western Germany.

The reason is that between 1938 and 1944 the construction of new plants in Hitler's Germany was greater than the vast air raid destruction after 1940. Since the equivalent capacity of 1938 had been greatly enlarged by five years of war preparations, Germany therefore still has a far larger industrial plant than when Hitler took power. Many experts believe that if Germany were allowed to resume production without restraints, within ten years she would again be economic overlord of Europe.

There remain, however, some potentially serious obstacles in the way of the present reduced reparations program. German workers, naturally, dislike seeing machinery that formerly gave them jobs crated up and carted away to other lands—despite the fact that Allied policy and lack of raw materials preclude the reopening of the factories. Their protests have some weight with people who fear unrest in Germany. But more serious is the opposition of powerful forces in America and Britain which hold that the best way to revive Europe is to restore German industry.

Certain British and American groups have been waging an intensive campaign against reparations, asserting that the program is destructive and costly. America is the focus of the conflict between those who want German reconstruction first and those who want reconstruction for Europe as a whole. The influence of the "Germany firsters" in this country has alarmed some nations whose industries were stripped by Germany during the war.

The confusion is due to misconception of the reparations problem. Some Americans believe that the concept of reparations is based on revenge and wonder if this is a practicable way to treat Europe's ills. Others have the impression that only Russia has benefited to any great extent from German reparations. This is primarily because Russia has helped herself freely to reparations from her own zone of Germany. Also, there was a short period when, for technical reasons, the American zonal authorities gave priority to the shipment of a small amount of equipment to the Soviet Union, a situation that resulted in such misleading headlines as, "Russia Obtains 95 Per Cent of Reparations From U. S. Zone."

The facts refute these misconceptions. The collection and distribution of German plant and machinery are directed by the Inter-Allied Reparation Agency, or IARA, which was created early in 1946 and has headquarters in Brussels. IARA's function is to divide the reparations from Western Germany, released by military authorities in Berlin, among eighteen participating nations, each of which is represented on IARA.

Allocations to these countries have nothing to do with revenge. The distribution is based upon the statement in the Act of Paris, signed in January 1946, that German industrial plant should be distributed in accordance with "the urgency of each claimant country's needs . . . to rehabilitate, reconstruct or restore to full activity" its economic life.

Moreover, the bulk of industrial reparations from the western zones has gone and is going to Western Europe. Under the Potsdam Agreement, Russia and Poland were to receive 25 per cent of the industrial reparations from the three western zones, as well as all such reparations from Russia's eastern occupation zone. In return Russia agreed to treat Germany as an economic unit and to supply the IARA nations with food and raw materials equal to three fifths of the value of the industrial reparations received from the western zones.

But in May 1946, the American zone commander, Gen. Lucius D. Clay, announced that the plan had broken down. On the grounds that economic unification had not been carried out, he stopped Soviet reparations from the American zone. The British zone commander followed suit.

The Russian share of plants from Western Germany, even under the most harmonious conditions could not exceed the 25 per cent agreed upon at Potsdam.

IARA's function has no relation to Soviet needs or demands. The only nations among the so-called Russian satellites sharing in its distribution are Czechoslovakia, Yugoslavia and Albania. The respective shares of the eighteen nations were determined by the Act of Paris and vary greatly in size. For example, the United Kingdom, with a share of 27.8 per cent, is entitled to 278 times more reparations than the Union of South Africa, and about eighty times more than Albania. The French share is 22 per cent; that of the United States is 11 per cent, and the Netherlands gets 5 per cent.

When General Clay stopped the Soviet reparations—which also put a temporary stop to all other industrial reparations from Western Germany—only seventy-two plants had been definitely earmarked for release to the agency. The IARA Assembly, composed of delegates of the eighteen nations, waited five months for a change of heart in the Berlin military headquarters. Then it addressed a strong resolution to the Big Four Council of Foreign Ministers requesting action on the problem.

The move brought an invitation to send representatives to the Moscow Conference, held in April 1947. Jacques Rueff, president of IARA, and Nigel Sutton, the secretary general, vigorously stated the attitude of the agency at the conference. Mr. Sutton, in a report issued a few weeks earlier, had summed up the attitude:

Nations entitled to substantial amounts of German industrial capital and equipment as reparation cannot adequately plan their national reconstruction until they have at least an approximate idea as to how much equipment they are likely to receive from Germany and when. They cannot afford to delay essential industrial projects for years in the hope of some day receiving German equipment.

Thereafter the military authorities resumed the allocation of factories to IARA and work was speeded on the removal of the equipment to the various nations. The process, however, is sometimes excruciatingly slow in comparison to the need.

Before an individual plant can be moved a complete inventory, giving specifications of every piece of equipment, must be prepared by the commander in the zone where the factory is situated and forwarded to IARA in Brussels. The conflicting claims advanced by member governments for the factory are studied by the IARA's secretary general and his technical staff, who take into consideration the over-all percentages allowed the various countries.

The secretary general than may recommend the award of the plant to the nation whose claim seems the strongest or divide the equipment among several nations. The Assembly of the IARA then passes on the recommendation. Thereafter the government which has received the award works directly with the zone commander to have the factory dismantled and transported.

Each idle factory put into production in another country makes a solid contribution to the reconstruction of Europe.

For example, in the town of Esslingen, in the British zone of Germany, there stood earlier this year a large factory known as Indexwerke, which contained some of the finest heavy machinery in Europe—machinery which makes precision machine tools, which, in turn, make consumer goods of all kinds. Before the war the biggest customer of Indexwerke was England, whose industries imported more than a third of the total output of this plant.

Although bombs did little damage to Indexwerke, with the coming of peace the great factory stood idle and forlorn. A large percentage of the skilled workers had been dispersed and the power and essential raw materials needed to operate the plant were lacking. Even if Indexwerke could have gone into production, there was nobody in Germany to buy its output, owing to the general dislocation of the economy.

But in England there was a burning need for the very machines which Indexwerke had once produced. In England the needful supply of skilled labor could be found. In England there were enough raw materials and power to put the factory to work.

The reparation mechanism went into action. In Berlin the zone commanders decided to make the plant available for reparation purposes. In Brussels IARA came to the conclusion that the British had a greater need and better claim for this plant than any other nation. German labor proceeded to dismantle the plant efficiently, crate the machines, transport them to the coast and put them on boats for England. Today the Indexwerke plant, renamed, is in operation on British soil, turning out machines of the kind which England and Western Europe as a whole urgently need for industrial recovery.

The real value of reparations to European reconstruction is progressively being revealed. Last year France, desperate for electric power, was awarded a 32,000-kilowatt steam generating plant known as Grosskraftwerke, then located at Mannheim, in the American zone. The Germans in the existing conditions of their economy, were unable to make effective use of this plant, but today, installed in France, it is helping to fill one of the great gaps in the French economy.

The Hensoldt plant at Herborn-Dilkreis, in the American zone, made excellent optical equipment before the war, most of which was exported to the Netherlands. The plant was undamaged by the war, but the Germans were not in a position to operate it. The Dutch urgently needed a supply of optical goods to meet consumer needs and to sustain the workers and manufacturers, wholesalers and retailers who had formerly thrived on this trade in Holland.

The factory, awarded to them as reparation, was dismantled and shipped to the Netherlands, where it is now going full blast. Germany lost an idle factory. Holland gained a busy factory and Western European production as a whole received the benefit of the exchange.

Most Americans do not realize how much their own country stands to gain from reparations. It is true that we are currently putting nearly one billion dollars a year into Western Germany in the effort to feed the German people and restore their economy. This has often led to the hasty assumption that we ought to make an end to reparations, since we are pouring money into Germany with one hand and helping to give away German assets with the other. But this is a superficial view of the matter.

General Clay has recently pointed out that Germany's supplies of coal, manpower and raw materials are so small that it will be four or five years before it can utilize in full even the plant capacity left there under the new plan. It is better, the General maintained, to ship plants in excess of this permitted level as quickly as possible to other European countries which have more resources with which to utilize this industrial machinery in the critical years immediately ahead. He expressed the opinion that if the plants scheduled for reparations were to be left in Germany many would fall to ruin through disuse. Additional economic waste would, in his view, result from the fact that by the time Germany had sufficient coal and raw materials to use this capacity—it might be ten to twenty years in some cases—the machinery in some plants would be outmoded.

The removal of idle machines does not materially hinder Germany's revival or add to the burdens of the American taxpayer. Ernest Bevin, England's Foreign Secretary, has stated that the reparations program will affect only 50,000 German workmen in the British-American zone, which has a 40,000,000 population. The German workers must be shifted to other employment in any event, and the sooner idle German machines can be put to productive use in other European countries, the less will be Europe's demands for American aid.

American industry at this time is not in a position to supply all the industrial equipment needed to speed European reconstruction. We can put up the dollars, but that does not mean that we can actually put into European hands the means of new production. Aside from some machinery that can be obtained from Sweden and Switzerland, the largest ready source of modern equipment is still Germany.

Moreover, there is another way America benefits from reparations. We ourselves are receiving some extremely valuable machinery from Germany. An example is an aluminum foil factory at Tenningen, in the French zone, which was made available as reparations last spring and was eagerly sought by France and England, which need aluminum foil for electrical equipment, building insulation and other reconstruction purposes. But the United States also needed machinery for making aluminum foil, owing to the wartime wear and tear on that type of machinery here. So America put in an urgent claim and IARA awarded it the plant.

The competition for industrial reparations is especially intense at this time. There is hardly a nation whose industrialists are not keenly interested in each machine that comes out of the German reserve.

STRENGTH THROUGH INDIFFERENCE [9]

At some not too distant date in the future, a peace treaty will be signed with a recognized German government—denazified, decartelized and demilitarized—and Germany will be granted sovereignty. Allied occupation forces will gradually be withdrawn and some continuing supervision of the economic and military activity of the new Germany will be undertaken by a Control Commission.

What can we expect from Germany after such a treaty is signed? If the past is any guide, we shall come up against organized German attempts to frustrate its terms. If we let matters go as we did last time, we shall encounter (a) an effort to turn military defeat into economic victory, (b) an active spirit of resistance to any thoroughgoing continuation of disarmament, and (c) an intensive drive to build up Germany in the eyes of Western nations as the only bulwark against communism.

These were Germany's three dominant campaigns in the years after World War I. Although a proportion of German

[9] By Robert Wohlforth, wartime head of a Justice Department economic intelligence unit and member of its Anti-Trust Division. *New Republic*, 116:30-2, March 10, 1947. Reprinted by permission.

leftists dissented from one or the other of them, Germans of the Right were wholly behind them, and this program was taken up by Gustav Stresemann's People's Party.

It succeeded remarkably. Germany evaded her reparations, avoided the economic consequences of her defeat and rebuilt her industrial power within 10 years. The efforts of the Allied Commission to enforce the disarmament provisions of the Versailles Treaty were almost wholly nullified. Germany's key war plants, instead of being dismantled, migrated all over Europe. By flaunting the Red Menace in the troubled period after the Kapp uprising in 1920, and for many years thereafter, the German Government won concessions from the Allies that ranged from postponement of army reductions and substantial increases in the armed police to the strengthening of fortresses on Germany's eastern frontier.

Leaving aside the general considerations of European politics between World Wars I and II which impinged upon the disarmament of Germany, the bare control picture spells out a pattern that may well be encountered again. The problem last time was that the Versailles Peace Treaty gave Germany sovereignty and left the Inter-Allied Control Commission created under it with supervisory power only. The 300 Allied officers of the Control Commission assigned to the task of eliminating Germany's war potential spent seven years on a job that was expected to take three months. They were "military men without arms, diplomats without mandates."

In all attempts to compel compliance with the treaty, the Control Commission met antagonism and opposition from the German Government and from the German people alike. It became a matter of patriotism in Germany to hinder the application of the treaty. German courts ruled that German citizens were not bound by its provisions. Brigadier General John H. Morgan of the British delegation stated that he "met with every kind of resistance that German ingenuity could devise."

In order to determine how far Germany was disarmed, for instance, the commission had to know just what the German army had at the time of the Armistice. But no such records could be found. German liaison officers gave advance notice to

Reich army units about to be inspected by the commission, and aided in transferring military equipment from one garrison to another in order to conceal excess material and prevent accurate checking of stocks.   Large quantities of German rifles and machine guns were hidden in false walls and floors: one factory in Saxony contained 600 new howitzers of large caliber, enough to equip 33 divisions, walled up in its cellars.   (The treaty allowed Germany 84 of these howitzers.)

How Germany rebuilt her air forces under the cloak of commercial aviation and by means of subsidizing the industry is well known.   Less well known is how the German army developed tanks, poison gas and heavy artillery.   By the treaty, Germany was forbidden to manufacture armored cars and tanks.   But within two years, Germany persuaded the Allied powers to permit the production of small armored cars for police use and for the Reichswehr.   Using this concession, Germany went on to experiment with tanks and tank tactics.

For another instance, Germany was forbidden by the treaty to make poison gas, but was allowed to study means of protection against gases.   According to German military logic, it was impossible to study gas defenses unless the attack was studied also.   In order to study the attack it was necessary to have gas.   So Germany made the gas.   Again, Germany was forbidden to manufacture heavy guns, but was permitted to retain heavy artillery on fortresses and ships.   It was only a short time before secret gun factories, such as those of the Rhein-Metall-Borsig firm, were operating with government support.   Didn't the German army have to have replacements, spares and parts to keep the guns in operation?

Meanwhile, as soon as the treaty went into effect, German arms plants scattered all over Europe.   The great military optical plant of Carl Zeiss, forbidden to manufacture devices for the German army and navy, set up a plant in Venlo, just a step across the Dutch border.   The Dornier Airplane Company, formerly in Friedrichshafen, moved across Lake Constance to Switzerland.   The aircraft factory of Heinkel moved to Sweden and continued producing military planes.   Junkers set up a plant in Russia and Fokker moved to Holland. German submarine experts went to work in Spain.

But it was in Russia that the closest cooperation on armaments was received. While table-thumping officers like General Ludendorff tried to persuade the Western Allies—and especially the British—to let Germany rearm in order to serve as their protector against Russian Bolshevism, German interests were busy establishing munitions factories in Moscow, Leningrad, Kuibyshev, the Don Basin, the Kerch Peninsula and elsewhere. Krupp cooperated with the Soviets by leasing them fire arms plants. Krupp also erected a Russian submarine plant and staffed it with German naval experts. The Hugo Stinnes concern, the great chemical firm of I. G. Farben and other important German industrial units directed or owned plants in Russia. In Russia the Reichswehr organized and directed training and experimental centers for tanks, flame-throwers, mortars, poison gases, artillery and aviation.

The world remembers pretty clearly how the German Government got around the treaty's restrictions on the size of its army, by such devices as setting up paramilitary "police" forces and civilian "defense" formations on the side and by giving its blessing to free-booting "Free Corps" and veterans' leagues and "athletic associations" bent on military drill. By 1923 the German defense minister admitted that all these outfits took orders from the regular army and numbered more than one million men in all.

But less well remembered is the record of postwar German heavy industry. Although the treaty had ordered the dismantling of war factories, the Control Commission never was able to make up its mind as to the difference between a machine or factory that manufactured for war and one that produced for peacetime use. The Krupp plant, with its worship of large lathes for producing heavy caliber guns, was also suitable for the manufacture of large tubes used in the Haber process for making ammonia. So the plant remained. While closing down gunpowder and explosives plants, the commission did not require the destruction of plants producing the components of explosives —for these components had important industrial application.

Thus the nitric-acid and the nitrogen-fixation plants of I. G. Farben were untouched; electrolytic chlorine plants, constructed to produce poison gas during the war, were ignored.

Yet all this was only part of the story of rapid German resurgence. Perhaps the shrewdest German efforts of all were directed at escaping the economic penalties imposed by the victors. For instance, Germany was required to deliver to France seven million tons of coal annually for ten years. Less than six months after the treaty was signed, though, Germany was already in default on deliveries. The Allies, accepting the plea that German miners were unproductive because undernourished, agreed to pay Germany five gold marks for every ton delivered during the next half-year, the sums to be used to feed the miners.

But these five gold marks were just the beginning. Because of a provision in the treaty that enabled Germany to get certain loans based on the difference between the German domestic coal price and the export price (a difference in favor of Germany of about 40 gold marks a ton), what happened was that a total of 45 gold marks began flowing into Germany for every ton of coal delivered as reparations. Under these circumstances the German coal miners suddenly became very vigorous and productive and in the next six months delivered a tonnage that netted Germany about $100 million. Germany thus got as much for her reparations coal as she would have done if she had sold it for cash.

With this nest egg in hand, by the end of 1921 Germany turned to the economic rearmament of her own industries. Two years later the British delegate on the Control Commission commented on how Germany was subsidizing key industries, promoting state factories for the manufacture of synthetic ammonia and aluminum and setting up vast electric-power stations. In the meantime Germany again defaulted on reparations—this time especially on deliveries of coke to France.

The great German monetary inflation of 1923 had disastrous effects on the mass of German people, yet at the same time government and industry turned it to profitable use. As Germany's internal debt was wiped out, German industry now won an advantage over industries in other countries that had to go on making tax payments on their own national debts. As a result, shortly after the Dawes Plan loan made Germany solvent again, the American trade paper, the *Iron Trade Review,* reported that "Germany's plant is completely modernized. During the inflation period when no other saving was possible, everything was poured into equipment, as though into a savings bank. Inflation was the sponge also, which wiped out the old mark indebtedness. The workers are on hand and the wages are relatively low. All that is needed to lubricate the rusting machinery is credit."

Credit was quickly forthcoming. United States investors put about $100 million into the Vereinigte Stahlwerke, the great German steel trust, in 1925, and other huge sums were poured from abroad into the German chemical and electrical industries. The great German industrial mergers and consolidations that now began paved the way for Hitler.

In 1925, only five years after the signing of the treaty, the Allies were distinctly worried. A British White Paper declared that Germany's defaults in respect of the treaty, "if not promptly rectified, would in the aggregate enable the German government eventually to reconstitute an army modeled on the principles of a nation in arms." But the defaults were not rectified. General C. M. E. Nollet, the French delegate and chairman of the Control Commission, declared "it was no longer in the realm of possibility to hinder this secret work of reconstruction."

It was impossible because the victors had already lost the strength of concerted action and had fallen out among themselves. This time, if we make the same mistakes, we have at least been forewarned.

GERMANY'S CARTELS ARE AT IT AGAIN [10]

Once again in our lifetime Germany is on her way toward turning military defeat into economic victory. For in the past two and a half years I have been in Germany and watched it happen. During most of that time I was one of the officials

[10] By James Stewart Martin, formerly head of Economic Warfare Section of Department of Justice, investigating economic systems of Axis countries; chief of Decartelization Branch of Military Government and United States Control Officer for the I.G. Farben combine, stationed in Berlin, 1945-1947. *New Republic.* 117:13-19. October 6, 1947. Reprinted by permission.

who gathered around General Lucius D. Clay's conference table every Saturday morning to discuss problems and progress in carrying out United States policy in Germany. Before that I had spent three years in Washington helping to plan steps by which the United States and other Allies might prevent the Germans from doing it again. But instead of going through with those steps, for the second time in 25 years we have watched Americans contribute hundreds of millions of dollars to prove to the German people that crime does pay.

What has happened is that within a period of two years United States policies for the treatment of Germany have changed their course by 180 degrees. Now in all important respects they coincide with what the German financiers, industrialists and politico-militarists have wanted us to do ever since they surrendered.

The official interpretation of our about face on Germany was given in a broadcast on August 16, 1947, by Willard L. Thorp, Assistant Secretary of State for Economic Affairs. He stated that the aim of the United States Government in setting up a far-reaching program of aid to Germany was simply to close the gap between the lagging recovery of that country and the more rapid recovery of the other Western European nations—which Germany had occupied and looted for five years.

Not two weeks later a London communiqué announced the results of the conference among Britain, France and the United States on the future of German heavy industry. The Americans and British had decided to disregard French fears of a strongly rebuilt Germany and to raise the level of permitted production of iron and steel in the Ruhr from 5.8 to 10.7 million tons. This will require keeping German coal in Germany instead of increasing shipments to France and the Low Countries, which need it for their own recovery, and inevitably means furthering the economic hegemony of Germany over Europe.

At the same time we have agreed—partly through default of a firm policy and a mere desire to "get things going," and partly through a desire of key groups in this country to do business with Germany—to the thesis of big-time German industrialists that the economic power of a revived Germany should be concentrated in their hands. These are the same hands that twice in one generation built Germany into a world threat.

To understand how this has come about, one has to go back to 1945, when it all began. In that year we were vowing, in speeches of government officials and in editorials throughout the country, not to repeat the mistakes we made after Germany's collapse in 1918. We told ourselves that it would take at least 25 years before Germans could be accepted as bonafide participants in the world's affairs without supervision or control. We were determined that they must show by actual conduct and not by pious talk that they had broken away from their previous adherence to any authoritarian leadership that promised new power, and had learned how to conduct their national affairs peaceably and without promoting conflict.

We warned ourselves that the Germans' discredited financial, industrial and militarist leadership would take every opportunity to promote and exploit disagreement among the Allies. We warned ourselves that the pseudo-democrats of the Weimar regime had proved to be just as aggressively pan-German as any Nazi. We reminded ourselves that after the First World War we had poured in United States and British capital to save Germany—over French protests—and that our reward had been default and German saving for new aggression. We kept in mind the fact that from the time of the Austrian Anschluss in 1938, the German economic high command had organized the key industries and resources of a large part of Europe into a continent-wide, German-dominated system, and we were intent on breaking up that "new order" for good.

This American point of view found its expression in the Potsdam Agreement of the victorious Big Three, whose economic clauses—today largely annulled—provided for the following:

1. Germany was to be treated as a single economic unit in the sense that common policies should be established to govern industry, agriculture, labor, imports and exports, finance, reparations, transport and communications.

2. In organization, however, the German economy was to be decentralized for the purpose of eliminating the excessive

concentration of economic power exemplified by cartels, syndicates, trusts and other monopolistic arrangements.

3. In organizing the German economy, primary emphasis was to be given to the development of agriculture and peaceful domestic industries.

4. Heavy industry was to be restricted to that necessary for Germany's peacetime needs, which were defined as the maintenance of living standards not to exceed the average of the surrounding European countries.

Though the Potsdam Agreement did call for a considerable reshaping of the German economy in the course of rebuilding, it lacked the destructive features usually attributed to the "Morgenthau Plan." Given reasonable efforts on the part of United States officialdom to carry it out, there was no reason for supposing that German reconstruction could not be guided along the prescribed lines.

Even before these Allied policies had been proclaimed, however, influential Germans had begun to undermine them. I have seen letters exchanged between Germans at home and Germans or their friends in the United States, congratulating one another on how well this attack was prepared in 1945. Their first propaganda effort was toward restoring the German economy along its prewar lines, with emphasis on heavy industry. Their second effort was to retain Nazis and other former leaders in key positions in an economy that was to remain centralized. Their third effort was to organize sympathy for Germany and to divide the occupying powers. All this seemed quite understandable as a German point of view. But while in 1945 it was still possible to refer to it as German propaganda, in 1947 some ingenuity is needed to distinguish it from official United States policy toward Germany.

It is easy to trace how the German attack on the Potsdam Agreement developed; but it is not necessarily safe to assume that the shifts of United States policy were German-inspired, or were engineered by German sympathizers. We have to avoid the mistake of looking for conspirators behind every development that entrenches the German position. As we found out during the war in the case of the German cartel system, the very motivations which operate American big business and finance are often enough to guide events the way the German negotiators want them to go.

The ink was scarcely dry on the Potsdam Agreement before some United States experts were arguing that it was unworkable, especially in its requirements for increasing food production and expanding light industry while prohibiting unusually large rehabilitation of heavy industry, machinery and tools. They won a ready hearing from Major General William H. Draper, the former member of the international banking house of Dillon, Read who had become director of the Economics Division of United States Military Government. As early as October 1945, one of Draper's principal advisers, Dr. Don D. Humphrey, began putting forth a series of recommendations that advocated revising the Potsdam principles.

The burden of these recommendations was that while Military Government was "for the moment" under a directive to the contrary, actually the best way to get German industry going and to produce exports sufficient to balance necessary imports would be to concentrate upon production of the most valuable forms of product: that is, to export complex machinery and machine tools rather than coal; to export complex chemicals and pharmaceuticals rather than coal tar and potash; and, in fact, to place the greatest emphasis first on reviving those very forms of industrial production which the occupying powers had decided to restore only to the minimum necessary to maintain the agreed average German standard of living.

Later, as the monthly statistical reports began to show that German heavy or capital-goods industries were actually recovering more rapidly than light industries, the explanation given was that the light industries, being in need of capital equipment, machinery and so on, were for the time being lagging behind the heavy, but that the trend could be expected to reverse itself after the light industries gained momentum. But the trend did not reverse itself, and then the talk shifted toward justifying the need for greater heavy industry as such.

Behind this shift toward the idea of swiftly reviving German heavy industry lay many pressures, and of these one of the most formidable was food—or rather, the failure to produce food adequately and the Germans' skill in producing hunger propaganda instead. During the summer of 1945, we Allied officials wondered at the droves of industrial workers and their families sunning themselves along the river banks in the Ruhr Valley while standing fields of grain grew overripe for lack of the labor to harvest them. That fall, German cries of "starvation" began. Along about January 1946, we waited apprehensively each week around General Clay's table for the report of the Public Health Division; but with mild weather and the reserve food stocks the Germans had accumulated during their occupation of the rest of Europe, the reports showed no epidemics and no increase in the death rate.

The fact that food supplies did thereafter become seriously short was due in part to the failure to reform German agriculture so as to achieve maximum production. Shortages of farm labor, failure to reallocate the use of land and absence of a positive program to stimulate production were in turn blamed. Personnel cuts in the Food and Agriculture Branch of our Military Government, the lack of a green light to carry through reforms and the failure to permit seed and fertilizer imports, all served to hamstring an able American staff while the major responsibility was shifted to the Germans themselves, in the United States zone, through the food and agriculture ministries of the several *Länder*.

By March 1947, the facts about what the Germans were doing began to roll out. With only twelve United States inspectors to watch the agricultural and food-distribution activities of the German agencies, food collections were running at only about 50 to 60 per cent of the estimated actual crops raised; the black market in food was flourishing; crop estimates by the German agencies were reported in some cases to be off as much as 62 per cent; and, to top it all, in the British zone the system of accounting for imported food had broken down so completely that of the first three million tons of grain arriving from the United States, some 300,000 tons had unaccountably vanished.

In the meantime the announcement of a ration cut in March 1946, had brought about an immediate collapse of coal mining in the Ruhr. ("Sabotage!" was one comment. "Teaching the occupying powers a lesson," was another.) Under pressure to produce coal, the Americans and British promptly began to send in food and to accept the feeding of Germans as their responsibility. And this in turn raised the question of how Germany was to pay for these food imports. With exports, of course. But what kind of exports?

At this point enter Herbert Hoover and his mission to Germany, sparkplugged by the German economist Gustav Stolper. The recommendation with which Hoover came back was that Germany should exchange primarily the products of heavy—rather than light—industry for food. (The idea of expanding German agriculture took a minor place in the Hoover report.)

Here was support from an elder statesman for the emerging doctrine of building up German heavy industry—a doctrine whose original authors had been German industrialists themselves. These Germans, having seen the initial eagerness of the victor powers to produce Ruhr coal for Europe's economy, had suavely tied the problem of expanding coal production to proposals for reviving Germany's leadership in heavy industry. You can't move coal to industry without transport, they argued; you can't improve transport without steel; you can't even mine coal without more steel for replacements.

Meanwhile, what about light or consumer-goods industries? The Germans maintained that to expand them would be impracticable. They chose to overlook the fact that the United States zone in particular is peopled with Germans who have been distinguished mainly for their handicrafts and for skilled craftsmanship in ceramics and precision and optical work. They also ignored the fact that Germany's huge existing heavy-industry plant was largely the result of planned overemphasis after the First World War, built to the detriment of agriculture and light industry and justified in the main on the grounds of military self-sufficiency.

That this German heavy industry was fairly uneconomic was proved by the fact that the American loans advanced to build it up after the First World War were largely defaulted. Indeed, this field is not even dominated by that highly specialized know-how which only Germans are supposed to possess. At the Leipzig Fair this year, for instance, the exhibits were particularly disappointing to expert observers in the heavy-machinery field, because most of the machines were 10 years out of date.

Like the Germans, Hoover did not stop to consider these points. But when he argued that the recovery of German light industry and agriculture must depend upon reviving heavy industry first, he was also overlooking what was happening just across Germany's borders in other Western European countries whose soil and climate are similar to her own. Not only was agriculture reviving with surprising speed in France and the Low Countries, but many manufactured items of consumer goods had begun to show up in their shops as early as the end of 1944, even though these countries had been systematically looted of their materials during five years of German occupation. Even little Luxemburg, the whole northern half of whose territory was ravaged by the Battle of the Bulge, had become 90 per cent self-sufficient in food by 1947.

While American economic policy in Germany was thus moving gradually into line with the Germans' own program, two other things happened that sped the process. First, the Germans themselves were put in charge of allocating coal and scarce raw materials to industries within the United States zone. Second, American officials took to encouraging centralization of control in the hands of "leading" German financial and industrial groups.

The two circumstances hang together. Under the Germans' own coal-allocation system, the pump-priming of heavy industries continued, to the embarrassment of the export-import program. (Although the Bizonal Agreement of 1946 had set a goal of $350 million of exports from the combined United States-British zones of Germany in 1947, only $60 million of this was achieved in the year's first half.) This storing up of productive power in the form of capital equipment, instead of putting it out in the form of exportable products, has greatly helped German over-all postwar plans. First, it paves the way for very substantial loans by seeming to show that without such loans the export program can never get off the ground. Second, the low export figures lend support to German drives for "efficiency"—meaning stronger centralized control.

And here is an example of how these drives are being aided by Americans. On July 3, 1947, we received copies at Berlin of a proposed statement of policy to be sent from the British-United States Bipartite Economic Control Group to the economic officers of the military governments in all *Länder* of the two zones. The document was prepared over the name of A. S. Barrows, who was formerly president of Sears, Roebuck, then serving as export-import chief for the combined zones. It would have required the economic officers to put pressure on the German allocation authorities in the *Länder* to close out small, "inefficient" industries by denying allocations of coal, iron and steel, and to concentrate industrial production to the greatest possible extent in the larger, "efficient" plants. This particular directive was for the time being suppressed after the Decartelization Branch raised objections to it; but its very existence is significant as revealing American sympathy for German big management—which, by and large, means Germany's old management.

Undoubtedly the Germans have had compelling reasons of their own for wanting to retain Nazis and especially members of their prewar financial and industrial leadership in key positions, and to retain a centralized economy in which their control can again become effective. The close alliance of Junkers, General Staff, financiers and industrialists has been a feature of the German social structure since the time of Bismarck.

The men who decided Germany's economic policy and created and managed her combines, cartels and syndicates, were the men who joined the Junkers and militarists in supporting the Nazis and maneuvering them into a position to take over the government. And if they or their nominees continue to have access to cartels or other forms of highly integrated organization, they will again be able to circumvent the terms of surrender.

Naturally they are bending every effort to stay in control. We were scarcely surprised, for example, when we found in the fall of 1946 that the German manager installed by the German authorities of Hesse to operate the Höchst plant of the I. G. Farben combine was meeting quietly with the ousted

Farben management. As United States Control Officer for I. G. Farben, I discharged the manager—doing so over the objections of our Economics Division for Hesse, which considered him a good production man—only to find him turning up in a private capacity at meetings of the Chemical Association for Hesse, where he was accorded the same respect as before. Since no law made it a crime to keep the old Farben gang together, nothing further was done.

Such rebuilding of German organizations under the noses of the occupying authorities is not something new. It happened after the last war too. One of our first investigations at Düsseldorf in May 1945, led us to Rheinmetall Borsig A. G., the huge armaments firm that was for a time integrated with the Reichswerke A. G. Hermann Goering. In one room we found research records and working papers dating back to 1922, when the office was set up right under the noses of the French occupying forces to design and manufacture artillery.

Other records led us to an installation at Unterlüss on the Lüneberger Heide, just off the highway from Hanover to Hamburg, which had evidently served as an artillery proving ground for Rheinmetall during the period when the Inter-Allied Commission was trying to suppress military construction and research and at a time when the new Weimar "democratic" Germany was developing.

The only noticeably novel feature of German tactics this time has been their success at convincing some occupation authorities—and apparently to a considerable extent our government—that the cumbersome, sluggish, red-tape administration of a centrally managed economy is more efficient and can achieve greater production than a decentralized one. From the standpoint of the desire of the dominant clique of Germans to retain control where they want it, the move is intelligible; but from the standpoint of the occupying powers, especially in view of the poor production record of the Germans in the past two years, it is not.

Yet we are hearing more and more in American circles about the allegedly serious inroads on German management made by the removal of Nazis, and of the need for retaining the old, experienced leadership.

Thus, in May of this year, a group of 14 "leading" American businessmen whom the War Department had sent on a tour of Germany released a report which recommended curtailing or postponing the program to reorganize the major cartels and combines that had dominated the German economy. The reason given for this was that the program represented "economic principles quite new to the German mind and to the past industrial development of the country." They declared their belief that "the strict adherence to the law in its administration" would be harmful.

Later, in a conference with the Secretary of War, the group of businessmen went into specific denunciation of the American denazification policy as well. It was their opinion that we could not get the German economy going unless we used the first teams of German management, which were either being denazified or awaiting trial. Another of their suggestions was that a group of American investment bankers should be sent to Germany.

Along with their campaign for retaining the former German leaders and their centralized forms of economic control, the German financial and industrialist cliques have continued to argue that Germany either is or must again become the economic hub of Europe. In this they have a small but highly influential group of willing supporters in certain large-scale manufacturers of durable consumer goods in the United States and Britain.

These manufacturers want two things to result from our control of Germany: first, a potential supply, at low rates, of capital equipment and semi-finished products, which they can then process and sell in their own protected and carefully allocated markets; and second, the powers to guide and channel the production and distribution of potentially competing products so as not to upset their already settled marketing arrangements. These are the business groups which would be most affected by the uncontrolled development of production in the Low Countries and France, with the possibility of an outbreak of competition in world markets.

Still another small but powerful group furthering the German game in the United States and Britain are those with investment-banking interests and sufficiently good connections to assure control of loans to Germany.

It has, of course, been a little difficult to maintain the "Germany-is-the-hub-of-Europe" theory in the face of her low production record and the well organized recalcitrance of the Germans, especially in the Ruhr, in getting to work for their own recovery. Ruhr coal production has been lagging far below its prewar and wartime performance: instead of 300,000 tons per day, production has hung around 225,000 tons, gradually creeping to 243,000 under the latest group of incentives. At the same time, iron and steel production have been hovering around the rate of 2.5 million tons per year, as against the old permitted rate of 5.8 million tons.

Yet, even though the Germans had not yet reached a full 50 per cent of their permitted iron and steel production, the United States and British governments have now raised the permitted level. What this means is that even if we succeed in stepping up Ruhr coal production, all or most of this increased coal will have to be retained in Germany in order to serve the new iron and steel levels—and undoubtedly to go into other correspondingly increased steel-processing industries. And thereby we shall find ourselves underwriting that complex of heavy industry which German financiers and industrialists have been hoping to reconstitute since 1945. At Potsdam we said we were not going to let them reconstitute it any more than absolutely necessary. Now we say that it is necessary, not for Germany alone, but for the benefit of Europe as a whole. What are the facts?

Belgium, Luxemburg and France are producing iron and steel at a rate of about 10.4 million tons a year between them. But they have an existing and undamaged capacity to produce immediately at least 16.7 million tons per year if they could get the necessary coking coal or coke. Now if we were really talking about benefiting Europe as a whole and not simply Germany, we might be impressed by the fact that an additional six million needed tons could be produced immediately by supplying these Western European nations with German coal. Instead of that, we are embarking on an extensive rehabilitation program for the reopening of the damaged steel plants of the Ruhr. What makes this decision even more illogical and uneconomic is this: If the Ruhr is to be the hub of the new production, we shall have to move three times as much ton mileage of ore *eastward* from the ore fields of Lorraine as the tone mileage of coke which we would move *westward* from the Ruhr or the Aachen basin if France and the Low Countries were the hub of steel production.

The effect of our policy of Ruhr rehabilitation is to turn the clock back to the period after World War I. Remember that on the eve of that war the French steel industry, *minus* Alsace and Lorraine, was equal to the German, *plus* Alsace and Lorraine. Yet after that war the combination of successful German hold-backs on Ruhr coal production and big American and British loans for building up German iron and steel production effectively whittled down the standing of the Western European steel industry. The result was that by 1926 the German industry, *minus* Alsace and Lorraine, had become greater than the French industry, *plus* Alsace and Lorraine. And this German advantage was solidified when, with the help of United States and British steel interests, the German steelmasters set up the International Steel Cartel as a device for maintaining, through alternate agreements and threats, their artificially acquired domination over the iron and steel industry of Europe and of foreign markets.

It is of the greatest significance therefore, that the International Steel Cartel, which maintained a shadow existence during the war and acted as an intelligence agency for the German General Staff, has resumed discreet but active operations. Various subgroups of the cartel have been meeting since at least October 1946, mostly in Brussels, in order to start working out new private agreements and quotas to govern the international trade in steel and steel products. For the present, since Germany cannot yet be formally represented at these meetings, this development is only an indication of things to come.

In two short years we have gone a long way—in reverse. We have forgotten how Nazi Germany organized the key industries and resources of a large part of Europe into a continent-wide, German-dominated economic system. War damage and defeat broke the immediate chain of dependence, and left the other countries of Europe free to shift for themselves and make their own readjustments. This they have done for two years, with such success that the Assistant Secretary of State for Economic Affairs points out that the United States must throw its greatest weight behind Germany's lagging recovery. To close the gap between Germany and the others, we are set to reconstitute the Ruhr heavy industry, under its prewar leadership, as the hub of Europe, to push the surrounding countries back into their state of dependence upon German economic well-being, and, in fact, to do for the New Order what it was never able to do for itself.

Beginning in late 1945 and on through 1946, a constant stream of German political and economic leaders regained prominence by denouncing the lack of any definite United States policy for Germany. Actually, this was the only period during which we had the semblance of a German policy. Now that the Potsdam policy has disappeared in a welter of conflicting purposes, we have nothing to take its place and we really do not know what kind of Germany we want to see emerge from the transitional state of military government. To make matters more difficult, an unwritten law has now decreed that all United States foreign-policy statements must be acceptably bipartisan. In practice this means that statements of policy sent to Germany now talk in two directions at once and furnish no practicable guide for Military Government action.

The vacuum is being filled by default—by economy-minded congressmen, visiting efficiency experts, sentimentalists, pan-German propagandists and United States businessmen with irons in the fire. Our confusion of purposes is illustrated by the fact that while we are trying at Nuremberg to make an example of a few dozen members of the German leadership which launched the war, we are actively reemploying or allowing continued power to other members of the same clique.

In spite of all this, our situation in Germany is not so hopeless as it seems. The main thing needed is a clear-cut determination to cease apologizing for or retreating from American points of view whenever they happen to run counter to the views of German "experts" or of United States businessmen with a personal interest in the outcome. We need to reassert a policy for Germany. If we can make up our minds to order a forthright reorganization of the German economy along truly democratic lines, there are hundreds of able and intelligent people still employed in Washington and in the Military Government organization who would know how to go to work and take the necessary steps. If we are going to rebuild Germany, we must first make sure that we are going to build the kind of Germany that will keep the peace.

EXCERPTS

The problem of restoring the European community inevitably raises in acute form the problem of Germany. The restoration of Europe involves the restoration of Germany. Without a revival of German production there can be no revival of Europe's economy. But we must be very careful to see that a revived Germany could not again threaten the European community.

I am not speaking of the revival of Germany in a military sense. There can be no question of the absolute necessity of keeping Germany disarmed and demilitarized. Today Germany is completely disarmed. Measures have been proposed by the United States and supported by the United Kingdom and France to insure the continued demilitarization of Germany for forty years. Thus far the Soviet Union has, in effect, rejected that proposal by wholesale amendments of its purpose, but the offer still stands.

The revival of German militarism, however, is not the only important factor involved in the relationship of Germany to a restored Europe. There is an imperative necessity for safeguards to insure that the economic power of Germany shall not be used by a future German government as a weapon for the furtherance of exclusively German policies. This poses admittedly a complicated and difficult problem. An attempt artifically to limit German peacetime economy could easily prevent the essential revival of German production to an extent that would render impossible the economic revival of Europe.

The answer to the problem would appear to relate primarily to the future role and functioning of the great industrial complex in the Ruhr. The United States believes that safeguards must be set up to insure that the resources and industrial potential of the Ruhr, particularly in respect of coal and steel, should not be left under the exclusive control of any future German government but should be used for the benefit of the European community as a whole.

The charge has frequently been made that the United States in its policy has sought to give priority or intends to give priority to restoration of Germany ahead of those of the other countries of Europe. The truth is that far from having been accorded a preference over any Allied country, German recovery has lagged so far behind that of the other countries of Europe as to retard the whole effort for European recovery. At the present time industrial production in Western Germany is less than one half that of prewar. The food supplies are seriously below the minimum requirement for health and efficiency, and German foreign trade is only a small fraction of its former dimension. In fairness to the American taxpayer who has been contributing hundreds of millions of dollars annually to support the people in the American zone, Germany must be made self-supporting as quickly as possible. With safeguards against any revival of German militarism and with measures to assure the utilization of the basic products of the Ruhr for the good of the European community as a whole, I believe that Europe and the world will be adequately protected against the danger of future German domination. In these circumstances it should be possible to proceed to the establishment of a provisional central authority in a federated German state and to the final framing of a peace settlement.—*George C. Marshall, Secretary of State. Address at Chicago, November* 18, 1947. *Department of State Bulletin.* N. 30, '47 *p.* 1027-8.

There is no question that the victims of German aggression are entitled to the greatest possible amount of reparations, even though Germany has already paid in territories and seized properties more than any nation has ever paid before. There is likewise no doubt that short-time payments in capital equipment are preferable to long-drawn-out reparations from current production, which could only repeat the consequences of such a program following the First World War.

But we submit that such payments are limited by two factors which should take precedence over other considerations. The first is that even under the Potsdam Agreement reparations payments are supposed to leave Germany enough resources to subsist without external assistance, which is not now the case, and that a self-supporting and viable Germany is the key to European recovery, as recognized in the European Recovery Program itself. The second is that the dismemberment of Germany and the loss of her eastern breadbasket—which . . . comprises not only the Soviet zone but all Eastern Germany unilaterally annexed by Poland and Russia—have completely changed Germany's population and production picture. As a result the new level of industry, under which plants are still being dismantled as "surplus," has become a snare and a delusion which can cost us and Europe dearly.

What the makers of the new reparation program have not yet faced up to, we think, is the fact that Western Germany has become another Britain, with approximately the same population living in an approximately similar area, with coal as the only important raw material, and with an ability to produce only about half the food needed. Yet Britain, with an unimpaired production apparatus and complete freedom to produce and trade, with vast resources in her Empire which more than offset her Empire obligations, and vast American aid already given, is able to live only under the severest kind of austerity on a diet which, while still twice the total calories the Germans usually receive, is nevertheless considered to be close to the danger point. How, without any of these advantages, Western Germany is not only to live but also to contribute to European recovery, under a program which would leave her only 75 per cent of the per capita production capacity of 1936 (when she produced more than 80 per cent of her own food) is an unexplained mystery for which we can see only one solution, and that is continued American subsidies to Germany and to Europe.

As regards the claim that the plants scheduled for dismantling can serve European recovery better if transplanted to the victor countries, we must point out that the dismantling and transplantation takes years and the labor of many thousands of men who could better be utilized in immediate production to relieve Europe's needs. And if it is said that the plants cannot be put into operation in Germany because of lack of skilled labor and raw materials, then we can only point to the fact that labor is withheld by the victors themselves through the retention of German war prisoners and that the raw materials are withheld by the Allied policy of economic strangulation. That is attested not only by such experts as John Hynd, former British Cabinet Minister in charge of the British zone, and others, but also by the constant revision of the program itself, even to the extent of reactivating industries forbidden under the Potsdam Agreement. —*Editorial. New York Times.* F. 21, '48. *p.* 12.

The United States position has been that German industry should remain in German hands, though "some special provision for the overseeing of Ruhr resources may be advisable."

If the industry of the Ruhr is to be left in German ownership, it is now generally agreed that effective means must be found of preventing its use as a basis for future German aggression. A large number of possible controls to this end have been suggested both here and abroad.

The present policy of prohibiting certain industries—arms, munitions, military equipment, explosives, nuclear fission—will almost certainly be made a part of the peace settlement, if and when such settlement is reached. As for the restricted industries, such as steel, the increase in capacity by surrounding countries of Western Europe will redress the European balance of war potential.

Control of the German war potential might also be effected by a selective control over imports into Germany of crucial materials such as iron ore, bauxite and oil. To the extent that Germany might be made dependent on outside sources of electric power, as from generating plants outside her borders, effective control of industrial expansion might be attained.

Within Germany cartels and other monopolistic arrangements have been prohibited for the occupation period by the Potsdam Agreement and Occupation directives. Such private organizations were useful in building Germany's relative strength in the years before the war. If ways could be found to enforce anti-cartel regulations after the end of the occupation period, here would be one more way of hindering German rearmament.

It has been suggested that control of Germany's commercial policy would also be effective. When an International Trade Charter is agreed on, its terms might be made mandatory for Germany, as might the terms of the International Monetary Agreement. Enforcement of the requirements of these pacts would prevent a resurgence of the autarchic commercial policy pursued by Germany in the years before the war. A Report of the Council on Foreign Relations says:

By insisting that the German trade be conducted on a multilateral, non-discriminatory basis (with countries willing to reciprocate), the Allies could prevent Germany from using her trade as a means of bringing smaller countries into political subjugation. More important still, through the expansion of her foreign trade Germany would become increasingly dependent on other countries, particularly with respect to the supplies of food and essential raw materials, and hence increasingly vulnerable in case of war.

Control over Germany's external assets would be helpful in preventing the use of German funds in other countries to build up research laboratories and develop war potential outside of her borders.

Enforcement of Allied controls by the use of (a) inspection arrangements to discover violations and (b) an international military force to punish violations is the proposal offered by the United States in the "Draft Treaty on the Disarmament and Demilitarization of Germany" submitted by Secretary of State Byrnes to the Council of Foreign Ministers at Paris in April 1946. By this treaty the United States, the United Kingdom, the USSR and France would agree that for a period of twenty-five years (or forty years) Germany would be kept disarmed by their joint action on inspection and military sanctions.

Experience in the 1920's has shown that a treaty of this kind would be effective only so long as the Allies remained in agreement on what controls there should be and what measures they were willing to take to enforce them. Allen Dulles, president of the Council on Foreign Relations, has said: "Adequate safeguards against German rearmament were written into the treaty after World War I.   Germany was able to aim for new aggression because the Allies were divided among themselves and were unwilling to assume the burden of enforcing the treaty by timely action.

Whether or not four-power agreement can now be reached on control of the Ruhr and of Germany, the possibility of agreement among the Western powers offers an alternative.   The proposal of Foreign Minister Bevin, January 22, for a series of treaties among the Western powers for economic cooperation and mutual defense may provide the answer to the security needs of Germany's neighbors.—*F. L. Van Schaick. "Rehabilitation of the Ruhr." Editorial Research Reports.* F. 18, '48. *p.* 120-2.

The only practical course for the harassed occupying forces is to foster German industrial production, and German exports, by way of exchange for necessary imports of foodstuffs.   The industry is there, requiring little to put it into production.   It would be a rare military governor who could resist so easy and so obvious a solution for his most pressing problem, the feeding of his charges.   Upon the urging of our occupation authorities, the United States is now well launched on a program of industrial recovery in Germany, financed by the Reconstruction Finance Corporation and other agencies of the American Government.

There is another sense in which the program of deindustrialization of Germany is unrealistic.   The industrial capacity of Europe is a valuable asset for all of Europe and the world.   It is one of the world's important accumulations of productive capital equipment, trained labor, and the complex interrelations of supply, transport, and management which make modern industrial production possible.   This is an impoverished world, which is passionately determined not only to restore but to outstrip prewar standards of living.   Every bit of available productive capacity is needed.   Europe above all cannot afford to scrap German production.   If a further disastrous decline in the economic welfare of the European peoples is to be avoided, the German industrial economy must be used for social ends, not destroyed. German industry is not necessary, as Secretary Morgenthau points out, to the mythical "economic equilibrium of Europe." It is essential, however, to assure prompt and dynamic reconstruction in Europe. Both in the Soviet zone and in the western zones, deindustrialization has given way to re-industrialization, and for the same fundamental reason.

More generally, a policy of expensive self-sufficiency for Germany is not one of economic progress in any sense. We need more specialization and more trade, not less. We should by all means abolish the protections and subsidies of many kinds which helped establish German industry. But it is hard to see our interest in wasting the valuable productive assets to be found in Germany.

There is also a strong political objection to the policy of economic self-sufficiency for Germany. A self-sufficient economy in Germany, under the central controls required to make it work, could again become the economic basis of a National Socialist program. We would be better off politically to make Germany part of an interdependent network of world politics and world trade. The faint hope of a democratic development in Germany requires a weakening of central controls, and the development of a life which depends at many points on continuing connections with the West.

One thing is certain. The disarmament of Germany cannot be guaranteed by any form of inspection or internal industrial controls. They have long since proved inherently unworkable, even during military occupation. Secretary Morgenthau, the great advocate of deindustrializing Germany, admits that this is the case, and puts his hope in controlling Germany's foreign economic relations, particularly in the realm of finance. But such remote controls can be evaded. And they miss the main point, which is that the technology of war changes so rapidly that new war methods would almost surely be developed independently of any German industries we might try to supervise or suppress. It is a striking footnote to the long wrangle over the permitted level of German steel production that the experimental rockets reported flying over Sweden are said to be made of non-ferrous metals.

Reliance on economic demilitarization of Germany is a snare and a delusion, which can easily distract our attention and energies from more promising remedies. The premise of the Potsdam plan was that we would be safe if German industrial capacity were cut down to norms of her peacetime needs, in terms of an approved standard of living for Germany. Are we to assume that the Germans would not again choose between guns and butter, but would be docile if allowed only enough capacity to produce civilian butter? We have come far enough since the summer of 1945 to see that even if we wanted to do so, we shall not in fact be able to destroy the accumulated capital of the last century and a half in Germany. Whatever the conceivable merits of the plan of economic disarmament, we are not following it. We never agreed to deindustrialize Germany, and we are not doing so.

Furthermore, the population of Germany is large. German war casualties were less than in the first World War. The German Army did not fight to the last man, by any means. The Allies took over six million German prisoners in the last few months of the war. The German birth rate has been the highest in Western Europe. And the Allies have pursued the almost inexplicable policy of sending German minorities from every other part of Europe back to Germany, to enlarge the German population, and to create prodigious difficulties of adjustment which accentuate all the Germans' resentments.—*Eugene V. Rostow, School of Law, Yale University. Virginia Quarterly Review. Winter. '47. p. 25-8.*

DENAZIFICATION AND REEDUCATION

DENAZIFICATION LAW AND PROCEDURE [1]

Denazification has uniformly been accepted as one of the primary responsibilities of American Military Government in Germany under both United States and quadripartite general occupation policy statements. The United States has assumed preponderant responsibility for leadership in promoting and developing the denazification program in Germany, first through the establishment of a comprehensive program in the American zone and later by inducing the other occupying powers to accept much if not most of this program in quadripartite regulations approved by the Control Council at Berlin.

Specific denazification regulations applied by United States Military Government in the initial period of the occupation were issued by the combined United States-British headquarters known as SHAEF (Supreme Headquarters, Allied Expeditionary Force). These regulations were founded largely upon, and were therefore in substantial agreement with established American occupation policy, as prescribed in the "JCS 1067" series by the Joint Chiefs of Staff, which was responsible for the basic directives to the American Theater Commanders. When SHAEF was dissolved early in July 1945, and American and British Forces were free to develop individual occupation programs in their respective occupation zones, the United States Theater Headquarters known as USFET (United States Forces, European Theater) issued new denazification directives. These, however, were little changed from those previously in use.

Meanwhile the US Group CC (United States Group, Control Council for Germany) was activated as a planning and operating staff of the American Military Governor in his participation in the quadripartite control of Germany, and, commencing late

[1] From article by Elmer Plischke, Chairman, Social Science Division, DePauw University. *American Journal of International Law.* 41:807-27. October 1947. Reprinted by permission.

in 1944, Military Government planning of the American branch of SHAEF (and later of USFET) was fully coordinated with the US Group CC. A number of divisions were established within the US Group CC organization, including a political division, to which responsibility was assigned for coordinating denazification policy and directives. In March 1945 it was decided that this political division should draft a single denazification policy paper incorporating the various elements of the program provided for in a variety of military government laws and regulations. This was undertaken by the present author, and was designated "Annex XXXIII (Denazification)" to the US Group CC "Basic Preliminary Plan: Allied Control and Occupation of Germany (Control Council Period)."

The Control Council (comprising the four Military Governors of Germany) did not convene in Berlin until mid-summer 1945, immediately following the Big Three conference at Potsdam. By the time it did convene, however, substantial general agreement had been reached by the Big Three powers as far as general denazification policy was concerned. At Yalta, in the "Joint Report of the Crimea Conference," on February 11, 1945, they agreed "to destroy German militarism and Nazism," to "wipe out the Nazi party, Nazi laws, organizations and institutions," and to "remove all Nazi and militarist influences from public office and from the cultural and economic life of the German people." These very general provisions of policy subsequently were augmented at the Tripartite Conference at Potsdam, promulgated in the Joint Report known as the "Potsdam Agreement" or the "Berlin Protocol," released on August 2, 1945. Its provisions are cited in some detail below. These agreements constitute the basis of the denazification measures adopted throughout the four occupation zones of Germany today.

The most immediate requirement for denazification that confronted our occupation forces was the wholesale eradication of the Nazi organization. To this end the Potsdam Agreement requires the Control Council "To destroy the National Socialist party and its affiliated and supervised organizations, to dissolve all Nazi institutions, to insure that they are not revived in any form, and to prevent all Nazi and militarist activity or propaganda."

When the Big Three met at Potsdam in the summer of 1945, such liquidation of the Nazi organization already was provided for by "Military Government Law No. 5" in the United States zone. This law, entitled "Dissolution of Nazi Party," requires the liquidation of the Nazi party and fifty-two specified Nazi organizations, and prohibits their activities. Dissolution also is required for eight Nazi party paramilitary organizations. . . . The Nazi party organization was rapidly dissolved in accordance with this law, and there have been no visible indications of its attempted revival in a large-scale organized Nazi underground, although there have been small-scale attempts at sabotage and visible remnants of Nazi fanaticism from time to time. . . .

The Potsdam Agreement is binding upon all four occupying powers, not the United States alone. The Control Council was persuaded by the American member to establish a quadripartite denazification dissolution program, designed to achieve uniformity throughout occupied Germany. On October 10, 1945, "Control Council Law No. 2" was therefore issued, "Providing for the Termination and Liquidation of the Nazi Organization," published simultaneously in the four zones on October 12, 1945. This law is very similar to U.S. "Military Government Law No. 5," referred to above. It declares that the Nazi party, together with "its formations, affiliated associations, and supervised agencies, including paramilitary organizations and all other Nazi institutions established as instruments of party domination, are hereby abolished and declared illegal," and the reconstitution of any such organization under the same or different name is forbidden. . . .

Nazi ideology and concepts are being uprooted from the German legal system. The Potsdam Agreement requires that "All Nazi laws which provided the basis of the Hitler regime or established discrimination on grounds of race, creed, or political opinion shall be abolished. No such discrimination, whether legal, administrative or otherwise, shall be tolerated."

Accordingly on September 20, 1945, the four Military Governors adopted "Control Council Law No. 1," entitled "Repealing of Nazi Laws." It provides for the repeal of twenty-five specified fundamental laws enacted after January 30, 1933, when the Nazi regime came to power, together with all supplementary and explanatory laws, ordinances, and decrees. . . . On January 30, 1946, a law sponsored by the United States, purging the German Criminal Code of Nazi and militaristic provisions, also was approved by the Control Council. . . .

According to the Potsdam Agreement, "Nazi leaders, influential Nazi supporters and high officials of Nazi organizations and institutions and any other persons dangerous to the occupation or its objectives shall be arrested and interned." When our occupation forces entered Germany American Military Government arrest program plans called for the detention of two groups of Germans. The first included all those who fell within certain prescribed arrest categories and who were arbitrarily arrested simply by virtue of the positions they held in the Nazi party or the German Government. Their arrest was based on the position held, not the particular culpability of the individual occupying the position. The second group, however, included those who were prescribed in the Allied Arrest Blacklist and were individually sought out by name. Many Nazis, of course, fell into both groups.

In general, automatic arrest of the following groups was initially required under these regulations: All persons who held office in the Nazi party organization, down to a low level; all persons who held commissions, down to and including the equivalent rank of major, in the paramilitary organizations; all officers and senior noncommissioned officers of the SS; and all officials in the higher ranks of the German Civil Service.

A revised mandatory arrest directive was issued on February 4, 1946, by OMGUS (Office of Military Government for Germany—United States, which replaced US Group CC in the fall of 1945). The new directive reduced the arrest categories, and the amended list—which was authorized by the United States Joint Chiefs of Staff in Washington and concurred in by the United States Chief of Counsel for the war criminal trials at Nuremberg—provided for the internment of members of organizations and groups contained in the following seven specific categories:

1. Gestapo and SD (*Sicherheitsdienst* or Security Service) of the SS.

2. Officers and non-commissioned officers of the *Waffen* (Armed) SS and *Allgemeine* (General) SS, and officers of the SA holding the rank of major or higher.

3. The leadership Corps of the Nazi Party, including Nazi officials down to the rank of *Ortsgruppenleiter* (Local Party Leader).

4. Members of the Reich Cabinet since January 30, 1933.

5. Members of the General Staff and High Command of the German Armed Forces.

6. War criminals.

7. Security suspects.

It was found to be very difficult to establish early estimates of the total number of Germans affected by the initial arrest program. This was due, in part, to the large shifts of German population occasioned by the military situation and the subsequent transfer of peoples, and also to the fact that arrests were based largely upon the positions held rather than upon the individuals themselves so that it was impossible to estimate accurately the percentage of overlap, that is, the cases in which one individual held two or more of the positions whose incumbents were subject to arrest. However, the figure 600,500 was given in September 1945 as the total number of arrestable persons in all Germany under established categories, and it was further estimated that approximately one third, or 200,200, arrests would be made in the American zone. The largest single group included among the arrestable categories was the Nazi party leadership corps, which, it was believed, would constitute 50 per cent of the total, or some 100,000 individuals.

In actual practice arrests averaged 400 to 500 per day prior to the revised directive of February, totaling about 100,000 in the first eight months of occupation. A substantial number of these arrestees did not actually fall within the arrest categories, however, but were detained because they came under suspicion for one reason or another. The above figures on the other hand, do not include all prisoners of war who fell within the arrest categories; when German prisoners of war were about to be released they were screened in order to weed out those subject to continued detention under the arrest categories and were simply transferred directly from P.W. enclosures to arrestee detention camps. . . .

Perhaps the most controverted phase of denazification is the so-called "removal-from-office" program. The Potsdam Agreement requires that:

All members of the Nazi party who have been more than nominal participants in its activities and all other persons hostile to Allied purposes shall be removed from public and semi-public office, and from position of responsibility in important private undertakings.

This is a similar, but somewhat less severe, statement of the general removal policy already provided for in the American removal directive, issued on July 7, 1945, and entitled "Removal of Nazis and Militarists." This directive, quoted directly from "JCS 1067," required that:

All members of the Nazi party who have been more than nominal participants in its activities, all active supporters of nazism or militarism and all other persons hostile to Allied purposes will be removed and excluded from public office and from positions of importance in quasi-public and private enterprises.

Considerable controversy has been evoked in defining an "active Nazi" under these provisions. It was decided to interpret it in the American zone as embracing all those who had:

(a) held office or otherwise been active at any level from local to national in the party and its subordinate organizations, or in organizations which further militaristic doctrines; (b) authorized or participated affirmatively in any Nazi crimes, racial persecutions or discriminations; (c) been avowed believers in nazism or racial and militaristic creeds; or (d) voluntarily given substantial moral or material support or political assistance of any kind to the Nazi party or Nazi officials and leaders.

Under the initial American directives removal from public and semi-public office was either mandatory or discretionary. Mandatory removal was required for the upper levels of Nazi leadership, including officials of the party and its affiliated organizations, for those who received certain Nazi party decorations, and for certain higher levels of the German Civil Service. . . .

All persons used by our occupation forces in public or quasi-public office were required to fill out a detailed six-page personnel questionnaire called the *Fragebogen,* containing questions intended to make the individual reveal his personal history, employment record, experience, military service, membership and role in all types of organizations, and especially the Nazi party and its affiliates, writings and speeches since 1923 when Hitlerism was being organized, income and assets since the party first achieved power, travel and residence abroad, and the like.

When the *Fragebogen* was completed the applicant signed and certified that the answers were true and that he understood that he would be prosecuted in an American Military Government court for falsification. . . .

Over 1,613,000 Germans—or one out of every ten persons in the American zone—were processed under this procedure by June 1, 1946, when a new procedure was adopted as described below. This in itself was a tremendous undertaking, achieved during a period of rapid redeployment of our troops. It entailed not only the perfunctory completing of the questionnaire and its evaluation, but also as complete a check, field investigation, and personal interview as possible. Of the cases examined, 373,762, or roughly 23 per cent, resulted in removal or exclusion from office, the remaining 77 per cent being cleared by this procedure. These figures tell only part of the story, however, since the elimination of the German national government and the mandatory abrogation by Military Government of numerous Nazi-created agencies, such as *Gau* units (the largest Nazi party administrative districts) and the DAF (German Labor Front), has resulted in the automatic group removal of many more thousands of Nazis from German public and administrative life.

The above figures, moreover, include only a small proportion of removals from business enterprises. It was early discovered that satisfactory results were not being achieved in removing active Nazis from private enterprises under this procedure. Inasmuch as the eradication of Nazi economic power and influence also has been conceived to be of prime importance, a supplementary regulation was promulgated and became effective on September 26, 1945. Designated "Military Government Law No. 8," . . . it rendered unlawful employment by any business enterprise of any member of the Nazi party or of its affiliate organizations in any supervisory or managerial capacity or otherwise than in ordinary labor, except as expressly authorized by

Military Government. Such authorization could be granted, upon appeal to Military Government, only to those persons, discharged or refused employment under the law, who claimed that they were forced to join the party and never were actively engaged in any of the activities of either the party or its affiliate organizations. Their appeals were heard by local German Review Boards composed of reputable non-Nazis appointed by the local mayor and approved by Military Government. The Review Board recommended to the local Military Government Office whether or not the appellant should be reinstated, but the final decision rested with Military Government.

Any business enterprise desiring to open for business, the law further provided, had to certify that it had no Nazis in its employ. A business open or operating with any person employed in violation of the law was required to discharge such person immediately, failing which it was closed by Military Government. Local German Labor officers were responsible for enforcing compliance on the part of business establishments.

Law 8 thus was expected to accord a priority acceleration to the denazification of the economic affairs of Germany. It prohibited former active Nazis from exercising influence in the economy of the Reich or dominating others through economic power. Germans falling within the purview of the law were not deprived of a minimum livelihood, but they were restricted in the type of position they could hold in the business field.

A quadripartite directive also was negotiated by the Control Council providing for removal from public office and from positions in private enterprise. This was approved on January 12, 1946, and was issued as "Control Council Directive No. 24.". . .

Once Nazis have been arrested or removed from office it is necessary to replace them with suitable politically reliable German personnel. The Potsdam Agreement provides that the selection of replacements shall be made from among "persons who, by their political and moral qualities, are deemed capable of assisting in developing genuine democratic institutions in Germany." The difficulty of locating trained and competent substitutes, free from Nazi taint, has been one of the greatest obstacles to immediate and peremptory denazification. Shortages were particularly acute in the initial days of the occupation, and were especially significant in the upper public office brackets, in the technical services, and in the teaching profession.

Difficult administrative problems resulted, but no breakdown —as was freely predicted by Germans whose self-interests were affected—occurred because of such removals. In the early days of the occupation, owing to a fear of resultant decrease in efficiency of operation, there was some reluctance on the part of Military Government to remove occasional officials whose removal or non-employment was required under our denazification regulations. But suitable non-Nazi replacements were found in most cases, and in the remaining cases new employees have been trained to fill the positions vacated.

In order to prevent the use of former Nazi economic resources for underground purposes or for the promotion of a Nazi revival, all property and funds of the Nazi party and its organizations were ordered to be immediately seized and held by Military Government as each new area was taken over by our Military Forces. This was required under our "Military Government Law No. 52," entitled "Blocking and Control of Property." However, in "Control Council Law No. 2"—the quadripartite regulation concerned with this matter and which has been referred to above—it subsequently was agreed not only to seize, but also to confiscate, all such properties. This multipartite law applies not only to the assets of the Nazi party but also to all formations, affiliated associations, and supervised agencies prescribed in this law.

Under these provisions Military Government seized accumulated Nazi wealth, but this was no mean task. It involved great financial and economic empires such as the DAF (German Labor Front), which was the sole organization of labor permitted under Nazi law in the Reich, and which, through a series of confiscations and sequestrations, developed into an enormous economic combine with an evaluation variously estimated between $1\frac{1}{2}$ and 2 billion Reichsmarks. In our zone Military Government was instructed in July 1945 to take over all DAF properties and assets. Some of these assets will be returned to the former organizations and individuals from whom they were taken by the

Nazis, while others may be dealt with as reparations. In any case, great care is being exercised to see to it that this economic wealth is not returned to any disguised Nazi organization, and it is so broken up that its combined economic and political power has been shattered.

Since it was deemed insufficient merely to liquidate the economic might of the Nazi organizations "Military Government Law No. 52" also was applied against the property and funds of the individual Nazi leaders and German militarists. Private transfers of their property were prohibited and their bank accounts frozen, so that they and their families could withdraw only minimum amounts necessary to maintain a livelihood. Law 52 applied to those Nazis who fell within the arrest categories or who were subject to removal from office. It is estimated that these aggregated over 400,000 families in the American zone.

The elimination of Nazi ideology and control from public information media is one of the more difficult and certainly one of the most important aspects of denazification. The Potsdam Agreement requires the Control Council to "prevent all Nazi and militarist . . . propaganda." To this end, German information services, including the radio, press, books and periodicals, films, theaters, concerts, and other forms of entertainment, were early placed under strict Military Government supervision in the American zone. This was undertaken in accordance with "Military Government Law No. 191," issued by SHAEF and entitled "Control of Publications, Radio Broadcasting, News Services, Films, Theaters, and Music and Prohibition of Activities of the *Reichsministerium für Volksaufklärung* and Propaganda."

This control is designed to eliminate information media which propagate anti-democratic ideas or Nazi policies including racism and race hatred, which constitute an incitement to riot or disorder, or which interfere in any way with the process of Military Government. As conditions have permitted, fuller scope for self-expression has been turned over to reliable Germans, but not until it was certain that such information services would not be used for Nazi and militaristic purposes.

All German information services initially were placed under direct Military Government management. Publishing houses were closed down until active Nazis could be eliminated and reliable Germans with democratic leanings licensed to replace them. Constant controls are exercised over the materials published. Nazi literature has been removed from the shelves of German bookshops and its display and sale prohibited. Initially all German newspapers were required to cease publication. Then certain papers were published by Military Government, and, as suitable German personnel was recruited and cleared, to whom could be entrusted the rebuilding of a free press, the papers gradually were licensed and turned over to such Germans and published under Military Government supervision. Nearly fifty papers were licensed during the first fifteen months of occupation and are currently published in the American zone. The radio, perhaps the information medium most thoroughly infected with Nazi ideology and personnel, has been the last to be returned to German management, and six German stations are now in operation in our zone. For the most part information services currently in existence in Germany are new, those existing under the Nazi regime having been dissolved, and virtually completely new German personnel has been utilized. As a result Military Government has exercised little more than policy supervision since the summer of 1946.

Although confiscation of Nazi and militarist literature in private libraries has been deemed undesirable and impracticable by the Control Council Coordinating Committee, comprised of the four Deputy Military Governors of Germany, nevertheless there is a general "Control Council Order No. 4," providing for "Confiscation of Literature and Material of a Nazi and Militarist Nature," approved May 13, 1946. This general order was amended on August 10, 1946, to permit the preservation by zone commanders of a limited quantity of copies of such prohibited documents, to be retained in the interests of research and scholarship under strict supervision.

In the field of education the purely Nazi schools, such as the Adolf Hitler Schools, the National Political Education Institutes, and the Nazi Leaders Colleges have been closed down permanently. Ordinary schools and educational institutions, originally closed by Military Government, on the other hand, have been reopened, but only after they were purged. This entailed the elimination of objectionable courses of instruction, the screening of teaching staffs, and the revision of textbooks. Today the teaching program is oriented towards developing democratic and humanitarian principles and values, and toward the eradication of Nazi and militaristic influences or doctrines, especially instruction giving support to the "Führer" principle, aggression, nationalism, militarism, and discrimination on the basis of race and religion. This is in accordance with the provision of the Potsdam Agreement requiring that "German education shall be so controlled as completely to eliminate Nazi and militarist doctrines and to make possible the successful development of democratic ideas."

In the field of religious affairs denazification was largely a matter of removing Nazi restraint on the freedom of religious belief and worship, of reviving an independent religious press, of protecting shrines from damage due to Nazi-abetted disrespect, of abrogating Nazi laws and decrees providing for religious discrimination, and of using religious groups and leaders for the reeducation of Germans through emphasis on moral values.

But it also involves the screenings of the clergy. Church authorities were instructed to discharge clergy whose Nazi backgrounds placed them within the application of the provisions of the removal-from-office directives. Military Government itself investigated the personnel constituting the church administration, in order to weed out both Nazis and militarists. Priests and pastors who preach nationalist or Nazi principles are treated as are laymen. The purging of the clergy and the church hierarchy has been deemed essential by Military Government because investigations established some collaboration with the Nazi organization. Military Government has proceeded slowly with church denazification, however, in order to allow the Germans to do as much as they could to set their own religious affairs in order. . . .

With the close of 1945 the denazification program in the American zone had largely reached its initial objective. The Nazi party and its affiliated organizations were dissolved. Former active Nazis had been removed from leading positions in government and business and their financial wealth taken under control. German authorities, purged of known active Nazis, were functioning at all but the national levels. Nazi pomp and color had been swept out of existence. Yet the American denazification program was so far largely an interim program designed for the initial period of occupation. The time, it was believed, had arrived for effecting a comprehensive long-range denazification program.

A Denazification Policy Board therefore was established within OMGUS to undertake a complete survey of the entire program. In its report of January 15, 1946, it concluded that every person who exercised leadership in support of the Nazi regime should be deprived of influence or power, and those responsible for the wrongs and suffering caused by the Nazi regime should be punished. The actions to be taken in carrying out this program, however, must commend themselves to fairminded men, and denazification should not be carried to the point of preventing the building of a democratic society in Germany. The Board further held—and this is of prime significance—that the German people themselves must be allowed to participate actively in denazifying their country.

In December 1945, the *Land* (or state-level) Ministers of Justice of Bavaria, Greater Hesse, and Würtemberg-Baden submitted to Military Government a German draft proposal to be adopted as German law in each *Land*, incorporating denazification as a regular part of the new German program of political and economic reconstruction in the American zone. Based in part upon suggestions made in this proposed German law, and as a result of extended deliberation by the Denazification Policy Board, a new "Law for Liberation from National Socialism and Militarism" was approved and issued by OMGUS on March 5, 1945, and was reissued as German law in each *Land* in our zone.

This denazification law calls for the registration and classification of all former members of the Nazi party and specified affiliated organizations, influential Nazi supporters particularly in the business field, and the more active militarists. When classified, such Nazis fall within the following groups:

Class 1. Major Offenders (*Hauptschuldige*).
Class 2. Offenders (*Aktivisten*)—or Activists, Militarist, and Profiteers (that is, active participants or supporters, or recipients of excessive or unjust profits).
Class 3. Lesser Offenders (*Minderbelastete*)—or probationers.
Class 4. Followers (*Mitläufer*)—those who, though party members, were never more than nominal Nazis.
Class 5. Non-offenders (*Entlastete*)—or persons exonerated.

The removal categories prescribed in the quadripartite removal agreement referred to above are fitted into this classification in an Appendix to the law. . . .

Military Government headquarters early estimated that under this new denazification law the German courts would be required to hear some 3,000,000 cases. This would mean a hearing for every five inhabitants in our occupation zone. An optimistic estimate was that at the 1946 rate of progress the tribunals would not be able to complete their task until June of 1948, while less optimistic reports indicated a belief that the task is virtually endless.

In order to hasten the tempo of denazification and to shift attention from the Nazi small fry to the more important members of the organization, two amnesties have been granted in the American zone in 1946. The first exempted from denazification trials all youths born after January 1, 1919, except Major Offenders (Class 1) and officers in the Hitler Youth movement.

The second, proclaimed in his 1946 Christmas address by the Military Governor of the American zone, provides for a general amnesty, but only for the Nazis who are not chargeable as Major Offenders or Offenders (Classes 1 and 2) Those benefitted are the "little men," including only those whose annual income during the calendar years 1943 and 1945 was less than 3,600 marks ($360 at present rates of exchange) and whose taxable property in 1945 did not exceed 20,000 marks ($2,000). Also exempted from prosecution under this amnesty are Nazis who are more than 50 per cent disabled, if they do not fall within Classes 1 and 2 of the denazification law. . . .

A total of approximately 12,000,000 Germans registered under the denazification law of March 1945, of which 11,000,000 (92 per cent) had their Nazi status legally determined according to established procedures. Of the latter 8,735,000 (73 per cent) were found to be not chargeable and therefore were completely exonerated, while the remaining 3,290,000 (27 per cent) were chargeable. Of the total number of chargeable cases, over 2,308,000 (70 per cent) have been completed, so that some 982,000 (30 per cent) remain to be considered. . . .

As of June 30, 1947, the total number of internees held under custody in German enclosures under the denazification law totaled 47,656, including about 26,200 SS members, 12,150 Nazi party leaders, and 1150 Gestapo agents.

At the present time the American Military Governor and the German denazification authorities are considering a new denazification law to further speed up the program. If approved, this new law will free about half (some 350,000 to 400,000) of those still awaiting tribunal hearings. This will be achieved by summary procedure, and will entail merely the payment of a nominal standard fine. Crowded tribunal dockets will thus be cleared, permitting the authorities to concentrate solely on those Germans whose offenses, on the record, are so bad that they must be classed as criminals.

Denazification thus is a comprehensive program intended to liquidate Nazi political and economic organization and power in Germany for all time, and it is founded upon both multilateral (or quadripartite) and unilateral Military Government laws and directives. In the United States zone it has been viewed as one of the primary phases of our initial occupation program. There are those who claim that it is not at all unreasonable to expect that, if properly enforced, the broad objectives of our denazification regulations are not impossible of achievement.

But the real test of denazification lies rather in the extent to which it contributes towards the achievement of our fundamental, over-all occupation objectives. If it helps to pave the way for the establishment of a stable government based upon democratic institutions and procedures that guarantee fundamental human rights, a realization that the German state is the servant of the people, and a consciousness of moral and political responsibility for German policy and action both at home and abroad—then it may have served a very useful purpose. A great deal of thought and energy have been given to denazification in order to direct it towards this end. It now is up to the more important, positive elements of the occupation program—democratization and reeducation.

AMERICAN MILITARY GOVERNMENT AFTER TWO WARS [2]

The duty of the military is properly military; that is, to support the civilian authorities and to keep down disorder. When the army moves into enemy territory, it must perforce exercise direct administrative functions for the time being; but the recreation of permanent civil government should be in the hands of civilians—perhaps civilians in uniform, but men without the military viewpoint. There is no doubt that the army must be present in Germany for some years, but the actual reestablishment of civil government should be supervised by civilians. On November 14, 1946, Anthony Eden made a demand in the House of Commons that the government send to the British zone "a Minister, who should be of Cabinet rank, who has had experience of administration, and who has good political judgment, to assist the Commander-in-chief in his most onerous task." Saul K. Padover, after returning from service with MG, suggested in the *Nation*, December 22, 1945, that Congress establish a civilian Occupied Lands Authority (OLA) under the direction of men like Harold Stassen, Milton Eisenhower, and Herbert Lehman. Padover declared that while military occupation is necessary, military government is undesirable.

Aside from exile, which is usually self-imposed, unwanted elements may be removed from the political scene by various

[2] From article by William A. Russ, Jr., Professor of History and Social Science, Susquehanna University, Selinsgrove, Pennsylvania. *Social Studies.* 38: 207-17. May 1947. Reprinted by permission.

methods, running from disfranchisement (the mildest) to imprisonment (more drastic) to execution (the most extreme). . . .

In the case of the Nazis, all three forms of punishment have been employed. The top men and the worst criminals were tried and executed. No constitutional provision for a jury trial prevented the Allies from convicting the ring-leaders at Nuremberg, as well as others by military commission. Some high-ranking ones like Hitler liquidated themselves. Exile, which saved the Kaiser, was not possible after World War II. Others have been imprisoned. The *Philadelphia Record*, January 29, 1947, commented on the fact that in the year and a half since Germany's collapse "the United States, which controls one third of Germany, has executed [only] 221 Germans." Inasmuch as it is estimated, continued the editor, that the Nazis murdered more than 6,000,000 Europeans, of whom probably 2,000,000 lived in what is now the American zone, executions have amounted to one for 9,000 murders. "During the war," however, "allied leaders, including our own, promised that those guilty of mass murder would be punished by death. . . . We still have a long way to go even to begin to eliminate the top leaders of the most vicious government of all time.". . .

Denazification has been carried out by the German courts with considerable despatch and efficiency; they are much more businesslike in the matter of punishing wrongdoers than were the courts of the Weimar Republic which were supposed to deal with "criminals" of the German Empire. As *Life* said on November 11, 1946: "If anything, the Germans are stricter and certainly more discriminating denazifiers than we were before we gave them the job." In one respect they are more severe than were the Allies. When the Nurmberg tribunal acquitted Franz von Papen and Hans Fritzsche, they were tried by a German court at Nuremberg.

Meanwhile the task of creating more permanent regimes had been undertaken in the American zone, partly to train the Germans in self-government, partly to relieve American administrators—whose ranks were being depleted as men left for home—of the details of civil administration. Roughly speaking, reconstruction of civil rule in the American zone and reconstruction in the South after 1867 were of a similar pattern. First came disfranchisement of the undesirables and then the new electorate was expected to create a new regime. The procedure in Württemberg-Baden was told by Moses Moskowitz, formerly with MG, in the *Political Science Quarterly*, December 1946. . . .

After hostilities ceased in Germany, there were immediate attempts to remove the outright Nazis from local posts if less tainted ones or if democrats could be found. The process of denazification made the task of American supervisors even more difficult, for, in many cases they had hardly gotten things going in certain towns through the use of Nazi officials before these men had to be evicted and green ones chosen. . . . Nevertheless the use of Nazis, even temporarily, angered many Americans. Padover was very critical about the employment of Nazis in local areas. In Aachen the German administration as set up by MG was almost entirely Nazi. This was also true in Bavaria until, in Padover's words, the Bavarian government was "kicked" out by General Eisenhower.

Just as happened during Reconstruction, the question arose as to how many undesirable Germans could or should be shelved; and if disabled, how long they could or should be kept out of politics. After all, a complete blood bath or purge went counter to democratic and humanitarian sensibilities. Only totalitarian states, like Communist Russia after 1917 and Nazi Germany after 1933 were bloodthirsty enough to attempt liquidation of the entire opposition. In the postwar South there were thousands of "little rebels" who were not worth punishing, even by disfranchisement; by the same token there were thousands of "little Nazis" who could not be taken out of circulation—at least not for long. Thus on the day before Christmas 1946, General Joseph T. McNarney "amnestied" about 800,000 of the "small-fry" Nazis. These were "little men" who had incomes less than 3,600 marks between 1943 and 1945, or who had taxable property worth not more than 20,000 marks in 1945. McNarney's act can be compared to the amnesty measure of 1872.

The rapid change from vengefulness to forgiveness on the part of American administrators in Germany was hastened by the dollar sign, just as it was hastened in 1867-1868 by the party purpose. It soon dawned upon British and American taxpayers that they were being given the dubious honor of standing the cost for the occupation of Germany. The deficit in the British zone was estimated at £80,000,000, or £100,000,000 if the British portion of Austria be included. For 1948 President Truman asked $725,000,000 for government and relief in occupied areas. This sum was about the same as in 1947. The decline of vengeance, in part because of the high cost of vengeance in pounds, was expressed by Winston Churchill in a speech to the Commons on November 12, 1946:

> We and the Americans continue to rule and administer the German people in our zones at extravagant and almost unbearable cost . . . to ourselves, and with increasing dissatisfaction to the Germans. . . . We are all agreed that the proper course is . . . to make the Germans earn their own living, and make them manage their own affairs as soon as possible, and give them all possible aid while preventing every form of rearmament . . . There must be an end of vengeance and retribution . . . It is my hope that we shall presently reach the end of executions, penalties, and punishments. . .

This declaration was a far cry from some of the vengeful statements that were made by many leaders during the war. Churchill went on to say that since the Nuremberg and other trials had punished the criminals, it was time to call a halt:

> We are told that thousands yet remain to be tried, and that vast categories of Germans are classed as potentially guilty because of their association with the Nazi regime. After all, in a country which is handled as Germany was, the ordinary people have very little choice about what to do. I think some consideration should always be given to ordinary people. Everyone is not a Pastor Niemoller or a martyr. . .

In other words Churchill was saying that thousands of Germans could not be blamed for siding with the Nazis because they had no other choice. This attitude was similar to that which some radicals soon reached; namely, that the ordinary people could not be punished, even with disfranchisement, because they had no alternative but to accept Confederate authority once Federal power vanished in the South.

Denazification has not been as thorough as many extremists might like; nevertheless the sizable number who have been removed from German politics presents a potential danger. They are the leaders who have the know-how of German government, who have the education and experience, and who, trained in National Socialist intrigue and subversive tactics, understand how to start trouble. Some former MG officers, now returned to civilian life, have expressed a fear that these disfranchised persons constitute a future menace. Removed from seats of local and even national power, they will doubtless be ready material out of which to create undergrounds which later may cause disorder. Seeing former "no-accounts" ruling over the *Kreise* and the *Länder,* remembering the days of their former glory and disliking to take orders from democratic officials who are supported by American arms, they promise to be untractable material out of which to make a new peace-loving, democratic Germany.

It is worth noting that the nationalists, Nazis, and militarists had the same attitude towards the Weimar Republic during the 1920's. Even though not disfranchised or otherwise disadvantaged by the Republic, men like Hitler and Ludendorff scorned the upstart, low-brow democratic officials, who, according to haters of democracy, were weaklings and miscreants who had stabbed Germany in the back. These dissident elements detested President Ebert because he had been a saddlemaker. They felt a little better at the election of Hindenburg to the presidency because he was a real aristocrat and Junker, although they did not like the democratic system even with Hindenburg at its head.

Furthermore, the inculcation of democracy in Germany is handicapped by the fact that it is being imposed from above by foreign arms. A conquered people is likely to be cool towards an outside system even though that system be good. That MG understands this fact is evident from the words of Colonel William W. Dawson, regional military commander in Württemberg-Baden, who was quoted by Moskowitz as saying:

. . . democracy has not become the passionate ideal, because it was not fashioned in the crucible of fire and sword. It is a gift of the conqueror. There is no reason to fight for it, because its existence is not threatened. It is safeguarded by the power and might of the armies.

That it is difficult to keep a large disfranchised group of people down—particularly if they have experience and intelli-

gence—is proved by the opposition on the part of the disfranchised Southerners after 1867. The underground of that
era was the Ku Klux Klan, many of whose members were disabled "rebels."

So far there is no evidence of any concerted movement by
the displaced Nazis to start disorder, although rumblings are
heard. Denazification offices have been bombed, and the
"Odessa" gang of ex-SS men had a veritable arsenal at their
headquarters in Stuttgart. On January 23, 1947, MG gave all
Germans in American zone ten days in which to turn in hidden
weapons on pain of death.

Aside from the possibility of subversive movements and
perhaps open disorder, both of which may develop, the decline
in the political ability of officeholders must be taken into consideration. The Nazis saw to it that, by execution and by exile,
the democratic leadership was extinguished. In the words of
Moskowitz:

> . . . the best of the anti-Nazi leadership was gone. Emigration and
> the concentration camps took a heavy toll. The handful who came out
> alive from the torture chambers and the larger number who spent the
> twelve years of Nazi rule in retirement were, for the most part, tired
> men, discouraged and disillusioned. They faced a new generation that
> did not know them, and they were discredited in the eyes of those who
> knew them.

The few democrats still living in exile would not be numerous enough to help matters, even if they were willing to return; and, in addition they could hardly be welcomed by resident
Germans who would look upon them as carpetbaggers. And so,
most of the individuals who have been raised to places of authority in the American zone are untrained men who know
little about government and who are likely to receive no more
cooperation from former Nazis than is necessary. Having belonged to the politically ostracized groups during the heyday of
the Nazis, they were able to secure no administrative experience.
How long it will take for them to learn the art of governance—
and above all to win the allegiance of the disabled persons—
is a question; but it is obvious that the removal of the undesirable
but experienced people from the political scene caused a lower-

ing of official ability. That very thing happened with dire results after the disfranchisement of Southern leaders. This is not the place to repeat what the present writer has already said in *The South Atlantic Quarterly,* January 1945, about the price paid for disabling Southern Confederates but the price was high, not only for the South but for the country at large. . . .

About all the new electorate could employ to maintain itself was Union troops. When military support was removed, the radical elements were helpless. It was not long before the Negroes, Scalawags, and Carpetbaggers were dislodged, and the white Democrats were restored to authority. If such is not to be the outcome in Germany, then military occupation for some time to come will be the only preventive; yet, paradoxically enough, the longer military occupation continues, the more likelihood there is of trouble.

The denazified elements were submissive enough for some time after the end of the war—so were the Southerners just after Appomattox—but, unless prosperity comes quickly to Germany and unless the occupation authorities can speedily train good democratic leaders who will make democracy popular, difficulty lies ahead. The International Committee for the Study of European Questions believes that denazification is already a failure: ". . . during recent months former members of the Nazi party and of the SS have been circulating again in uniform in the various zones of occupation both in public and at private gatherings, particularly in Lower Saxony and Bavaria, and have received open manifestations of sympathy from the German people." One hears the estimate that Germany must be occupied for at least ten years; and yet, even after ten years of military reconstruction in South Carolina, Florida, and Louisiana, the new electorate fell from power and the older elements returned. Can a different result be expected in Germany?

It is generally agreed that the answer centers around education. If enough Germans can be educated to see the value of democracy, there is hope that the new groups will be able to maintain themselves. Chief reliance is placed upon education of the young, because it is felt that most of the people who grew up under Hitler are hopeless. In a sense education was also the key to success in radical reconstruction. If the Negroes could have been quickly taught at least the three R's, the radical experiment might have shown better results. But the recently liberated blacks, now voters, could not be educated that quickly, in spite of efforts of Northern teachers who were sent to the South by the churches and by the Freedmen's Bureau. As a result the Reconstruction governments were so corrupt and venal that even many radicals in the North became disgusted. As Professor Sageser said: "The political reconstruction had wrought havoc in the South. Intelligence had been disfranchised; ignorance infranchised." The very wickedness of uneducated radicalism brought on its own undoing.

The problem in Germany is not one of educating a totally illiterate people in the three R's; it is rather the problem of educating a highly literate nation into support of democracy. Germans must be de-educated out of nazism. The era of radical reconstruction would indicate that this will be a delicate task. . . .

It is clear that educating Germans into democracy cannot be done either by foreign teachers or by German exiles. In reference to "Axis Reeducation," W. B. Langsdorff says correctly: ". . . first . . . education cannot be coercive from the outside; second . . . it must represent the national culture and be under the direction of national leaders; third . . . it cannot be provided by 'missionary' [read carpetbagger] teachers from the United States or others of the United Nations." If Southerners after 1865 did not welcome "do-gooders" from the North (who were their own fellow citizens), Germans will be even more opposed to the ministrations of outside educators. . . .

Above all, Americans should set a good example. But setting a good example is one of the difficulties. Necessary as the army is for the control of Germany, it is education's worst enemy. After all, education in democracy means more than formal schooling and denazified textbooks. Example is even more important and yet many American soldiers in Germany are not the best exemplars of democracy. Black market operations, drunken sprees, sex looseness, and even looting, are not the finest arguments in German eyes for the worth of democracy. The original American invaders were usually careless enough about their actions, but returned soldiers admit they were disturbed at the caliber of the replacements.

A German economist told Shepard Stone: "In recent months many of the best Americans have gone back home. Who, with a few exceptions, have remained? Those Americans who had small jobs at home but big ones here. And others, who think they can make a good thing out of their stay here." Stone gives many instances of the unfortunate actions of some Americans. In one case, " . . . eighteen Germans have had to give way to two Americans who wanted a house for themselves and their girls; furnishings have been looted." Stone's conclusions about success in swinging Germans to democracy are not too optimistic. Most Germans, he reported, have not changed psychologically, and too many Americans are "feathering their own nests, living high-handedly. They are a bad example to Germans and a discredit to the their country."

Military occupation is a thankless task and has always led to ill will and hatred between troops and civilians. If this friction does not produce a "Boston Massacre," it results in some species of "woman order" such as General Butler issued in New Orleans, or non-fraternization rules which were tried in the early part of the American occupation of Germany. If the Germans are to be given an education in the delights of democracy, the army must be kept out of sight as much as possible, although ready for any emergency.

The success of American administrators in creating a stable, democratic Germany, in the United States zone at least, depends a great deal upon a frank recognition that a social, political, and economic revolution has been taking place in Germany since 1945. Displacement of thousands of Nazis and favor shown to the democratic elements are evidence of the social and political phases of this revolution. The economic aspect includes denazification of trusts and cartels. This process, if kept in the right groove, is desirable; in fact the victors are responsible for it because they have aimed at permanently unseating the militarists, Nazis, and other enemies of democracy. This time the revolution must really do the job. For, as has been observed many times since 1918, the revolution of that year stopped in midstream and did not go far enough. Instead of pulverizing the militarists and nationalists forever, the revolution resulted in a weak compromise which Hitler easily overturned.

The Russians in their zone are carrying the revolution to its logical conclusion by a wholesale uprooting of the Junkers and by the division of their estates among the common people. The American-sponsored revolution aims to stop far short of this; indeed the Americans are frowning upon the socialization of the chief industries by the British in their zone. Furthermore, the rise of a spirit of forgiveness, already discussed, would indicate that the Americans have gone about as far as they intend. Have they gone far enough? Only time will tell.

The *sine qua non* is to maintain control of this revolution and to keep it going in the direction of democracy. It must be protected from sovietization by the extreme Left and from counter-revolution by former Nazis. This is of the essence if the American experiment is to succeed. The International Committee for the Study of European Questions declared that the chief danger lay in counter-revolution by the Nazis who would use for their own purposes the very democratic governments that are being set up, just as they did with the democratic processes of the Weimar Republic. In the words of Mallory Browne, summarizing the report: "The Nazi party has recovered from the first shock of Germany's defeat and is quietly reorganizing for return to power through control of democratic institutions set up by the Allies." MG at once denied the existence of any subversive activities. MG is probably correct in saying that no widespread movements have so far been started. But in a similar way, the displaced Southerners, after 1867, working under the very constitutions which the new electorate had established for its own defense, recaptured the state governments from the radicals.

The basic reason for the failure of military reconstruction after 1867 was that it could not be kept within reasonable limits and that it went into the extremes of Negro rule and vicious government. The pendulum then swung to the opposite extreme of Negro disfranchisement. Whether the Americans have the skill and experience to accomplish their middle-of-the-road goals or whether circumstances over which they have no control will prevent the realization of those goals in Germany it is too early to say.

THE AMERICAN DENAZIFICATION PROGRAM IN GERMANY [3]

The military government detachment which was assigned to take over the administration of Aachen was probably fairly typical of military government detachments. Its officers included a variety of types and backgrounds; some were abler than others, but the average was not low. Like most other military government officers, the officers assigned to Aachen knew comparatively little about Germans in Germany. They were under considerable pressure to get a German government started at the earliest possible moment in order to deal with the emergency. Apparently they were impressed by the cordiality of the local German bishop and relied heavily on his advice as to the local inhabitants suitable for staffing that government. Unfortunately they chose as *Burgermeister* a German business man who turned out to have a bad Nazi record and with his assistance they mired in more deeply by filling the other key positions with Germans whose pasts more often than not could not bear examination.

Of course the anti-Nazis expressed their indignation and the newsmen, given the cue, began to investigate the past records of the men used by military government to operate the local government. What they found was enough to fill many dispatches sent to their papers and to cause literally thousands of the most sensational headlined stories to appear throughout the length and breadth of the United States. Being newsmen most of them were of course looking for stories rather than attempting to report the routine operations or depict the over-all difficulties. A tremendous wave of indignation, anger, disappointment, resentment, bitterness, and even horror developed in the United

[3] From article by Harold Zink, Hall Professor of Political Science, DePauw University; consultant on reorganization of German Government, U.S. Group, Control Council for Germany. *Journal of Central European Affairs.* 6:227-40. October 1946. Reprinted by permission.

States, especially on the part of the Jews and others who had to bear the brunt of the Nazi crimes. Military government, which had enjoyed the status of a favorite child, became anathema; the pressure that descended on Washington caused even the strongest to quail.

The combination of the delay in getting the denazification plans to the military government officers and the hornet's nest stirred up by the news stories from Aachen was, if not fatal, certainly most unfortunate. It got military government in Germany off to a bad start. Moreover, it immensely complicated the denazification problem. The Joint Chiefs of Staff in Washington, stung into action, issued a directive which, though somewhat vague in certain particulars, seemed to have the effect of barring all who had Nazi affiliations from holding public positions of any type, even if they were clerical or mechanical in character. When this JCS paper was received in the ETO it led to virtual paralysis in the denazification program for a time because no one on the ground in Germany could see how it would be possible to organize a German system of government under its ban on all Nazis. Not that many officers had a brief for any German with the slightest Nazi contact; it would have been far more desirable to use only those who amid all of the Nazi orgy had managed to keep themselves entirely unsullied. But the question was where to find such Germans.

The Nazis had not contented themselves with organizing a political machine, such as is familiar in the United States; they had aimed at integrating every possible phase of German life under their control. Teachers had to belong to the Nazi teachers' association or surrender their positions; doctors and lawyers were compelled to join the Nazi organizations for doctors and lawyers if they wished to practice; artists, who were writers, painters, musicians, and actors, could only engage in their art by affiliating with the Nazi culture organization. Laborers were brought together in the Nazi Labor Front; civil servants into the Nazi civil servants' group; railroad, steamship, postal, and communications employees into Nazi organizations designed for them. Young people were regimented into the youth groups and into the students' association, while housewives found it difficult to remain out of the women's organizations. German business men were of course not neglected in this mania on the part of the Nazis to engulf the entire German population.

It would not be accurate to state that there were no Germans in Germany who had managed to keep themselves free from the Nazi contamination. Jews were of course not permitted to enroll or become affiliated and those Jews that remained after the Nazi regime were available for use by military government, but their number was not large and their misery was frequently so great that they were consumed by it to the exclusion of anything else. The inmates of concentration camps might or might not have kept entirely aloof from the Nazis; some of them had started out as Nazis but failed to get along as time passed. Many of those who had refused to be assimilated and consequently had gone to concentration camps had been so brutally dealt with by the Nazis over a lengthy period that they were physical or mental wrecks or both. Business men perhaps succeeded in keeping free from formal Nazi affiliations in larger numbers than any others, but they had rarely kept out of bankruptcy unless they had carried on business dealings with the Nazis and these seemed as contaminating in many instances as formal membership in certain Nazi-affiliated groups. The proportion of the German population with Nazi records has been variously estimated. Some would place the figure as high as 90 per cent; others consider two thirds or three fourths a more accurate proportion. A good deal depends on the definition set up as a basis for classification. But the fact remains that a very large majority of the German population from whose numbers public officials, civil servants and teachers would ordinarily be recruited had to be labelled as "Nazis" of a sort under any definition. . . .

In comparison with the British, Russian, and French denazification programs the American effort has been by all odds the more comprehensive and energetic. The Russians started out with more of a dynamic effort in this field and ruthlessly liquidated numerous Germans whom they regarded as dangerous. But they have never been interested in an elaborate denazification organization. More has been left to the discretion of the local military commanders in their zone; less attention has been paid to the past records of individual Germans and more to the prospects of whether these individuals would contribute to the Russian goals of the future. Neither the British or French have seen fit to expend anything like as much of their energy on denazification as the Americans. The British have used lists somewhat similar to those prepared by the United States, but they have not revised these at intervals so as to include more and more Germans, because there has been far less in the way of pressure arising out of public opinion in England. The British and French attitudes have stressed the big fellow and more or less ignored the little fellow on the ground that the latter was a victim or pawn who could not be blamed too severely because his very life and livelihood depended on submitting to the Nazis.

There is some basis for concluding that the United States has not been as wise as it might have been in devoting so great a part of its military government energy to the one problem of denazification. It is probable that no other single problem, whether it be democratization, education, economic reconstruction, or food has received as much attention over so long a period from both higher headquarters and field echelons as denazification. Denazification represents primarily a negative approach to the German situation; it harks back to the past more than it points to the future. The preoccupation with carrying out the campaign to get rid of Nazis even at the lowest levels has perhaps partially blinded the American occupying authorities to the very great importance of the constructive problem of filling the key positions with those persons who have both ability and democratic sympathies. That is not to say that no attention has been paid to the recruiting of able men with democratic beliefs, but this effort appears as a dwarf alongside of the giant denazification program.

The experience of the First World War in Germany seems to indicate that it is more important to fill key positions with the strongest available men than it is to get rid of followers of the conquered regime, important as the latter may be. In that earlier occupation the Allied authorities ousted the supporters of the Kaiser, but they left in their stead bureaucrats who espoused other nationalistic cults and had little or no love for democratic institutions. It is a matter of record that the German bureaucrats did little to resist the scuttling of the Republic when the Nazis brought their guns to bear. The question remains to be answered whether a similar mistake has been made in the American zone this time as a result of the concentration of attention on the negative approach as represented by denazification. If that should prove to be the case, the blame will in large measure be attributable to public opinion in the United States which was focused on this aspect of military government in Germany far above any other and demanded an expenditure of energy out of all proportion to such positive activities as democratization and reeducation. In fairness it should be added that many of the most ardent proponents of a denazification program that would seek to extirpate every root of National Socialism regard such an effort as an absolute prerequisite to any worthwhile attempts to establish a democratic system or a sound educational program in Germany.

DENAZIFICATION OR RENAZIFICATION? [4]

In the early stages of denazification, mass arrests were its most spectacular feature. The number of those arrested in the American zone, and often interned in the concentration camps of the defunct Gestapo, reached a peek of 100,000. Protestant as well as Catholic leaders in Germany protested. A dispatch to the News Service of the National Catholic Welfare Conference, dated May 6, 1946, gave the following details about the background of the protests:

Blueprint patterns thus are applied perfunctorily even to people who have produced dependable witnesses and ample evidence to prove their consistent hostility to and active resistance against the Nazi regime. There are instances of Catholics and even members of religious orders, who were interned months ago under American, British or French military orders without ever having been given a hearing and

[4] From article by Ferdinand A. Hermens, Professor of Political Science, University of Notre Dame. *Forum*. 108:257-64. November 1947. Reprinted by permission.

often without being granted the privilege of communicating with their families and friends. Agencies such as the Army's Counter-Intelligence Corps, sometimes operating with methods that senior military government officers have termed caustically as those of "junior G-men," frequently have perpetrated arrests wantonly. Commanding officers have admitted to this correspondent that people often are hired as special agents who lack experience and a sense of discretion, and even people motivated by petty instincts of revenge and personal hatred who hardly had gone through the most elementary training for so delicate and responsible a job.

These facts may come as a surprise to many of the readers of this article. It should, however, be borne in mind that arrests without warrant, and without *habeas corpus* were and still are quite "legal." The Potsdam declarations—preceded, in this respect as in others, by a corresponding provision in the final version of JCS 1067—provided that the military authorities could arrest not only members of certain groups, but also "any other persons dangerous to the occupation and its objectives." Thus anyone could be arrested without redress. Strange incidents occurred. There was a provision that people arrested as members of a certain group were not to be released under any circumstances. In this case as in others, some arrests were due to mistaken identity. When the facts were uncovered, the military authorities first professed to be helpless, and changed their attitude only after a well-known American journalist threatened to publicize the errors made. The situation is unsatisfactory even in the case of those who were arrested for good reason. Tens of thousands of them have now been held for more than two years. During this time no effort was made to re-educate those who might have proved redeemable. All, including many able-bodied men, were kept in idleness and fed at public expense, in spite of the fact that a scarcity of labor developed, and that properly supervised reconstruction work was the least which those really guilty could have done in expiation for their deeds.

Removals from office were, of course, more numerous than arrests. At first, they were, for the most part, limited to public employment where they did not fail to produce their share of unexpected results. In one Bavarian district it was found, for example, that more than 90 per cent of the judges were members

of the Nazi party and had as such been summarily removed
from office. This, of course, implied that they could not be
employed except as ordinary laborers, and that they might be
expelled from their homes. The high percentage of party members seemed strange to the legal division of the Military Government. Investigation revealed that the Nazi boss of this particular area had wanted money in order to build himself a
palatial office building. So he went to see Hitler, and after his
return he called a meeting of all court employees from janitors
to judges. He told them: "Our beloved Führer is very pleased
with the work which we are doing in this district and, as a
result, he has conferred upon all of you the honor of membership in the party. Heil Hitler!" All had to pay their initiation
fees and their dues, and the palace was built. The prompt action
of the legal division of the Military Government secured redress
in this instance; the case of each justice was investigated sep-
arately, and a decision made upon his personal merits, which
made possible the reinstatement of the majority of the
judges. . . .

Examples testifying to the detrimental effects of [Military
Government Law No. 8.] could be multiplied. Inasmuch as coal
production is of such crucial importance not only to Germany,
but to all of Europe, it is interesting to note that the report of a
British parliamentary committee which visited Germany in the
summer of 1946 contains this sentence: "No man, for instance,
who has been a Nazi can in 1946 be a technician in a mine,
whereas, in 1945, no man could be a technician in a mine unless
he was a Nazi." Or take the fact that in the American zone
more than 10,000 railroad employees, mostly technical personnel,
such as engineers and brakemen were dismissed on the same day.
It was generally anticipated that the result would be a lowering
of both the efficiency and the safety of the railroads, a fact which
must be evaluated in combination with the circumstance that, in
the summer of 1947, the bottleneck in transportation became as
bad as, if not worse, than, the bottleneck in the production of
coal. Besides, even if a locomotive engineer or, for that matter,
a postman, had been a Nazi (provided that he was not a criminal, or a notorious Nazi) is that reason to expect political danger
from his continued employment?

So far as the professions are concerned, consider the example given by Lord (formerly Sir William) Beveridge in his booklet, "An Urgent Message from Germany:" "A British officer concerned with public health named as one of his difficulties that nearly all the best surgeons and medical specialists in his region were behind our bars. The best occulist in Hamburg is no longer allowed to save people from blindness." Lord Beveridge concludes: "The policy of denazification that we accepted in Potsdam is a policy fit only for a totalitarian state." Another observer, Dr. Hans von Hentig, an exile from Nazi Germany, who is now teaching at the University of Iowa, commented: "Former surgeons now make chairs; former judges paint dolls; university teachers pluck hops or repair fences. The ones hardest hit, on the basis of party membership, are the grade school teachers. Hundreds of thousands of them have sunk into a sub-proletarian existence."

It will be said that the entire program of denazification has now been handed over to the Germans, and that it is up to them to administer it in such a way as to exclude injustice. Essential provisions, however, of the so-called "Law for Liberation from National Socialism and Militarism" were not contained in the German draft; considerable pressure had to be brought to bear on the German leaders before they could be induced to accept the American program. The German objections, which are shared by a great many of our own officials, center on the following provisions: first of all, in the appendix of the law there reappears the large list of organizations and categories which had been drawn up in Washington at a time when wartime passions had reached their peak. Some of these groups do not belong there on any count; others should be eliminated because the task involved cannot be handled properly as long as it is not reduced to reasonable proportions. The *Spruchkammern* can handle tens of thousands of cases, but not millions. Second, those covered by the provisions of the law are presumed to be guilty unless they prove themselves innocent. This is contrary to the rules of criminal procedures prevailing in countries where the common law applies. In other countries, to be sure, the opposite rule obtains, but then this is hardly a commendable feature of their legal system, and besides, in the past (always, of course, excluding dictatorships) the practical handling of indictments and trials greatly mitigated the evils inherent in this rule. Careful investigation of every single case preceded an indictment. In the case of denazification, indictment is brought against millions without previous investigation. Third, when a German *Spruchkammer* classifies people as mere followers, or as anti-Nazis, the special branch of the military government may review their cases and often does. This prolongs uncertainty, and is contrary to the professed intention of "dumping it all into the laps of the Germans."

A great many additional details could be mentioned, and some of the oddities characteristic of the operation of the law could be related. Suffice it to say that the task handed to the *Spruchkammern* is so vast that some have calculated that their work will not be completed before the year 2000. Optimists are willing to cut the time in half, but those deprived of their positions, their homes, and of higher rations, may be forgiven if they are not impressed with the difference in the estimates. Irrevocably, harm has already been done. . . .

The point has now been reached where diplomatic necessities have added their weight to that of the arguments set forth above. In August, an order was issued by the supreme commander of the Russian forces in Germany, which not only stated that denazification had been completed in the Russian zone, but provided that the vote was to be restored to all former Nazis who had not "participated in crimes against the peace and security of other peoples or in crimes against the German people." It was, of course, known that the Russians did not take denazification too seriously—in fact no one took it quite seriously except the Americans—but this particular order went a great deal farther than could have been expected. It can hardly be understood except as a diplomatic move against the Western powers, whose own countermove was slow to materialize.

What should be done? Aristotle, in his *Constitution of Athens* reports that, after the overthrow of the tyranny of the Pisistratidae, "the Athenians, with the usual leniency of the democracy, allowed all partisans of the tyrants who had not joined in their evil deeds in the time of troubles, to remain in the city," where, apparently, they were left undisturbed. It might be argued that this policy of "denazification" was eminently successful, assuming that the ultimate aim is "democratization," for Athens was afterwards, with two brief interruptions, a democracy for 170 years.

In the case of Germany, it would indeed be wise to give immediate attention to major offenders and have them brought to justice. This task is now delayed by the necessity to clear the great many little people who will have to be cleared some time; if a general amnesty were granted in their favor a concentrated effort to deal with criminals and the leading supporters of the Nazi system would become possible. Criminals are easy to identify; in regard to those whose guilt consisted in political acts, a satisfactory definition is difficult. A solution might be found by letting the German authorities frame their own measures in regard to political offenders. They might not do too badly. When at the conclusion of the Nuremberg trials von Papen and Schacht were acquitted, a genuine wave of indignation swept over Germany, indicating that the majority of the people were guided by the right instinct. If such feelings can be translated into action, the problem can be solved. That it should be solved by action genuinely originating with the Germans would seem to be required by the fact that when nationals of a country have committed deeds as reprehensible as were committed by Germans under the Nazi system, a people has the duty as well as the right to purge itself of the responsible elements. Moral regenerations can, after all, not come from the outside.

There have recently been reports that General Clay was considering a change in denazification methods which would eliminate the bulk of the little people by having them pay a fine. The willingness to make a change is more important than the method proposed, which might or might not be satisfactory. These reports were immediately followed by protest from well-meaning people in this country who were afraid of leniency to real Nazis. They were not aware of the extent to which "denazification" as now handled has in reality contributed mightily to the renazification. A Congressional investigation, in the course of which all the cards could be laid on the table, would clarify the situation. The average American will not support the present form of denazification if he has access to the facts.

THE FAILURE OF THE REEDUCATION
OF GERMANY [5]

The attempt to reeducate the defeated Germans and to re-form the German schools, which the Allies are now making in the Reich, is unprecedented. Never before in history have victors undertaken to alter systematically the mind of a whole vanquished nation, particularly a nation which, before Hitler, had been one of the cultural and scientific leaders of Europe. It is important to keep in mind that the great majority of Ger-mans still feel themselves to be culturally at least equal to some of the occupying powers and superior to the others. As a rule, Germans regard the British and the French as more or less on the same *Kultur* level with them, and the Russians and Americans as considerably below them. These opinions are deep-rooted and widespread and are not necessarily connected with politics or nazism; they are part of the national folklore of Germany. Con-sequently, they complicate the whole problem of reeducation.

Reeducation is a matter of extraordinary complexity, for it involves not merely the youth of school age but the whole adult population. Obviously it is not possible successfully to imbue children with ideas which their parents find alien or objectionable, and, equally obviously, one may expect that the home environment will tend to undo the work of the schools. The first question to be considered, therefore, is the home en-vironment, or the German mind.

Here we are dealing with a double problem, that of the old-type Germanism and that of the more recent Nazi-fascism. In some cases these two have blended, and in others they have been in conflict. But from the point of view of the occupying powers,

[5] By Saul K. Padover, Lt. Col., United States Army, Psychological Warfare, 1944-1945. *Education in Transition*; Thirty-fourth Annual Schoolmen's Week Proceedings, 1947. University of Pennsylvania. School of Education. 47, no. 29: 21-31. Reprinted by permission.

especially the democracies, both contain extremely dangerous elements. Old-type Germanism or Prussianism and Nazi-fascism have in common the following:—hostility to democracy, that is to say, shared power; reliance on authoritarianism, whether in private affairs or in government; respect for force and acceptance of the military virtues; and belief in German superiority, cultural or racial. I think that the great majority of Germans, including the anti-Nazis, subscribe to some or all of these views. In fact, it is hard to see how it could be otherwise, since these doctrines have been official and current in Germany for generations.

The problem of reeducation, in brief, is not merely one of eradicating nazism, but also of eliminating authoritarianism, militarism, Junkerism, and racism. The evil work of Hitler, be it remembered, lasted only a dozen years, but that of his predecessors went on for generations. The occupying powers are now called upon to wipe out in a comparatively short period of time this age-old accumulation of dangerous notions. Clearly, the task is not easy.

Adult Germans may be divided roughly into four categories which cut across political and class lines. There is, first of all, the diehard Nazi-Fascist element which is fanatically loyal to the memory of Hitler and everything he stood for. Secondly, we have the militarist-nationalist group which consists of professional officers, Junkers, aristocrats, and a large assortment of big business conservatives. Thirdly, there is the middle segment, ranging all the way from moderate nationalism with an admixture of mild nazism to complete political indifference and apathy. Finally, there is the section of true democrats and proven anti-Nazis, among them many Social Democrats, certain Communists, and some intellectuals. The last category is a small minority—perhaps no more than 10 per cent of the population—without much power or drive. Moreover, most of the genuine democrats, that is, those who know the meaning of democracy and believe in it, are older people belonging to the pre-Hitler and pre-World War I generation. They have no great following among the youth; only about 10 per cent of the Social Democratic party, for example, consists of young people, and they are Socialists usually because their parents are. The real drive and dynamism in Germany, to some extent actual but more so potential, is to be found in the first two categories: the Nazi-Fascist and the militarist-conservative. These have fanaticism, skill, and arrogant self-confidence. Nothing much can be done to alter the attitudes of these people, who constitute a permanent danger not only to the occupation authorities but also to the future peace of Europe. For the Allies, the only practical policy is to disfranchise the first two categories and to give active support to the democratic, anti-Nazi minority. The latter could then lead and help to reeducate the moderate and indifferent middle segment of the German population. This, however, has not been generally done. On the contrary, we have been too much in a hurry to permit the German people to vote, with the result that large nondemocratic and antidemocratic elements have slipped into power through lawful channels. Now power and influence is often in the hands of the kind of people who are friends neither of the Allies nor of the German people.

From this it becomes clear that the reeducation of Germany's youth presents some difficulties.

What kind of youth has Hitler left behind him? Despite much propaganda to the contrary, I should like to assert that by and large Germany's younger youth is the most hopeful element in an otherwise gloomy situation, that the young people are not universally poisoned with nazism, and that they are generally eager for a new life. Fanatical Nazis do exist among the youth, but they are a minority.

In this connection it is necessary to make age distinctions. In the United States zone there are approximately 17,000,000 people, and of these about one third—or nearly 6,000,000—consists of the young between 3 and 18. Around 4,500,000 of them are of grammar school and high school age. As a rule, one may say that the younger the individual the less nazified he is likely to be, and that the dangerous youths are to be found in the older age group, particularly among those who had served in the Wehrmacht and had been members of the Nazi party and its various auxiliary organizations. This leaves us the youth under 18, and especially under 6, as the field which we can cultivate with a good hope of producing a successful crop. In other words, if we apply ourselves devotedly and systematically to this young group, and if we stay in Germany long enough to do the job correctly, we may succeed in bringing up an anti-Nazi and prodemocratic generation.

The task will require immense effort and patience. For the youthful products of Hitler's school system, even when they are not Nazis, have a distorted view of the world and display certain attitudes which can lead to future trouble. For example, they know only a few carefully inoculated lies about the German Republic and nearly nothing about the meaning of a free society. Of German history they are familiar mainly with wars and military heroes. Concerning the outside world, their minds are stocked with the Goebbel's cliches, such as that Americans are uncultured, French degenerate, Italians cowardly, Englishmen hypocritical, and Russians barbarians. No one of all those interrogated could tell us, even in the most general terms, what kind of government the United States or Great Britain had, or what a parliament was, or a republic. The nearest any one of them ever came to a description of America was that its ruler was a Fuehrer like Hitler. I once asked an intelligent fifteen-year-old girl, who said that she loved to study history, whether she knew what a republic was. "Oh yes," she replied without hesitation, "a republic is when a country is torn into many states, like Germany was after the Thirty Years War."

They are polite children, sometimes over-polite, but it is a mistake to assume, as did so many of our soldiers, that they show deference merely to curry favor with the conquerors. The truth lies deeper than that. The German class system and hierarchical structure, which begins in the home where the father is the acknowledged master and the female members of the family are definitely subordinated to the males, creates a kind of politeness in the presence of the strong and an almost automatic obedience to authority. The German child learns obedience also in the classroom where the schoolmaster is a veritable drill-sergeant whose authority is as unquestioned as was that of

Hitler. In fact, Hitler had no difficulty in setting up his dictatorship based upon the "Leadership Principle" because every German is accustomed from childhood on to obey implicitly some given authority, whether it is the father or the school master. If we are ever to reorient the Germans into a democratic direction, we will have to begin with the eradication of this whole structure of authority and blind subordination.

I remember one noon in Aschaffenburg when about half a dozen youngsters carrying schoolbags surrounded my jeep with the obvious intention of making friends. I asked them why they were not at school; they replied that, owing to the lack of buildings, teachers and other facilities, they attended only three mornings a week. I asked what they did with the rest of their time. They shrugged and said that there was nothing to do. Didn't they have any sports or play any games? "No," they replied, "nobody had told them to play anything." I demanded, perhaps a little more sharply than I intended, "Why don't you organize a team and play games?" They suddenly stiffened and said that if "Mr. Officer" *orders* it they would do it. I said that it was not an order but only a suggestion. They looked a little bewildered and then the oldest, a lad of about ten, clicked his heels, bowed, and said courteously that if this was an order they would obey.

When you have children like these and want to turn them into self-reliant, democratic, self-starting individuals, how do you go about it? Obviously you need teachers who are self-reliant and imbued with the spirit of freedom. But unfortunately such teachers are hardly available in Germany. Even before Hitler, German teachers were not trained in the ideals of democracy but, on the contrary, they reflected the general national pattern of authority, hierarchy, and obedience. Among the many fatal mistakes of the Weimar Republic, be it noted in passing, one of the greatest was that the democrats then in power made no serious effort to train a new corps of teachers but permitted the educational ideas and institutions of the Kaiser to go on unhindered.

Hitler, of course, made the situation infinitely worse. Even the extremely conservative educational system was undesirable in his eyes, and he was determined to nazify it from top to bottom. Some time around 1937 the Nazis began to set up a large number of Normal Schools, *Lehrer und Lehrerinen Bildungs-Anstalten,* to train teachers in the Hitlerite spirit. The director of every one of these *Anstalten* had to be a loyal Nazi party member and the students, aged 14 to 19, were recruited only from families which the Nazis considered reliable. Those whose parents were liberals or democrats or had a priest in the family were refused admission.

The training lasted five years and, apart from the purely pedagogical courses, it was based on the principle of *Rassenkunde* (race science). Hitler himself had given the order that "No German child should leave school without a thorough orientation in *Rassenkunde*." This meant that all the young teachers were inspired to imbue their pupils with the idea of Nordic race superiority, a contempt for other peoples, and an abhorrence for intermarriage between Germans and other Europeans.

The first crop of these purely Nazi-trained teachers came out in 1942. I asked a superintendent of a large German school system what he thought of this new generation of Hitlerized teachers. He had been in the profession for forty years and his opinion was that of a highly experienced specialist. This is what he said. I quote:

The new teachers were infected with basic Nazi ideas, although I must admit that on a technical level they were as competent as the old ones. They were not religious and not cultured. They said that the Bible was neither binding nor sacred. As regards *Kultur*, they knew no Latin, no music, and very little history. Of course, they taught what they were trained to teach, and in such subjects as history it was either pure propaganda or plain tendentiousness. They emphasized the pre-historic German period and when they mentioned the Republic it was only to dismiss it as a contemptible and shameful period in German history. Their whole outlook was based on the Leadership Principle and Race Science.

Incidentally, this same old-time superintendent, though himself not a Nazi, said that he would not hesitate to employ these nazified teachers because, after all, they were German patriots and skilled professionals trained in the art of pedagogy. If they did not believe in democracy but in racism and authoritarianism, so what? The non-Nazi superintendent did not believe in democracy either and did not think it was the kind of government fit for Germany.

It is not surprising, therefore, that when we entered Germany we found that we could not use the great majority of the available teachers. The older ones were largely nationalistic and nondemocratic, and the young ones were nearly all Nazis. In one German city, I recall, we scrutinized a list of about 320 teachers and found that only some 24 were not Nazi, or militaristic, or ultra-nationalistic. In Berlin about 80 per cent of the teachers had to be dismissed in the denazification process. In the state of Thuringia 98 per cent were Nazis and the Soviet military government had to fire 9,000 out of the 10,000 teachers there; the other thousand were retained simply because there was no choice. All over Germany no less than half of the teachers had to be rejected, and many of the others were of dubious value.

Most of those who passed the denazification tests are past fifty (in Berlin the average age is fifty-nine) and are not always the right kind of instructors. Some have strange notions. I remember one day in the city of Bingen on the Rhine, in the French zone, visiting a partly damaged school while classes were in session. The teacher of the third grade was a kindly old lady who invited me to her classroom. As I entered, she said, "Children, we have an American gentleman for a visitor." They all popped out of their seats and shouted in disciplined chorus, "*Gruess Gott*," and spontaneously sat down again, folding their arms. I said to the teacher, "What nice children!" "Yes," she replied with a deep sigh, "they are indeed, but you know, Sir, even they are not entirely free of the Nazi disease." I looked at these well-scrubbed, shiny-cheeked children of nine or ten and said that I could not believe that these innocent youngsters could possibly be tainted with nazism. "But it is true," she insisted; "you see, they are not as obedient as children used to be in the old days."

From the beginning military government in all the four zones has had a hard time with the schools, particularly since so many buildings were damaged and so few desirable teachers were available. But somehow schools were opened and operated. In the United States zone, within the first year of the occupation, at least 80 per cent of the children between the ages of six and fourteen partly attended some kind of school, with classes averaging about eighty pupils per teacher.

One of the most challenging problems was the matter of textbooks. The glaringly and crudely Nazi texts, were, of course, promptly forbidden, but it was not easy to cleanse those that contained subtle militaristic propaganda or an indirect nationalistic slant glorifying German heroes. Moreover, it is almost impossible to draw a line between objective national history and one that arouses potentially dangerous nationalist pride. Take, for example, this sentence from the grammar school textbook, *Deutsches Lesebuch IV* (p. 110-114), which ends the story of Alfred Krupp—"His work remains as a blessing for hundreds of thousands of diligent hands, an enlightening example of national labor and a proud glory of our German fatherland." This seems innocent enough, except for the fact that Alfred Krupp built Germany's biggest armament works. The question is, should such sentences be left in or cut out? This one has been left in. Or take this sample from the history textbook, *Lehrbuch der Geschichte III* (p. 56), which, speaking of the Prussian defeat of 1807, says: "The successors of Frederick the Great were weak sovereigns and they missed the right moment for the inevitable war." Is this legitimate history or propaganda designed to keep alive the militaristic spirit? The answer is obviously not easy.

Unfortunately the superintendence of education, like that of political affairs in general, is not infrequently in the hands of ultra-nationalist Germans whose aim is to revive the nationalist spirit and keep fresh the military tradition. The man in charge of education of the Aachen area at the time when it was in American hands was an old miltarist clerical who, in conversation with me, revealed a furious hatred of the French ("our eternal enemy"), a biting contempt for the British, and an intense bitterness against Woodrow Wilson and the Versailles Treaty; he also, naturally defended Hitler's war. This man was in charge of textbooks, and it can be imagined what kind he favored. Incidentally, he was never a member of the Nazi party and therefore was eligible for office under the Allies. And today in Bavaria, Dr. Alois Hundhammer, the Minister of Culture in charge of education for this big province (9,000,000 people), is a violent reactionary and fanatical militarist. He believes in the subordination of women and in corporal punishment for grammar school children, and he personally supervises the revision of textbooks, one of which contains a notorious glorification of war.

The colleges and universities also reflect this general situation. To begin with, a large number of the higher schools and institutes have been physically damaged or destroyed. In our zone, Heidelberg and Marburg are intact; Frankfort and Munich universities are severely burned, and Giessen and Wuerzburg completely so. They are, nevertheless, all trying to function despite difficulties.

One of the early problems was staff. Even before Hitler, German universities had been centers of nationalism and class conservatism. The Nazis had no trouble in taking control of the seats of learning. It is a notorious fact that few colleges or professors resisted nazification; on the contrary, with some honorable exceptions, they succumbed without too much protest. As a result, we found that the great majority of college teachers and professors were tainted with nazism and had to be dismissed. When we opened Heidelberg, for instance, there were 201 members on the faculty, but only 92 could be employed, and even many of the latter were not above suspicion.

The students were another problem. While prominent Nazis and active party leaders and SS officers were excluded, ordinary members of the Hitlerite organizations were permitted to study. Most male students, being young people, are naturally veterans of the Wehrmacht and of the Hitler Youth movement. They are, as is to be expected from an age-group that spent its impressionable years under Nazi influence, heavily nationalistic and of course infected with various degrees of nazism, militarism, and racism. Some are less so, others more. Only about 10 per cent are believed to be strongly Nazi-minded, ready to follow and fight for another Hitler. The others are either lukewarm politically, indifferent, or open-minded. Extremely few are democrats or believers in democracy, and even fewer are ready to accept the idea of Germany's guilt for the war and the atrocities. When Pastor Martin Niemoeller at the University of Erlangen addressed the student body on the question of guilt, saying that all Germans, including himself, must share in the moral responsibility, the students booed, hissed, and then stomped out in protest.

Perhaps I should tell you about my visit to Heidelberg last spring. The university, which is completely undamaged, was overcrowded with 2,500 students, of whom 1100 were in the faculty of medicine, 550 in philosophy, 400 in law, 300 in natural science, and 150 in theology. About 10 per cent of the students were foreigners, supported by UNRRA, who have quarters and mess separate from the Germans. I asked some Poles and Yugoslavs how they were being treated. "Fine," they said. "Most German students are pretty friendly. Occasionally we hear nasty remarks about us, usually from some Nazi or militarist, but we pay no attention."

On the question of faculty denazification, this was the opinion of an elderly professor whom the Nazis had dismissed in 1933 because he refused to join the party: he said—"Sure, denazification causes some hardships among individuals, but what the devil! Did they have pity on us in 1933? Now they don't like it a bit. Some say that life is over for them, they feel suicidal; others are making adjustments and doing hard work, even manual labor." Another member of the faculty, the university administrator Dr. Ostfeld, told me that in general denazification did not impair the efficiency of the institution. He said that there were enough instructors and scientists to go around.

The students were hard-working, intense, and seemingly eager for some new guiding idea. It is significant that lectures on philosophy are literally mobbed. In Heidelberg they line up by the hundreds and then rush the doors to hear philosophy. I joined in one of these rushes and it was quite an experience. After the lecture I engaged several students in conversation. One said that while he himself was not a member of the Hitler

Youth, he believed that "Nazi party members have a right to study as much as anybody else." I brought around the conversation to the subject of democracy, and one young man said firmly, "We have never lived under a democracy. You Americans say it is good. We would like to see it for ourselves. If it is good, we'll adopt it." The others nodded in vigorous assent.

I have heard similar opinions expressed in many parts of Germany. The attitude of young Germans can be formulated something like this:—We are culturally at least as good as you are, but you beat us, so you are temporarily our masters and we have to obey you. You come to us with these alien notions about democracy. This may be Anglo-Saxon hypocrisy or there may be something to it. We don't know anything about it, but we'll wait and see. It's up to you to show us. If you don't prove what you say, then we'll be more convinced than ever that our way of life—the life of strict authority, of undivided Leadership, of established hierarchy, and of military discipline—is best for us.

Such, generally speaking, is the German youth's state of mind, and the question is what are we doing about it?

The occupation authorities have struggled with the reeducation problem to the best of their abilities, which of necessity were limited. They denazified faculties, cleansed textbooks, and set up a few three-month training courses for teachers. The army also gave occasional encouragement to the formation of sport groups and discussion circles among young Germans. Whenever our troops organized games for German kids, the latter showed themselves to be enthusiastic participants. Military Government has tried to encourage Germans to form youth organizations, wisely insisting that this be done voluntarily and not on order from above. But so far these efforts have not been very successful. In Wiesbaden, for example, only about 5 per cent of the city's youth joined voluntary sport groups. In general, the youngsters reflect their parents' suspicions of anything that smacks of politics and are leary of organizations and organized movements. They have had too much of this sort of thing under Hitler.

By and large, in so far as reeducation is concerned, it must be said that the occupation has been a pretty solid failure. This is true of our own zone but even more so of the British and the French.   As for the Russian zone, the chances are that the failure there has been as great as in the West, but we do not have sufficient data to generalize.

Two main reasons account for our failure in Germany.   One is that we had no consistent, carefully thought out, long-range plan for reeducation of the youth and reorientation of the people.   The other reason is that we did not entrust Germany to a corps of trained and specialized civilians but to the army. Troops are good for fighting and policing, but it is most unfair to them to expect them, as we did, to carry out educational reforms and psychological changes.   Since nobody in Washington bothered to set up a civilian agency for the control and reformation of Germany, the army was forced to take over this job, and the results have not been happy.

Last summer a State Department mission, headed by Dr. George F. Zook, President of the American Council on Education, spent a month in Germany investigating educational conditions and policies.   The mission made the disturbing but not surprising discovery that nowhere in the United States zone, or any of the other zones for that matter, did conditions exist in which "the democratic spirit can develop and democratic institutions be established."   It, therefore, recommended a thorough revolution in the whole German school system.   The mission's statesmanlike report proposed the abolition of the prevailing class system on all school levels, a change in the methods of teaching, a widening of the social sciences, a transformation of the universities from aloof centers of research to institutions for the assistance and improvement of the whole community, and a democratic training of teachers and a broadening of their outlook by sending some of them to study abroad.

The mission stressed the long-term obligations of the United States and warned that the responsibility for the reeducation of Germany was not merely a matter of the government but of the American people.   I quote—"We have committed ourselves to a program in which education plays a critical role.   There must therefore be no turning back in our support of that program so vital to the enduring peace of the world."

So far the American people do not seem to have realized the immensity of the German problem nor the difficulties involved in trying to change the mind of a whole nation. There has not been a sufficiently enlightened public opinion to bring proper pressure upon the government in Washington for the creation of a civilian occupation authority that should concern itself with Germany for at least a generation. There has been no long-range systematic program. And above all, there has been no strong movement to replace army control with that of specially qualified civilians.

The task that faces us in Germany is heart-breaking enough, and perhaps under the best conditions it may not be possible to alter the German mentality, but we will never know until we really try. This immense experiment can be carried out only by civilian educators, psychologists, sociologists, and other social scientists. The next step, therefore, is up to you, to me, to all of us, but especially to you who are concerned with education.

UNITED STATES POLICY IN THE REEDUCATION OF GERMANY [6]

The present policy of the United States in the reeducation of Germany is based on the Potsdam Agreement. Therein the victors decreed that "German education shall be so controlled as completely to eliminate Nazi and militaristic doctrines and to make possible the successful development of democratic ideas."

Education Officers in Military Government in the American zone have pursued earnestly both the negative and positive implications of this directive. Negatively, they have denazified the teaching profession at all levels, eliminated Nazi and militaristic textbooks, destroyed the vast educational press of the Nazis, purged German administrative personnel in education, and screened all educational films and all school libraries. On the positive side, they have, to date, reorganized the three ministries of education and cults in our zone, reopened the schools

[6] From an address by William M. Landeen, Professor of History, State College of Washington; delivered at the Institute of World Affairs, Riverside, California, December 11, 1946. *Institute of World Affairs. Proceedings.* 23:141-9. December 1946; *World Affairs Interpreter.* 18:148-60. July 1947. Reprinted by permission.

at all levels, authorized the beginnings of a new educational press, fostered a program of adult education, drawn up a comprehensive program of sports for the youth, examined and approved a large number of once-used textbooks, as well as new manuscripts, and developed long-term objectives for the guidance of German educational authorities.

A few figures may serve to illustrate what has been accomplished. On October 1, 1945, elementary schools were reopened with 1,118,564 children between the ages of six and fourteen in attendance, and 12,849 teachers. By May 1, 1946, the attendance had risen to 1,895,706 and the number of teachers to 23,825. Of the latter, 4,421, or 18.6 per cent, were the product of emergency teacher-training courses, started during the summer of 1945. Since they were untrained and inexperienced, they were assigned, as far as possible, to seasoned teachers as school assistants. While their work in the schools was often unsatisfactory, nevertheless they did materially help us overcome the acute shortage of teacher supply. The most competent of them will be retained and given a regular course of study with a view to permanent appointment.

The secondary schools were the next to open, and by July 1, 1946, the student enrollment was 187,853 with 6,219 teachers. By May 1, 1946, vocational schools reported 139,521 students and 2,063 teachers; and special schools, such as for the blind, deaf, and dumb, had 4,751 enrolled with 188 teachers. The universities, last to reopen, showed an attendance on May 1, 1946, of 20,040 for the six institutions in the United States zone. Technical education had also begun, with the four colleges of engineering in the United States zone reporting 7,302 students in attendance and the two agricultural colleges 536. Six research institutes, really branches of the College of Engineering at Karlsruhe, have reopened lately. Research of all kinds is supervised by a Research Control Office at Military Government Headquarters and is regulated by the provisions of Allied Control Council Law No. 25, drawn up with the view of liquidating the German war potential.

The Nazis had virtually destroyed theological training, with the result that the churches were sorely in need of clergymen. During the summer of 1945 a survey was made of the theological institutions in the United States zone. Requirements for re-opening were explained to the various church authorities, teaching staffs were screened, the necessary application papers processed, and in October of last year virtually all of such institutions were given permission to resume their instructional activities. A few were unable to find teaching staffs and have not reopened to date.

At all levels of German education the most acute problem encountered was the shortage of acceptable teachers. In the United States zone there were about 36,000 elementary teachers, of whom 65 per cent were eliminated under the terms of denazification policy. On the secondary level the situation was even worse, and the universities presented a problem all of their own, with militarism and nazism strongly entrenched in most faculties. In one university the whole faculty of law was dismissed and in the large faculty of medicine only three teachers survived the denazification process. Further, those who did survive were older men and women. Thus the average age of elementary teachers in the United States zone is between 55 and 60.

To meet this situation Military Government has encouraged an extensive program of teacher training. More than forty teacher-training colleges and institutes are now functioning in the United States zone, and it is expected that by January 1, 1947, about 8,000 new elementary teachers will have passed their first teacher examinations and will have entered service. This group, together with the fairly large number of teachers expelled from the East who are being employed in the United States area, should materially serve to overcome the shortage until such time as lasting patterns of teacher-training curricula shall have been developed and fully trained teachers graduated. In the secondary and higher levels the task of developing new teachers is more difficult still and will require years of patient and constructive effort.

When United States Military Government took over temporary control of German education all textbooks were frozen. To provide the most necessary texts as quickly as possible a three-fold program was instituted. The first involved the emergency reprinting of elementary school texts from the Weimar period, to be used until new and better materials were available. Preliminary work on this program had been completed before the invasion of Germany, and with the capture of Cologne and Bonn in the spring of 1945 temporary printing presses were set up in those cities immediately and an edition of 40,000 sets of approved texts was produced. However, textbook requirements in the United States zone were far in excess of this limited printing, and so a much larger edition was produced in Munich in the summer of 1945. By October 15, 5,328,616 copies of these texts had been distributed in the United States area of occupation. The series consisted of 20 small volumes—eight readers, five arithmetic texts, three history books, and four volumes on nature study. The initial cost was assumed by the Bavarian Government, which in turn was reimbursed by the other *Länder* under United States control and by Berlin. The cost of the books varied from ten to thirty pfennigs.

The printing of emergency textbooks, however, was regarded as an expedient to aid German educational authorities "over the initial period of reopening and reorganizing the educational structure until such time as better books could be found or produced." Consequently, German school authorities were ordered to search for texts that might still be of value and to submit them to Military Government for approval. In Berlin a commission on censorship of texts read the books submitted and divided them into three categories—"approved," "approved subject to change," and "rejected without qualification." By May 1, 1946, the commission had read 1,894 textbooks and approved 1,020 unconditionally, 386 with changes, and had rejected 488. The levels covered in this censorship included the elementary, intermediate, secondary, and special schools. German or other language classics and books used in professional schools or in the universities were not included in those examined. That the commission was thorough in its work is indicated by the fact that such books as catechisms and Bible histories used in the schools did not escape scrutiny.

Meanwhile, the German Ministries of Education were directed to create committees to encourage the production of new textbooks. German pedagogues responded well and to date approximately 220 manuscripts have been submitted to the commission on censorship. In general the manuscripts presented have been conservative in outlook and lacking in vitality and bold ideas. They reflect the shackling of creative thought and expression during the thirteen years of Nazi supremacy.

In the field of visual aids the three German Ministers of Education in the United States zone established on February 5, 1946, the Institute for Educational Films, with headquarters in Munich, Bavaria. Already several hundred educational films from prewar Germany have been submitted to Miliary Government for scrutiny and many have been approved. The rebuilding of the Visual Aids Service, so widely used in prewar Germany, is a task of enormous importance in the reeducation of German youth.

In Nazi Germany adult education was controlled by the Party and was operated through the organization "Strength Through Joy." Military Government has restored supervision to the various *Länder* and has encouraged an extensive adult education program. The Frankfurt Academy of Labor, closed by the Nazis because of its labor affiliations, has been reopened, and the well-known Hindenburg People's University at Nuremberg has been reorganized and given a new start. Among the numerous municipalities and local organizations that have taken up adult education may be mentioned the municipally owned street car company in Berlin, which has started a school for its employees and their families. Operating branches in various parts of the city for the convenience of those concerned, the company offers courses for two hours in the morning and for an equal period in the evening in order that its employees may attend regardless of their shifts of labor. As to subject matter, the morning and evening courses parallel each other. Costs are covered by a low student's fee and by subsidies from the company.

There is reason to believe that adult education may develop into a powerful factor for democratizing Germany. The people have responded eagerly to the opportunity of hearing something new. Courses in the English language and literature are particularly crowded. While practical necessity no doubt is responsible for some of this popularity, the fact remains that considerable interest exists for studying Anglo-Saxon culture and institutions as such. In this program the universities may take an important part. Thus the University of Erlangen is developing plans to function as a strong adult education center for the propagation of Anglo-Saxon contributions to contemporary culture. A "Forum Academicum" has been sponsored by the University of Frankfort, and its success as an attempt in adult education, with lectures and round-table discussions, has led the University of Marburg to establish a similar branch.

Thus far we have discussed the efforts of Military Government in the United States zone to start again the whole machinery of German education after having first denazified it. This task was done at first by a small group of officers and other military personnel to which was later added a number of civilians. In the course of the last eighteen months ministries of Education and Cults have been reestablished in the three *Länder* under United States control, schools have been reopened at all levels, and control over education has been turned over gradually to the German authorities until the function of education officials in Military Government has become chiefly advisory but with the important power of veto. We must now consider briefly the deeper aspects of the German educational problem as well as the various factors operating for or against the ultimate objective of Germany becoming democratic.

When the United States in the Potsdam Agreement pledged its aid to reeducate Germany to democracy and peace, it undertook an obligation the magnitude of which is scarcely yet understood by our government and certainly not by our people. Actually we undertook the obligation not only of helping the German people acquire those ways of life and thought most eminently vital to our democracy—in order that Germany might not constitute an ever-recurring threat to peace—but, as it has since turned out, we also committed ourselves to demonstrate that this democratic rebirth of Germany can be achieved under the most adverse economic conditions and in cooperation, or shall we say in clash, with other concepts of education and politics very different from our own. From having been a battleground of Allies, successful in crushing a common enemy, Germany has been transformed into a vast testing ground for extraneous and dissimilar ideologies, and in this competition of clashing ideas we are determined that ours shall not fail.

In the last analysis the United States military occupation can make the Germans neither democratic nor peaceful; they must make themselves so through the establishment of new cultural and political institutions. The problem is, first, how can German culture be reoriented under the present collapse of political and economic life and, second, how can the United States stand by with aid until new cultural and political institutions are firmly established? . . .

How, then, can the United States best aid in the reorientation of the German people toward national self-respect and democracy?

The most important aspect of this program, that of creating national unity for Germany, belongs to the realm of international relations and cannot be considered at this time. The economic union of the British zone with the American is only the first step in the solution of this problem.

Meanwhile, certain needs of the German educational authorities in the United States zone are so urgent and grave as to demand immediate action. This will require the combined resources of our government, of voluntary agencies, of institutions of learning, and of private individuals, all of which must be coordinated if we are to achieve maximum results.

First in order stands the need for intellectual intercourse between America and the United States zone. Religious and educational literature, such as papers, journals, books, and scholarly professional productions, should be admitted to Germany immediately, and the "Trading with the Enemy Act" should be interpreted so as to permit German church and educational leaders to subscribe to or purchase such materials as they may need. . . .

American scholars and educational leaders should be sent to Germany as visiting professors at German universities and teachers colleges, and German educators and scholars should be given similar opportunities in the United States. The latter is even more important than for Americans to spend time in Germany, since the Germans would see our institutions of democracy function in their own environment and would thus benefit more realistically from our experience in the training of their own youth, in the preparation of new textbooks, in the development of plans for adult education, and in the administration of education in their own country. . . .

Private efforts must be enlisted in this emergency. Churches, service clubs, trade unions, private schools, philanthropic-minded citizens, and professional educational groups should respond readily with quantities of books and educational equipment without cost to the Germans. These efforts should be coordinated with the agencies already at work under Military Government. . . .

That the German people can build quickly, from the ground up and out of economic chaos, lasting democratic institutions is a vagary of the imagination. They can, at best, and that only with strong aid from the United States and Great Britain, begin that long and arduous development toward a democratic way of life which will eventually make them a factor for peace and culture. And as long as the United States continues as an occupying power in Germany, it must encourage and use the instrument of education to attain its major purpose, the furthering of a democratic spirit and form of government. We have committed ourselves to a program in which education is the critical factor, and the sooner we devote to this task our varied and rich educational experience and our resources the greater will be the likelihood of our success.

DEMOCRACY IN GERMANY, IF . . . [7]

We, the people of the United States, can help the Germans develop a democratic country *if* we really want a democratic Germany; *if* we are willing to pay the price to achieve it.

[7] by L. Thomas Hopkins, Professor of Education, Teachers College. *Teachers College Record*. 49:10-18. October 1947. Reprinted by permission.

We, the people of the United States, *will pay the price* to achieve a democratic Germany *if* we realize how vital it is to the continuation of democracy here; and *if* we have pertinent information to guide us in making this decision.

I believe that up to the present time the people in this country have not been given the facts which would enable them to make an intelligent decision, and that two years of occupation have yielded unsatisfactory results in helping the Germans become a democratic country. Because of this belief I wish to suggest some bases upon which more adequate help can be given and greater development expected.

We must know what democracy is both in theory and in practice. The word democracy is used today in two sharply contrasted meanings. The first, or liberal concept, is the one which we accept. It is based upon the rights of the individual both against the church and against the state. The American tradition has grown up around freedom of worship; freedom from political domination by the church; freedom of business enterprise; a weak or laissez faire state and central government; a mobile but equalitarian society; control by the middle or bourgeois class; toleration of all dissentient opinions, even those hostile to democracy; a non-cooperative, laissez faire dynamics; democracy as a relative moral value, to be abrogated at any time by the will of the majority; the belief that democracy and dictatorship are political opposites. The laissez faire concept of democracy was born out of revolution against the church and the government. The philosophy underlying it was developed by Locke and his followers. It still furnishes the basic pattern of our political, economic, and social life. Liberal democracy must, however, develop a state with a more positive dynamic function if it is to survive in an industrial society.

The second, or totalitarian concept of democracy is the one accepted by Russia. It is based upon the right of the state to control the beliefs and actions of the individual. The Russian tradition since 1917 has grown up around domination of the religious and political behavior of the individual by the state; government control of business through planned economy; a strong central government, controlled by a few for the benefit of the many; an immobile equalitarian society dominated by the proletariat; toleration of dissentient opinions on specific issues *only* among those who accept the fundamentals of their totalitarian beliefs; acceptance of democracy as an absolute moral value to be maintained at all costs even to the extent of liquidating unbelievers and non-cooperators; the continuation of the revolutionary dynamics which brought totalitarian democracy into power; and the belief that democracy and dictatorship are one and the same thing, or at least are highly compatible. This concept of democracy originated with the ancient Sophists. In its modern version it is the product of revolution. Its spiritual father is Rousseau, who in his social contract identified society with the state and "posited an all powerful general will from which it was treason to dissent." Karl Marx pointed out that the revolution which ended in control by the bourgeoisie was not complete and must be finished by bringing the proletariat into power. Thus totalitarian democracy was born.

The major differences between the liberal and the totalitarian concept may be summarized in a few words. The liberal democracy assumes that intelligent individuals, in voluntary cooperation, will operate for the common good. The better the education of the individual, the higher his intelligence, the greater his freedom in using it, the more and better will he work for the interests of the social group. Therefore, the less interference he has from the state in his educational, religious, economic, and social affairs, the better it is for him and the state. The totalitarian democracy assumes that the welfare of the state is superior to that of any one person; that individuals, no matter how intelligent, will not voluntarily cooperate for the common good; that government must define for them the area and direction of such good; and that all individuals who refuse to accept this relationship shall be summarily dealt with by the state for its own protection and preservation. But the basic difference is whether democracy refers to a dynamic state directed by the cooperative thinking of a free people, or to a dynamic state directed by a few individuals through the secret police.

This totalitarian concept of democracy was first introduced into World War II by Marshal Stalin, who placed it in the forefront of allied war aims. In his broadcast of July 3, 1941 he spoke of the Soviet war against Hitler being "'merged with the struggle of the peoples of Europe and America for independence and democratic liberty." On November 6, 1942 he described the "restoration of democratic liberties" in Europe as one of the aims of the Anglo-Soviet-American coalition. Thereafter, references to democratic aims or nations or practices appeared frequently. At Yalta, in February 1945, the Allies announced they would meet the political and economic problems of liberated Europe in accordance with "democratic principles." At Potsdam in August 1945 the democratic principle was applied to Germany. German education was to be denazified and controlled so as to make possible the "successful development of democratic ideas." The judicial system was to be reorganized "in accordance with the principles of democracy." Local self government was to be restored "on democratic principles." All "democratic political parties" were to be encouraged. Thus the principle of democracy was to operate in the reconstruction of Germany. But which principle? Our government wants the liberal democracy. Russia is applying the totalitarian democracy.

Liberal democracy in Germany at the moment is in a precarious position for a number of reasons. First, there is no common agreement in the United States or among the American military and civilian personnel in Germany regarding positive dynamics. The old revolutionary drive which brought liberal democracy into being is gone. Mere freedom is not enough. It is too negative. Freedom must be used to achieve some common group ends in harmony with basic principles. Lacking these, the result is laissez faire, which means that interpretations of democracy vary with individuals. And this is very confusing to the German people. Second, the German tradition for the past four hundred years has been closer to the totalitarian concept than to the liberal concept of democracy. Control and regimentation from the top have permeated all aspects of the life of the people. They were dominant even in the days of the Weimar Republic from 1918 to 1933, and reached a climax under Hitler before and during World War II. The step to a new totalitarian control is much shorter and easier than it is to a democratic state based upon the free thinking of a free people. Third, the German people have never been educated to think effectively about their own problems of living. Those who controlled the culture turned the energy of the few into the making of academic minds which show just as little reality in dealing with immediate social problems as they did at the time of the rise of Hitler. They have some facility in academic learning which is more or less useless in interpreting human motives and human behavior. To tell such minds that they are free to do functional thinking on social problems by a liberal democratic process is to invite disaster. For they have neither the tradition nor the process for such action. And this is not to disparage the desire of the many and the ability of the few to accept our way of life.

We must develop the economic bases upon which democracy rests. Liberal democracy is the product of an adequate diet. It has flourished in countries which had sufficient food, shelter, clothing, and other economic goods to produce a high standard of living. It has languished in countries where the ration is 1200 to 1550 calories a day, derived primarily from carbohydrates. Totalitarian democracy thrives on low caloric rations and inadequate nutritional balance. To give or to take a life to support the all-powerful "general will" of the state for any reason at any time is in harmony with that theory of government. It is even more compatible with it when that life has dissentient opinions regarding fundamentals rather than minor specific issues. So we must help the Germans solve their economic problems and improve their general standard of living, if we want liberal democracy to grow.

Three proposals have been made for dealing with the economic situation. The first is to keep the population on a low caloric and inadequate nutritional diet for a long time as a penalty for the devastation which Hitler brought on the world. The Morgenthau Plan, if put into effect, would achieve this result. But it is rejected as not in harmony with our democratic viewpoint. The second proposal is to give the German people an adequate diet through a dole at the expense of the United States taxpayer. This is rejected as being an utterly inadequate solution to the problem. The third proposal is to help the Germans build up their economy to a self-sustaining basis under the advice and guidance of our own economic experts. This is the only sound suggestion. It means that Germany must develop as an industrial country. She must have manufactured products to exchange in the open markets for food and other necessities of life which she cannot produce in adequate amounts. This industrial rehabilitation can best be achieved in cooperation with the other allied governments in their respective zones.

But such cooperation has not yet been achieved and the proposal to restore German industry is not yet accepted by the people of the United States. Those who have argued against it are: (1) Morgenthau followers, who want to keep Germany an agricultural country; (2) American businessmen, who do not want German products to compete with those manufactured in the United States; (3) American labor, which does not want competition from the lower paid labor of Germany; (4) Americans who fear that German industrialists might convert their factories to the production of war materials as they did after World War I. There is some merit in all of these objections. At the moment we are one of the few countries who can afford to purchase the products of German factories and sell the Germans the goods they need to buy. And some competition with American goods must be expected. Yet the stake is bigger than a few products. It is liberal democracy. The Marshall Plan seems to be the best proposal yet made for rehabilitating Europe. Germany is a key country to the success of such a plan. A liberal democratic Germany is vital both to Europe and to the United States.

We must recognize developing liberal democracy as a long-time educational job. The evidence is clear that high officials in our government responsible for over-all policy in Germany do not believe that helping the Germans to develop liberal democracy is a long-time educational job. Some of the evidence is herewith presented.

These officials have not yet recognized the scope of the educational problem. It has two major parts. The first is to help the Germans reorganize their school system from the kindergarten through the universities. This reorganization includes all types of schools and related institutions, such as libraries, youth organizations, and adult education programs. The second is to help the Germans reorganize the basic structure of their total culture within which the democratic school system is to function, for the patterning and organization of the whole in achieving liberal democracy is more important than any of its component parts. A liberal democratic school cannot survive in a totalitarian culture.

From the outset the field of education was given and even now holds minor status in the Office of Military Government United States Zone (OMGUS). It is combined with religious affairs into the Education and Religious Affairs (E and RA) branch of the Internal Affairs and Communication (IA and C) division. It is of less importance than economics, finance, transport, internal affairs, law, and displaced persons, all of which are given higher status. Any adequate recognition would place education on a division status with all of the rights and privileges of participating in the top councils of general policy making.

The educational staff is far from adequate for the real work it should accomplish. In February 1947 there were 55 persons on the staff of E and RA in the central office in Berlin and in branch offices of the various *Länder*. In May the army cut personnel 10 per cent across the board, eliminating adult education members and reducing the total staff to fifty. In October adult education members were reinstated and total staff was increased to seventy workers who must assume responsibility for leadership of 23 million people in reorganizing schools and social institutions through their various representatives. Such a staff is inadequate for any one of the E and RA *Länder* offices. It would be inadequate for a high school of two thousand students in America.

There are few inducements to competent American educators to make a career of educational work in Germany. Apparently there is too much uncertainty in the future of education to offer long-time opportunities with adequate salaries, security of tenure, and reasonable provisions for retirement. Yet such inducements must be offered. To see the educational job through to reasonable completion may take at least fifty years, for approximately three generations of children must pass through the new schools. And this figure assumes that total cultural conditions will be favorable. If they are not thoroughly reorganized, our stay in Germany may be prolonged indefinitely.

There is too much reliance upon the reorganization of machinery of government or education to achieve democracy. Decentralizing the government of a country does not make it democratic, neither does the development of opposition political parties. There is a process of democracy which people must learn. Reorganizing the over-all administrative pattern of a school system does not make it democratic. There is an internal process which is far more important. The value of this process in both the political and the educational field seems to be overlooked. And it takes time to teach it to adults, even under the best conditions.

There is little recognition that education for democracy is a civilian, not an army responsibility. This is not to disparage the excellent work which the army has accomplished in Germany in the past. And all praise should be given to the present high command in Germany for a realization of this problem. As soon as possible a civilian administration should be inaugurated with the necessary military units holding the same general relationship to it as they do in this country.

Little leadership is given the groups who are the best potential for developing liberal democracy. Some of these are the youth groups, the elementary school teachers, the young soldiers, especially those who have been prisoners of war in the United States, the young women, and the farmers. These groups need help. Their spirit and attitude are excellent. They must be given hope, confidence, guidance in democratic action.

We must send to Germany individuals competent in theory and practice of liberal democracy. All members of OMGUS believe in democracy. They have taken oath to support liberal democracy, which is the basic belief and pattern of the United States. But belief and loyalty do not necessarily qualify a person to give leadership to the German people in establishing a liberal democracy of their own. Leaders should have a clear knowledge of the meaning and direction of democracy, an understanding of cooperative deliberative process, a long and well-established record of practice in the use of such a process in many and varied relationships with people, and recognition of leadership in democratic action in the United States. Everyone who is making direct contact with Germans in any important capacity should meet these qualifications. In the field of reorganization of the school system from the kindergartens through the universities, at least one thousand persons thus qualified are needed immediately. In the fields of business, economics, finance, government, religion, and many others, similar needs are evident. And the persons selected must have the ability to teach the Germans how the democratic process works in the solution of their own needs. They should not, under the name of democracy, show the Germans how to substitute American authoritarianism for their German dictatorship.

The present personnel of OMGUS seems to have been selected on the basis of a number of different criteria, such as the following:

1. Those who enjoy the preferred status which members of an army of occupation have over the native population.

2. Those who have a special subject matter or technical knowledge necessary to the maintenance of the various divisions of OMGUS.

3. Those who have facility in the use of the German language as a mother tongue or as a secondary learning.

4. Those who were refugees from the Hitler regime.

5. Those who preferred to remain in Germany after V-E Day for various personal and professional reasons.

6. Those who believe that the German people are responsible for the war and should have hard, uncompromising treatment.

7. Those who have always been Prussian in their personality patterns and see in the present situation an opportunity to practice them.

8. Those who once had but have lost preferred political status and power in the United States.

9. Those who believe that the future of liberal democracy in the United States will be determined by what we do in Germany.

10. Those who meet the qualifications for liberal democratic leadership which have been presented above.

In building such a vast organization to function immediately after Germany surrendered, it is to be expected that the criterion of democratic leadership would not dominate the selection of personnel. Yet over two years have elapsed since V-E Day, and still too many of the non-democratic criteria seem to prevail.

But where can we find the people in the United States who meet the criterion of democratic leadership? This is indeed a difficult problem. Examining it, one sees our whole educational, economic, social system in a different light. Administrators in colleges, secondary schools, or elementary schools are not a fertile source for democratic leaders. They are generally "promoted" for other reasons. Neither are college professors of education or of subject fields a promising group. They have risen to prominence for other reasons also. Most high school teachers are little concerned with democratic practices. They are more interested in their subject matter. That leaves only one large and valuable source of such persons—liberal elementary school teachers. And it is curious that a similar test applied to educators in Germany would lead to the same conclusion. But the elementary school teacher faces a difficult problem in giving leadership to persons of higher status in the school system of Germany. So the two choices are either to select the best of the elementary school teachers or other educators who meet the democratic criteria and give them preferred rank, or to select the best of those educators who already have preferred status and teach them the processes of democracy. And either one or both must be done rapidly. Yet the problem of personnel seems to be equally acute in other fields. Where can we find enough democratic employers, labor leaders, economists, financial experts, social workers, political scientists, practical politicians, theologians? Does the present need in Germany show us the shortcomings of our liberal democracy at home? And what will we do about it here?

We must demand liquidation of social, economic, educational, church systems that made a Hitler possible. The groups responsible for the rise of Hitler were the militarists, Junkers, and

industrialists. They operated through four great institutions—
the government, the social class system, the school system, and
the churches. Of these groups the militarists have been or will
be destroyed, the Junkers and their landed estates are gone, the
industrialists have been curbed and their highly organized industrial system is flat. The conditions that still remain to nur-
ture a new führer are the class system, the school system, and the
churches. From the beginning, a war aim of the Russians was
to remove all vestiges of nazism, including the groups and institutions responsible for its development. They are employing
various measures to eliminate the class system, to purge the
schools of Nazi ideology and to remove the church control over
the schools. The government of the United States had no such
clear-cut and definite war aim in relation to the forces which
brought the Nazis into power. When our armies were advancing into Germany, General Eisenhower issued a proclamation
promising freedom of religion and respect for religious institutions, but he said nothing about removing church control over
the schools and eliminating the effects of such control upon the
social and educational status of the people. Consequently, from
the very beginning of United States occupation the Military
Government re-established temporarily the status quo of 1933
in church-school relationships, assuming that the churches were
entitled to have their traditional rights and privileges respected.
And any change in the future should be made by the school
and church authorities. But little progress has been made, for
no church wishes to give up voluntarily a control which it has
so long exercised. Prior to 1933 the churches—Evangelical and
Catholic—were "in control of four fifths of the publicly supported elementary schools."

Through many years of state support and close association
with the monarchy, both churches cultivated conservation. They
were strong supporters of the crown, gave deep loyalty to cultural traditions, and operated in close alliance with the social
groups which supported such traditions. They built up an educational system which was differentiated by classes and gave only
the most traditional education even to the few who graduated
from the universities. Under the Weimar Republic (1918-1933)

the traditional relationship between church and state was maintained since religious bodies were allowed to be incorporated and were given the right "to levy taxes on the basis of the civil tax rolls." Thus the old order continued. And it was Hitler's attempt to break this order and to control the schools in the interest of his Nazi ideology that caused both the Evangelical and the Catholic churches to break with him early in 1937. To restore the status quo of the Weimar Republic of 1933 re-establishes the basic traditional educational controls and patterns. And thus little progress is made toward the achievement of liberal democracy.

The decision for the liquidation of the traditional control of the churches over the social and educational systems should be made by the Allies and not by the Germans. The surrender of such systems should be a war reparation just as is the machinery from the Nazi factories, the ore from the Nazi mines, or the millions of dollars worth of other products and services. And surrender of the church control system will in no way affect the freedom of religion of the people. For the two are not synonymous; in many respects they are not even related. A peace without removing such controls is no peace at all, but only a stalemate, as it was after World War I. We must complete the whole job now. Only as the schools are separated from the traditional viewpoint of the churches can the German people go forward to develop the functional intelligence which is so necessary for the success of a liberal democracy.

The United States can help the people of Germany develop a liberal democracy. It will take time, economic rehabilitation, reorganization of the educational system including the cultural controls, a large number of democratic leaders, and ample financial support. But this is really a small price to pay to insure the security of our democracy at home. The liberal viewpoint is on the defensive. Totalitarian democracy is on the march. Every spark of liberalism everywhere must be encouraged and supported. For our sake, for the Germans' sake, and for the good of the world, let us bring the work we are in to a just and lasting conclusion.

REEDUCATING THE GERMANS [8]

It is difficult to educate; it is more difficult to reeducate; it is well-nigh impossible to reeducate a foreign nation. To attempt to reeducate Germans by military government action is to attempt the impossible.

Now, by reeducation we may mean *all* measures designed to change the character structure of the German people, or we may merely mean such measures as affect either the educational institutions (schools, universities, youth organizations), or the media of communication (press, theater, radio, movies, books). Primarily we will deal here with education in the narrower sense, although some attempt will be made to analyze the problem within the broader concept.

The impossibility of reeducation by military government has been clearly recognized by the occupying powers, and the role given MG is accordingly much less ambitious. The Potsdam Declaration of July 1945 (III A 7) stated: "German education shall be so controlled as completely to eliminate Nazi and militarist doctrines and to make possible the successful development of democratic ideas." The responsibility of the victorious powers was thus at once a negative one, the elimination of certain dangerous traits, and a positive one, the creation of a soil in which democratic ideas could grow.

This Potsdam Declaration statement is, however, as ambiguous as all those other provisions that commit the powers to the destruction of nazism and militarism, and assistance in the creation of democracy. The ideological dispute over the meaning of such terms as "democracy" and "nazism" has its roots in differing analyses of these conceptions.

For the Western powers, nazism is essentially a political phenomenon that can be eradicated by the elimination of Nazis from power and by the introduction of democratic procedures. Democracy is conceived as a method of ascertaining the popular will in a free manner. To the Soviet Union, however, such

[8] From article by Franz L. Neumann formerly Chief of German Research Section, Department of State; author of *Behemoth* and co-editor of *Germany Under Military Government*. *Commentary*. 3:517-25. June 1947.

definitions are totally unsatisfactory. Nazism for her is merely the political form of an economic and social system—the ultimate form of monopoly capitalism; consequently, the eradication of nazism requires the destruction of that socio-economic system. As a corollary, democracy is defined as not merely a method of ascertaining the popular will, but as a society without exploitation, in which the equality of citizens is not confined to the legal and political spheres but is extended into the economic. For only in such a society, contends the Soviet Union, will democracy flourish and last.

The clash between these two different analyses determines the occupation policies of the powers in all respects and is most clearly reflected in their educational policies. In the Western zones, the western point of view has indeed produced a state of considerable freedom for the Germans; all the paraphernalia of democracy exist and the practices of political democracy are widely resorted to. But the ultimate outcome of this experiment is in doubt. The Weimar Republic points a warning that cannot be overlooked: that is, that political democracy may again give birth to a nazism, perhaps not while the occupation lasts, but once the vigilance of the occupying powers has been relaxed.

Consequently, from the Soviet point of view, measures have to be taken that make a repetition of the Weimar experience impossible. The socio-economic system has to be changed at once in such a way that those forces that have traditionally supported imperialism and reaction can never again gain the ascendancy. In carrying out these measures (land reform, nationalization, and the educational reforms described below) the Russians have, however, resorted to the assistance of a state party, the Socialist Unity party (SED), with the danger that once that party achieves complete political control, freedom will not be established even when the socio-economic reforms are carried out.

One could formulate the clash between the conflicting ideologies in terms of a dilemma: *In the Western zones, there is the presence of freedom with the prospect of a rising neo-fascism; in the Soviet zone, there is the presence of repression with only a vague prospect of getting democracy.* The choice between these alternatives is obviously no choice—there is neither a greater nor a lesser evil, there are two evils, and to be relieved of such a dilemma requires concrete action by the Four Powers. But so far this has been almost totally absent.

The Western powers have so far been presented as one unit. In all essential problems this is quite correct, yet an analysis of the differences in their occupation policies will help provide a better picture of their educational measures.

In the American zone the principle of indirect rule has been developed most successfully, if success is measured in terms of administrative efficiency. American policy favors turning over to the German people, through their democratically elected representatives, as many tasks as possible without jeopardizing the basic principals of the United States Military Government. In consequence of this policy, all three *Länder* (states) in the American zone have their constitutions, their parliaments, their responsible governments, and their ministers of education, who are in almost full charge of educational policies. MG is thus confined to *Länder* level. Lower MG echelons merely observe, analyze, and report to the *Länder* MG, but they no longer rule.

The second principle of the United States Military Government is the full transfer of all powers—whether formerly exercised by the Reich or by the *Länder*—to the separate *Länder*. There is in the American zone no zone-wide German authority that can be considered the keeper of the former powers of the Reich. The *Länderrat* (Council of States), composed of the minister presidents of the three *Länder,* is merely a drafting and coordinating body without legislative and executive powers. Its recommendations have to be enacted by the three *Länder* governments in order to become law. With the exception of a press law, the *Länderrat* has so far made no recommendations in educational and cultural matters.

The British Control Commission has adhered to the principle of direct rule much longer than the United States Military Government. In fact, not even now has the delegation of powers in the British zone gone as far as it has in the American *Länder*. Diets were elected only on April 20, 1947. In addition, former Reich functions have not been given to the separate *Länder* but have been preserved intact and established in the hands of the central zone authorities, formerly predominantly MG, now more under German control. Consequently, there is in the British zone a Zonal Educational Council under a former Prussian minister of education, Dr. Adolf Grimme; this council, however, possesses not legislative and executive powers but merely coordinating and advisory powers.

The French zone combines features of both the American and British zones. Like the American zone, it lacks a central organization to preserve the powers of the Reich and, consequently, to prevent the complete atomization of the zone into *Länder*. It does not know of a state council. It shares the slowness of the British zones in evolving a system of indirect rule. It differs from both other Western zones, however, in the supreme significance attached to cultural penetration and in the high caliber of French educational and cultural personnel.

Legally, the Soviet zone is not much different from the American. There are *Länder* with elected representatives and constitutions; in addition, as in the British zone, there is a German Central Administration for the whole zone, with a very extensive department of popular education under the direction of Paul Wandel, an SED leader. In theory, the Central Administration merely coordinates; in practice, however, it directs, simply by virtue of the fact that the Socialist Unity party holds the key positions in the Central Administration as well as in the *Länder*.

It is difficult to make the outsider realize the scope of the educational problem. Its physical aspect alone challenges the imagination of the planner. But this has been overcome, largely through the active assistance of military government. The moral and intellectual problem is, however, difficult and involved. It consists in creating conditions for democracy in a youth that has not known it, does not particularly want it, does not have teachers imbued with the spirit of democracy, and lives in an environment unpropitious to democracy.

There is, first and foremost, no traditional social and educational environment within which democracy can grow.

German education was and still is class education. Secondary school students (especially at the humanistic Gymnasium), university students, and consequently professors, came from the wealthier groups of society; they constituted in fact the reservoir from which the traditional ruling groups drew their intellectual strength. Under the Weimar Republic, 34.1 per cent of all university students came from the upper classes, 59.2 per cent from the middle classes, and only 5.9 per cent from the lower classes, workers comprising only 3.2 per cent of all university students. This class composition is essentially unchanged in the present Western zones of occupation. In Heidelberg the composition of the student body, as to parentage, is now as follows:

Academicians and professionals	32	per cent
Employers	24	" "
Middle civil servants	17	" "
Higher civil servants	13	" "
Workers	6	" "
Artisans	5	" "
Farmers and lower civil servants	3	" "

In Marburg only 2.6 per cent, in Göttengen less than one per cent, come from workers' families. All these institutions are in the American zone, but there is no reason to believe that the situation is different in the other universities of the Western zones. The problem has, of course, not escaped the attention of the political groups or of the military government.

Military Government has no power to act here, or rather it has deprived itself of its power. The basic Military Government Regulation 8-102, in implementation of the over-all policy stated above, specifically states that "the reform of German education will be left to the Germans themselves, subject to encouragement, supervision, and control by MG," and 8-216: "The Germans must reorganize their own schools and create a new school system out of their own intellectual and spiritual resources." The three *Länder* in the American zone have each solved the problem differently. The constitutions of Bavaria (Article 128) and of Württemberg-Baden (Article 35) merely promise more scholarships, but retain essentially the old structure; only Hesse, dominated by the Social Democratic party, envisages (Article 59) free education on all levels, including the university, subject to the power of the government to charge fees for the wealthy students.

The composition of the student body is further adversely affected by the problem of admitting Nazis and former officers. German universities were hotbeds of nazism under the Weimar Republic. This was true even, and especially, of the Bavarian universities. In Protestant Erlangen, in 1930, 19 out of 25 students were Nazis; and in Catholic Würzburg 40 per cent of the students voted for the Nazi party in 1930, while in the electoral district to which Würzburg belonged the Nazis polled only 12.1 per cent. The directive of the Allied Control Council of January 14, 1946 permits the enrollment of non-active Nazi party members, provided they do not exceed 10 per cent of the accepted students.

The admission of former army officers causes further deterioration of the student body. While in the Soviet zone active army officers are allegedly excluded and only reserve officers are permitted, the western zones do not make any distinction. According to American statistics, the student body in the American zone includes 3.1 per cent active officers and 16 per cent reserve officers; in the French zone, 1.5 per cent active and 15 per cent reserve; in the British zone, 3.7 per cent active and 20.07 per cent reserve. The officer groups in the Weimar universities supplied much of the leadership for the Free Corps and for reactionary industrial and agricultural organizations.

Soviet policy is totally different. Special admission committees screen aspirants not only for membership in the Nazi party and for army status, but also for social origin, and care is taken to admit students without secondary education. But, as a consequence of the overwhelming influence of the SED in the screening committees inquisitional methods are applied to give preference to SED members. Already, the result in the Soviet zone universities has been a destruction of the educational privileges of the wealthier classes. It is stated that 40 per cent of the student body now comes from the working classes, and special workers faculties (as in Leipzig) provide for the rapid training of the economists and lawyers so sorely needed by the state party.

It has been the pride of the occupation powers that they have been able to reopen all German universities. (Only Giessen has not and will not be reopened, but its medical and agricultural schools are operating.) The French have even created a new university in Mainz. Yet the hasty reopening of the universities is now producing quite disagreeable consequences because the second denazification wave tends to deprive universities of their teaching staffs.

Denazification proceeded in two stages. In the first stage, an attempt was made to remove members of the party and its affiliates. It proceeded on the basis of the famous *Fragebogen* (questionnaire), which compelled professors, under threat of punishment, to state their party affiliation. Relatively few professors were affected. But it soon became apparent that what was adequate for the ordinary Germans could not possibly be adequate for those to whom the education of the intellectual elite of Germany was entrusted. The authorities then began to scrutinize the publications of the professors and discovered that the majority of them had preached pro-Nazi, militarist, and antidemocratic doctrines—certainly no unexpected discovery for the initiated. A second wave of dismissals began, far more comprehensive than the first, a wave that actually threatened the continuation of many universities, especially of their law faculties. In Heidelberg, one of the most democratic of Germany's universities, 153 of 272 teachers were dismissed.

The mistake of hastily opening all universities, instead of opening a few with teaching personnel of unimpeachably democratic views, has now to be paid for.

The situation is aggravated by the caste system in German universities, the rigid separation of the university career from all others. Rare are the cases in which outsiders (such as practicing lawyers and recognized writers) were given university professorships. Universities complain of the lack of a new generation and yet they look only into their own ranks, their own *Privatdozenten*, for teachers and stubbornly refuse to renew themselves from outside. Anyone who knows the Germany of today knows that there are a great number of capable young men and women—lawyers, literary and art critics, historians, economists—who could be induced to choose teaching as a career if the universities so desired.

MG has again prevented itself from intervening, having re-established the principle of the autonomy of the university (MG regulations 8-320 and 8-330 of May 27, 1946). After approval of each university's charter it will, according to MG law, operate under this charter, subject only to the continued control of MG. Autonomy is a cherished dogma of German universities. The original intention was to preserve academic freedom from interference by the governments that maintained them financially. Under the Weimar Republic, however, autonomy turned into a device to permit the sabotaging of the republic itself without fear of retaliation. Autonomy was abolished by the Nazis and re-introduced in a situation which is essentially that prevailing under the Weimar Republic.

The over-all picture of university life is thus disheartening. In the Western zones, the Weimer Republic has been substantially recreated; in the Soviet zone, the universities have been transformed into institutions for the creation of a corps of technicians and administrators serving the state party.

The principles underlying German elementary and secondary school reform are again directly affected by the ideologies of the powers.

It has been American policy first and foremost to open all elementary schools as speedily as possible. Educational ardor and the military necessity of keeping the children off the streets have indeed worked miracles. The principles underlying American policy may be summarized as follows: (1) The transfer of MG authority to the Germans; (2) severe denazification of teaching staffs and elimination of Nazi and militaristic texts; (3) political neutrality of the schools.

The transfer of authority to the Germans has been completed (MG regulation 8-102; 8-216 of May 26, 1946) and the sole safeguard retained by MG, except for its supervision of denazification, is the clause stating that no school system is to be permitted "which would make it difficult for any person to realize a development commensurate with his ability" (MG regulation 8-101).

Denazification of teachers in the American zone (and apparently in the Soviet zone) has been carried out speedily, energetically, and successfully by MG, and about 50 per cent of the teachers of elementary and secondary schools have been dismissed. How many of these have been reinstated by the Germans, on the basis of clearance by the *Spruchkammern* set up under the Law for the Liberation from Nazism, cannot be ascertained. In the British and French zones, denazification has generally been laxer.

The transfer of the school system to the German authorities in the Western zones has not produced any basic changes because the major problem still remains: the old issue of secular versus confessional schools. True, there are a number of plans, such as those of the former Hesse Minister Schramm, the Bavarian Fendt, and Dr. Grimme. None of these, however, has gone beyond discussion. The major concern in the Western zones is the battle over the preservation or extension of church influence.

The school system of the Weimar Republic was based on a compromise (incorporated in Articles 143-149 of its constitution) between the secular Social Democratic party (joined by the Democratic party) and the clerical Catholic Center party. Three types of schools emerged from the compromise: the *Gemeinschaftsschule*, or community school (also called *Simultanschule*), comprising members of both religious confessions; the *Bekenntnisschule*, or denominational school; and the secular school (*weltliche Schule*). These schools were to be established according to the wishes of the parents. Private confessional and private secular schools were also permitted. Detailed regulations were foreseen in the Weimar Constitution but never enacted; in fact, the school question remained so sore a point that even a cabinet composed exclusively of right-wing parties (1927) could not agree on it.

American policy, as expressed in the directive of October 17, 1945 and the MG directive of May 27, 1946 (8-112), has been to refrain from interference and to permit private schools. The sole important legislation is the directive of the Allied Control Council of November 19, 1945 to the effect that no school drawing on public funds could deprive children of their opportunity to receive religious education or compel them to receive it. In its early stage, however, MG actually gave preference to the *Gemeinschaftsschule* with its separate religious instruction simply because the scarcity of school accommodations worked against confessional (as well as against secular) schools. The situation is now reversed. The confessional school has triumphed in Bavaria, has held its own in Württemberg-Baden, and is prevalent in Hesse, where the Social Democrats, in order to get the consent of the Christian Democratic Union to the nationalization clause in the new constitution, agreed to freeze the school system until 1950.

Consequently, the situation resembles that under Weimar, with all the stakes in favor of the confessional schools—the more so since, on the basis of a bargain between Social Democrats and Christian Democrats, all education ministries in the American and British zones are held by Christian Democrats, who in return conceded to the Social Democrats all ministries of economics.

Only in the French among the Western zones has a military government school reform been enacted with definite favor shown to confessional schools, which seem the best vehicles for instilling a particularist or strongly federalist spirit and thus promoting a pro-French cultural reorientation.

Needless to say, a far-reaching school reform has been enacted in the Soviet zone. The only school permitted is the public *Einheitsschule*. Private and denominational schools are prohibited. The *Einheitsschule* begins with eight years of secular foundation or primary school, in the seventh year of which the student chooses between a practical and a theoretical course. The practical course again divides into two years of vocational (*Berufsschule*) or two years of technical (*Fach*) school. The theoretical course leads to high school (*Oberschule*). Gifted students of the high or technical schools are admitted to the universities and the schools of technology.

At the same time the Soviet zone has abolished the difference in training of teachers. Pedagogical faculties at universities provide for the training of elementary school teachers, whereas in the Western zones they are still trained in special pedagogical schools of a definitely inferior status.

It is again the same divergences in philosophy and analysis between West and East that have determined the different school systems. The structure in the Soviet zone is definitely progressive. It fulfills the demands of progressive liberals and of the working classes, regardless of political affiliation. But the great danger is the use to which that system is put. For the Russians, education must be political, which in practice means the training of sycophants and functionaries for the state party.

The education in the West is "unpolitical," which, in view of the social and educational structure, means that it is actually or potentially reactionary.

Among the media of communication the press ranks first as an instrument in political education. The printed word still means more than the spoken one.

Newspapers are operating in all zones under different systems. But the results of the different systems are rather similar.

In the American zone about 40 newspapers are licensed (with a combined circulation of over 4,000,000; in the British zone 44 papers have a circulation of over 4,500,000; in the French zone 28 papers have over 2,000,000 readers; in the Soviet zone 80 papers have over 8,000,000 readers). The papers in the American zone are "unpolitical": their editors have been selected exclusively from a journalistic point of view, regardless of party affiliation—but after an extremely careful screening. The political parties have no newspapers, although they are permitted to publish small bulletins.

So far, MG has refused to license newspapers run by political parties or party representatives, believing that an "objective" press is a superior medium for a democratic education. It is backed up in this view by a series of public opinion polls conducted by MG's Information Control Division. While such anti-political licensing was undoubtedly the right policy in the initial period of occupation, it now tends to become a serious obstacle to the reconstruction of political life.

The present licensing system has already given birth to a new *Generalanzeiger* type of paper—that is, an allegedly neutral provincial paper, which in the past, under the guise of being non-political, insidiously fought democracy. The licensees, under the present system, enjoy a perfect monopoly, and, being fully aware that they owe their business to MG, are of course more easily manipulated than party newspapers would be. Yet to deny political parties the right to publish newspapers is to deny the very basis of democratic political education. There is no political life that does not center around political parties.

Political neutrality (in education as well as in the press) and education for democracy are thus, in Germany, mutually exclusive terms. German political parties are no accidental phenomena; they fulfill—no matter what their leadership and quality—the basic political needs of society. There are bound to be, in view of the class character of German society, labor parties (one Communist, one Socialist); there will always be an outspokenly right-wing party (so far not admitted in the American and Soviet zones), and there will always be a middle party trying to avoid and overcome the polarization of political forces between Right and Left. Political education consists in taking a stand for or against something with a political party. Meanwhile the public opinion polls simply express the desire of the bulk of the Germans to be left alone and to avoid taking a stand, the very attitude that a democratic political education should fight against.

This, of course, does not mean that the party press in the British and Soviet zones is superior to the non-political press in the American zone. They are equally bad. There are exceptions, the most outstanding being the *Tagesspiegel* (United States sector of Berlin), which, so far as I can see, is the only German newspaper that wages an unremitting fight against German smugness and unceasingly educates the Germans by a ruthless self-criticism. (This must be admitted in spite of the fact that the author is in almost complete disagreement with the positive policies advocated by the editor, Erik Reger.)

The most productive of all zones in papers and periodicals is the Soviet. This is because of the larger amounts of newsprint available there, but also because of the deliberate policy of the Soviet military administration. Here, of course, an intense politicalization of all the media of communication contrasts sharply with the political neutrality in the American zone. But, as can be expected, Soviet zone papers are overwhelmingly SED papers and thus merely stereotypes.

Less significance attaches to the role of the radio.

Since June 30, 1946, radio in the American zone has been turned over to Germans, supervised by small staffs of American control officers, though no German organization has yet been licensed. This is now being prepared. (The three major stations are at Frankfort-on-the-Main, Stuttgart, and Munich; there are smaller ones at Nuremberg and Bremen, and a wired wireless in Berlin.) According to the German News Service (Dena), the Frankfort Radio will be owned and operated by a corporation made up of the universities, churches, trade unions, chambers of commerce, farmers' and youth organizations, political parties, the Hesse government, and the management of the station. No such transfer is apparently taking place in any of the other three zones. And in the Soviet zone, even receiving sets are licensed (Order No. 78, September 27, 1945, allegedly relaxed in the spring of 1946).

It is a truism that there exists an intrinsic connection between education and the social, political, and economic structure of a country. This is clearly expressed in the American policy statement of August 1946 on the long-range aim of reeducation: "Reeducation of the German people can be effective only as it is an integral part of a comprehensive program for their rehabilitation." Yet there is always a danger that the present political-economic situation may defeat the long-range aim of education. Education aims at the future, but present social and political attitudes determine its present status and thus prevent basic changes in the future. Without an almost revolutionary act it is quite impossible to sever this vicious circle.

Present attitudes in Germany are far from encouraging. This is not only because of the Nazi system, it rather antedates it.

In university education Germany was already, under the Weimar Republic, on the way to losing her intellectual leadership, especially in the social and humanistic sciences. The German intellectuals were largely morally corrupt and their corruption clearly manifested itself under the Nazi regime. Their lack of resistance, their large degree of enthusiasm or at least of

conformism, were the natural results of an utter lack of democratic attitudes both among teachers and students. Even those
whom Anglo-Americans usually depict as the true representatives
of the German democratic spirit reveal themselves, upon closer
analysis, as basically conformists. (This is especially true of Karl
Jaspers.). . . The German intelligentsia of today follows three
key ideas: the first is "Western civilization," the second "the
Occident" (*Abendland*), the third "anti-fascism." The first
provides for synchronization with the Anglo-Americans; the
second with the French; the third with the Russians.

Conformism to the domestic regime and domestic tendencies
has been replaced by conformism to the occupying powers. Much
of this is inevitable and merely expresses the disappearance of
Germany as a political power. The extent itself of this conformism, however, is a daily surprise to anyone spending some time
in Germany. The three terms mentioned in the previous para-
graph are, so to speak, entrance tickets to the spheres of influence
of the three major powers.

Those who reject such conformism simply become nationalists.
Nationalism—or better, chauvinism—in Germany is again rampant. On closer observation, however, even nationalism is seen
to be merely a form of conformism to the great powers. Today
already, the major political parties announce their determination
not to sign a future peace treaty if it should violate the basic
needs of the German nation. The Left (especially Social Democracy) is as determined as the Right and, apparently, has not
learned that playing with nationalism leads of necessity into
reaction.

Simultaneously with the growth of nationalism, the attitude
of Germans toward nazism has changed. Denazification is no
longer a moral problem; it is no longer felt to be morally
detestable to deal with Nazis. They are merely irritants in the
body politic, to be dealt with as fast as possible and with as
much good grace as the situation permits (which is not much).
Denazification today is simply an administrative procedure, no
longer a problem of right and wrong. . . .

On the whole, the German intellectual world is dominated by
a gerontocracy that so far has successfully excluded outsiders.

Much of this is, of course, due to the isolation of German intellectual and political life. The isolation is practically unbroken. It has by no means been overcome by the educational officials of MG, who, on the one hand, do not represent the finest flower of American intellectual life, and, on the other, cannot, as parts of the machine of the occupying power, exert any influence on Germany's intellectual elite. The little that can be done by a foreign power should not be done by MG, but rather by America's outstanding scholars free from all controls by MG. American policy in this respect has been correspondingly formulated, but so far little has been carried out in this direction.

The rest has to be done by the Germans. The revival of democracy presupposes, however, a unified Germany, no matter what her constitutional structure. In a Germany divided or excessively federalized, intellectual trends will either be intensely chauvinistic or intensely conformist, according to the interests of the big powers.

Democratic revival requires, secondly, an understanding among the great powers. Lack of understanding will make the Germans pawns in a struggle for their affections. Such competition is intensely corrupting. (This was one of the key themes in the Stuttgart speech of former Secretary Byrnes.)

But even if there should be a unified Germany, there is of course no guarantee that Germany will become a democratic nation. The risk exists that Germany may again become imperialist, that racism may triumph, that the Left may prove itself again incapable of stemming the tide and creating a political and social democracy. To enable the Left to achieve this, basic educational reforms are vital: the destruction of education privileges, the elimination of the caste spirit in German universities, the secularization of education—all these are vital for achieving the long-range aims. But in order that these may be achieved, the present institutional arrangements must be changed by coordinated action of the occupants, along lines whose detailed description would go beyond the scope of this article.

THE FUTURE OF GERMANY: UNIFICATION OR DIVISION

IS A PEACE TREATY WITH GERMANY LEGALLY POSSIBLE AND POLITICALLY DESIRABLE?[1]

By its complete defeat, the surrender of its armed force, and the abolishment of its national government, Germany has ceased to exist as a sovereign state and subject of international law. By the Declaration of Berlin, June 5, 1945, the four powers occupying the country—the United States of America, the United Kingdom, the Soviet Union, and the French Republic—assumed "supreme authority with respect to Germany including all powers possessed by the German Government, the High Command, and any state, municipal, or local government or authority." This meant that the four occupant powers have assumed sovereignty over the former German territory and its population, though the term "sovereignty" was not used in the text of the Declaration. The four occupant powers exercise their joint sovereignty through the Control Council, established at Berlin as the legitimate successor of the last national government of Germany. All this is in complete conformity with general international law, which authorizes a victorious state, after so-called *debellatio* of its opponent, to establish its own sovereignty over the territory and population of the subjugated state. *Debellatio* implies automatic termination of the state of war. Hence, a peace treaty with Germany is legally not possible. For a peace treaty presupposes the continued existence of the opponent belligerents as subjects of international law and a legal state of war in their mutual relations.

The opposite doctrine, advocated by some authorities and governments, that Germany, in spite of the fact that there exists no independent national government, not even a "government

[1] By Hans Kelsen, University of California. *American Political Science Review*. 41:1188-93. December 1947. Reprinted by permission.

in exile," still exists as a sovereign state, that the four occupant powers are not the sovereigns in relation to the German territory and its population, that they only exercise Germany's sovereignty just as a warden exercises the rights of his ward, is manifestly based on a legal fiction. According to international law, a community is a state if, and as long as, a certain population is living on a definite territory under an independent government. If one of these three essential elements of a state in the sense of international law is missing, the state as a subject of international law disappears, or, in other words, the community ceases to exist as a sovereign state. No state can exercise the sovereignty of another state. State sovereignty does not permit representation or substitution.

Legal fictions should be avoided in clear juristic thinking. However, it is understandable that politicians should be inclined to use legal fictions if such fictions are politically advantageous. The legal fiction that Germany still exists as a sovereign state has no such advantage. On the contrary: if Germany still exists as a sovereign state, the occupation of the country must be interpreted as *occupatio bellica* under the Fourth Hague Convention; and many measures taken by the occupant powers constitute violations of this Convention, for which a future German government might hold the occupant powers legally responsible. Nonapplication of the Hague Convention is possible only under the assumption that Germany has ceased to exist as a sovereign state and that the occupant powers have extended their own sovereignty over the former German territory and its population. The argument that the occupant powers are not the sovereigns in relation to the occupied territory because they do not intend to "annex" it is of no importance; for sovereignty over a territory can be established not only for the purpose of incorporating it definitely into the territory of the occupant power, but also for that of ceding it later to another state, or of establishing on the territory a new state. It is the last-mentioned alternative which exactly applies to the occupation of the former German territory.

That Germany has ceased to exist as a sovereign state does not prevent the occupant powers from creating a new German state. But it is at least doubtful whether the new state would be

legally identical with the German Reich as it existed at the outbreak of World War II. There certainly will be no legal continuity in the relation between the German Reich and the new
German state from the point of view of German national law.
The legal order which will be the basis of New Germany cannot
come into existence in conformity with the constitution of the
old German Reich, which has definitely lost its validity. From
the point of view of international law at least, no direct continuity will exist, since between the German Reich defeated in
World War II and the new Germany there will have been a
period during which no German state as a subject of international law existed. New Germany cannot be the direct successor of old Germany; it will be the successor of the *con-
dominium* exercised by the four occupant powers as sovereigns
over the former German territory and its population. As to the
identity of the new with the old German state, the fact—important from the viewpoint of international law—must be taken
into consideration that the territory of the new state will be quite
different from that of the old state, since vital parts of it have
already been annexed by Poland and the Soviet Union and will
probably not be assigned to the new German state. Identity of
territory is—besides legal continuity—a criterion of the identity
of a state. Non-identity of the new with the old German state
must certainly be recognized in case no peace settlement with
respect to Germany as a whole proves possible, and Germany is
divided into two states according to the line separating the territory occupied by the Soviet Union from the territory occupied
by the other three powers. Neither of these two states could be
considered as identical with the German Reich; with neither of
them could a peace treaty be concluded. The four powers which,
for the time being, are the sovereigns over the former German
territory and its population may, it is true, conclude a treaty with
the new state; or the three Western powers may conclude a treaty
with the new state set up on the territory occupied by them. But
such treaty could not have the character of a peace treaty in the
true sense of the term. However, such a treaty could contain
the same provisions which a peace treaty with Germany, if it

were legally possible, would have contained with respect to territorial changes, reparations, and the like.

There can be little doubt that such a treaty is politically not desirable. The victors should not repeat the mistake, made after the First World War, of burdening the government of a democratic Germany with political responsibility for a peace settlement whose harshness had been made necessary by the guilt of a previous autocratic or totalitarian government. In Hitler's propaganda against the Weimar Republic, political responsibility for the Treaty of Versailles played the most important rôle. The responsibility which the new democratic government of Germany assumed by signing the Treaty of Versailles destroyed the Weimar Republic and opened the way to the Nazis. It is besides, very doubtful whether it will be possible to find an honest German statesman willing to sign a treaty by which vital parts of German territory are ceded to Poland and the Soviet Union and the forcible transfer of many millions of Germans from their homeland into the overcrowded remaining territory is recognized. A German statesman who signs his name to such treaty would certainly share the fate of Erzberger, slain for having signed a much milder treaty. There can be little doubt that, under the pressure of inevitable nationalistic propaganda, the German people would consider such a treaty null and void because enforced upon them, just as they considered the Versailles Treaty as "dictated" and consequently not binding. This reaction, from the point of view of international law, is certainly not correct; but what is the political value of a treaty when those committed to the execution of it consider themselves not morally obligated?

What, then, is the politically adequate legal form for settling the German question? Since the future German state will be a new state, it must be created by the governments of the states which have the sovereignty over the territory concerned. This is what in reality must and will happen. The new German state can come into existence only by an act of the occupant powers. They may, directly or indirectly, appoint a central German government or order general elections for the establishment of such a government, or of a constituent assembly empowered to create it. The creative act will always be a sovereign act of the occupant powers. It is of the utmost importance that the legal procedure which these powers adopt shall be in conformity with political reality. This will be the case if the new German state is created by an international agreement of the states which have the legal power to create it, since they possess the sovereignty over the territory and the population concerned. There are precedents in international law for the creation of a new state by international agreement. The most recent ones are the creation of the State of Danzig by the Treaty of Versailles and the creation of the State of the Vatican City by the treaty of February 11, 1929, concluded between Italy and the Holy See. To both of these treaties, the state to be created was not, and could not be, a contracting party. By both, international obligations were imposed upon the new state in spite of the fact that it was not a contracting party. A treaty by which a new state is created is one of the few exceptions to the rule that a treaty can impose obligations only upon the contracting states. Hence the treaty by which the new German state (or the new state of Western Germany) is created may contain all the obligations which the victorious states wish to impose upon the new German (or Western German) state.

The fact that there will be no (or no direct) legal continuity, and consequently no legal identity, in the relation between Nazi Germany and the future democratic Germany (or Western Germany) might facilitate the development of a new political philosophy as an ideological basis of the new state. The legal procedure here suggested has the further advantage that it would be in harmony with political reality, and particularly that conflict would be avoided between the idea of a treaty voluntarily entered into by a vanquished state and the fact that this state is forced to accept the conditions laid down in the treaty; and, finally, that since there will be no peace treaty at all, no separate peace treaty would be necessary, whatever political situation may exist with respect to the relation between the Soviet Union and the Western powers.

The act by which the new German state is to be created can be performed only by the occupant powers. It must be preceded by an international agreement entered into by these states, on the one hand, and the other states which were at war with Germany, on the other hand; and the purpose of this agreement must be to determine the obligations to be imposed upon the new German state by its creators. By this agreement, the occupant powers will assume responsibility for erecting the new German state as an international subject bound by the stipulated obligations.

THE PARTITION OF GERMANY AND THE UNITY OF EUROPE [2]

The debate over the future of Germany . . . presents the most dangerous of all the problems about which we and the Russians shall have to agree—the problem of the political organization of Europe. For the question of Germany is unintelligible apart from the question of Europe. The strength or weakness and the political direction of German policy are relative things. They depend on the strength or weakness and the political orientation of Germany's neighbors. Germany as a secondary part of a cohesive European Federation of States would be one thing. Germany as the balancing factor in a quarreling, divided, and frustrated Europe would be quite another. . . .

The most promising political idea now current in Europe is the idea of European union. It is the germ of a program which we and the Russians could pursue or approve together, as a peaceful alternative to continued quarreling over the ideological affiliations of Poland, Rumania, Greece, and Germany.

It is notable that Europeans were far more willing than Russians and Americans to consider yielding "sovereignty" to the United Nations. Many Europeans are convinced that nationalism is no longer a workable basis for the organization of states, at least in Europe. The idea of creating some sort of European union or association has real vitality. The Churchill-Monnet plan of 1940 for the joint citizenship of the British and the French, and eventually of the other nations of Europe, was an

[2] By Eugene V. Rostow, Professor, School of Law, Yale University. *Virginia Quarterly Review*. 23, no. 1:18-33. [January] 1947.

early expression of the goal. Most observers are sure that the idea will be revived. The customs union of Belgium, the Netherlands, and Luxembourg is close to reality. At this point projects for a closer political union of European states are being actively discussed abroad, although they have been little considered here. Léon Blum, the leader of French Socialism, champions the idea. So do experienced and conciliatory conservatives like Leopold Amery, the veteran British Cabinet Minister. An impressive list of thoughtful men and women, both among the active leaders of the resistance and among the surviving political leaders of the prewar period, are pressing the project.

Winston Churchill, who is as much a European as an Englishman can ever become, has been stumping the continent with speeches in behalf of European unity. That Elizabethan figure, with his magnificent style and his sure sense of history, has put new passion into a project which Britain has for centuries opposed. With the emergence of Russia and America as world powers, the plan of European Union has ceased to be a utopian dream. It now offers Europe its most promising road to independence, equality, and peace, in a world of changed dimensions.

There is a spirit of idealism and humanity in the conception which should not be lost. A vivid moment lights up the meaning of the plan. Georges Bidault, the President of the Provisional Government of France, was at the end of the war the head of the French Underground Resistance. One of his first public appearances after the liberation of Paris in 1944 was at a Paris hospital for wounded German prisoners. "I wish you good health," he said to the German soldiers, "as future citizens of a united and democratic Europe."

A European Union of States would rest on what Harold Nicolson has called "the inner nucleus of cohesion" of Europe's common culture. Proceeding from that inner unity, men could build a wider area of loyalties, and a more effective framework for their political and economic progress. A European Union could become an effective federal grouping. It should lack the threat of power implicit in centralized control. But it could end the absurdity of tariffs and other economic barriers which have helped to ruin the modern life of Europe. It could guarantee within Europe democratic forms of political life. It could provide the political setting within which the Europeans could together pursue their goal of democratic social development.

The practical place to begin building such a European Union is through the projected European Regional Council of the United Nations. The Charter of the United Nations contemplates the existence of regional bodies, to deal with both political and economic problems of specialized local character. A European Political Council and an Economic Council have in principle always been part of the program of the United Nations. Discussions have been held about the formation of such bodies, to meet permanently in Geneva, and to serve at the least as a forum for the discussion and reconciliation of European problems. Whether such a European Council of the United Nations ever comes into existence, however, and whether if created it will be made capable of serving the ends of orderly progress, depend largely on the attitude and agreement of the Big Three, and especially of the Bigger Two. Active support for the immediate organization of such groups would be one way to try to stop our menacing race with the Soviet Union for political influence in various areas of Europe. A European Council should have a good chance to achieve an independent authority and status. It should be able to put European problems into a new perspective, and to proceed towards their resolution on the basis of compromise and common action, not the endless and insoluble issue of yielding either to the East or to the West.

The project of European Union faces two practical difficulties of great magnitude. The first is that the plan might be affirmatively dangerous unless the German state created by Bismarck in 1871 is further divided into its component parts. Prewar Germany, even as reduced at Potsdam, is altogether too large a unit to be allowed into a European Union. The danger of German domination in such a Union would be too great. The second general difficulty of such a plan is that it might be construed by the Soviet Union as a hostile act, and a revival of the disastrous policy of the cordon sanitaire against Bolshevism. A European Federation including a large German state would seem like a plan to give defeated Germany the fruits of victory.

For one fact stands out plainly in the confusion of our experience with occupation: the Germans are utterly unrepentant and unreconstructed. The illusions of the war are fading, as we discover for ourselves what is going on within occupied Germany. We see that bombing and defeat have not eliminated the Germans, nor solved the problem which Germany has posed for her neighbors. The Germans exist, some sixty or seventy millions of them, living in central Europe between the Russians and the West. They live in a rich and productive country, full of the equipment of modern life. We have discovered that defeat has worked no magic change in the German culture. The Germans are the products of their education and experience. Their homes, their schools, and the other institutions of private and public life bear a familiar shape. The Germans have not accepted guilt, nor do they seek penance and forgiveness. Concerned with status and authority, aggressive and deferential, romantic and pedestrian, ruthlessly cruel and fantastically sentimental, the Germans remain the great problem of the peace of the world. They are and will continue to be intense nationalists and disciplined militarists. They are committed to the ideas of fascism. In our lifetime the Germans will be responsive to a policy of revenge. The concept of their own supremacy will attract them, and plans for another war of conquest will inevitably gain adherents if the opportunity should ever again emerge. Resentment at defeat and military occupation is a common and normal attitude among defeated peoples. With the Germans it is an obsession.

Despite bombing and defeat, Germany ended the war in a position of great potential strength. The Germany which fought off the whole world for three years still lives. Germany is and will remain one of the important industrial areas of the world. Recent official studies of the German economy have established the facts beyond a doubt. German industrial potential was not reduced 5 per cent by bombing, although her cities were wrecked. German industry today has the capacity to support a German army within a few months, and German economic life on the old scale within a few years. Except for the areas lost to Poland, the German economy at the end of the war had a greater capacity in all the crucial categories—machine tools, locomotives, steel and engineering—than in 1939. Wartime increases in capacity were greater than bombing losses. . . .

The existence of the Germans, their numbers, their geographical and economic position, and their state of mind are a major danger to the security of the United States. If we permit a unified German state to reappear, such a state would constitute the most serious of all threats to the relationship of the Soviet Union and the Western powers. A unified Germany would be ideally equipped to gain strength by playing the East against the West, and the Western Allies against each other. The relative success of such efforts is already apparent in our miserable experience with military occupation. Scattered and unorganized as they are at this moment, the Germans have found rich material in the mutual suspicions of the Allies. The Germans now have the Allies competing for their good will, contrasting conditions in each occupation zone unfavorably with those in other zones. By threatening us with communism, and the Russians with reaction, the Germans are blackmailing the Allies into more and more ambitious programs of aid for the German population and economy.

Manifestly, it is in the great and equal interest of all the Allies to prevent the reappearance in European and world politics of a German state capable of such a program. It is almost incredible that in advance of actual negotiations on the subject, both the Soviet Union and the United States have now declared themselves in favor of a unified German state.

The day-to-day impact of occupation policy, and our program for the next stage of development in Germany, should be in the direction of permanently dividing Germany into separate states. The unification of 1871, which was accomplished by force, should be undone. Poland has been enlarged at German expense. France should be likewise increased in area and economic potential. Three or four Germanic nations should be established, some Catholic, others Lutheran, some with strong French or British affiliations, other leaning more to the South and East. Such nations could safely be assured prompt restoration of their equal participation in the political and economic life of Europe. Within a Europe without tariffs, or with very low tariffs, and as part of a general security system, such states could facilitate the reintegration of the German people into the main stream of Western civilization. The partition of Germany is the only course which would permit the Germans economic recovery and political freedom, without constituting a military threat.

The first objection to such a policy is that it would create a rallying point of nationalist appeal for a new Hitler. Most commentators on proposals for partition go this far and regard their analysis as closed. The Germans would object to partition; therefore it cannot be done. It is an argument with startling implications. The Germans objected strongly and for all practical purposes unanimously to the defeat of Hitler. They object now to the separation of East Prussia, Silesia, and the Saar, or, for that matter, to their evacuation of Austria, Czechoslovakia, Poland, and France. In assessing this argument it should be recalled that each step in the nineteenth-century unification of Germany was accomplished by force. Germany existed ununified for centuries before Bismarck, and there is no historical imperative which makes it necessary to preserve Bismarck's creation.

But one should admit at once that the Germans would be against partition, and that partitioning Germany would feed nationalist sentiment. But violent nationalism will exist in Germany with or without partition. Partition will not create German nationalism, nor make it measurably more dangerous than it is. The strength and menace of German nationalism is one of the strongest reasons for partitioning Germany. The German past, and the shock of defeat in two wars, guarantee us the survival of an intense and provocative feeling of nationalism in Germany. Every party which has appeared in occupied Germany is a nationalist party and has expressly opposed the loss of the Eastern provinces. Until Mr. Molotov recently corrected their deviation, the German Communists were strongly in favor of revising the Eastern boundary, and are still violent proponents of German union. They were the decisive group in beating the proposal to call the head of the new Bavarian Government a "President" rather than a Prime Minister.

One can hope for the reorientation of this universal German nationalism into constructive forms only after a long time and a different kind of group experience. Separate German states could soon become members of a European Union, and of the United Nations. Within such a framework, one might hope slowly to counter the force of German nationalism. Participation in the councils of Europe with other small states would create non-German poles of political activity and association. The several German states would acquire a momentum of their own. Vested interests in jobs, institutions, and traditions could develop. There is no reason why Bavaria or Hanover could not become states as real as Czechoslovakia or Belgium—both in their time "created" by partition. The guaranty of the Great Powers should be enough to permit such a system of small German states to get a good start in the period of ten or fifteen years when combined Allied action could be presumed to be available.

At first glance, Winston Churchill's recent speech in Zurich, advocating European Union, seems to contemplate a single German state, which might dominate the Union, and wreck the peace. What he said on the subject, however, does not bear out such first impressions. "The ancient states and principalities of Germany," he pointed out, "newly joined together into a federal system, might take their individual place among the United States of Europe." The emphasis is significant. The starting point of a new political system in Germany, he is saying, is not the Reich of Bismarck, Ebert, and Hitler. By their political behavior, the Germans have lost the right to have a German state of such dimensions. What Churchill is talking about is the ancient German states. If those states are restored, we "might" safely consider their loose federal association, within a larger framework of European Union, and in close and stabilizing contact with France itself, the strongest cultural influence in Europe. Churchill's treatment of the German question gives emphatic recognition to the danger of a unified German state. His concept of German federalism means in effect that separate

German states, and not a Fourth German Reich, would be members of the European Union—a formulation of the problem which takes adequate cognizance of the abiding menace of German revenge, yet offers the German people direct and equal share in the common life of Europe.

A second generally stated objection to the political partition of Germany is that it would be economically wasteful. This, of course, would be a strong objection to the creation of tariff-ridden little Duchies in the territory of Germany. It is no objection at all to a plan for partitioning Germany within a wider European Union, which should itself become a continental economy, and a freely trading part of the world economy.

The attitude of the Russians, of course, presents a problem of a different order. The Russians, and their collaborators in all countries, might view plans for European Union with deep suspicion as an anti-Soviet plot. Although the Soviet Union strongly favored regional groupings some years ago, it has been wary of all such projects since 1943, and has seemed lately to prefer weakness and separatism both in Eastern and in Western Europe, on grounds of Russian security.

A great deal of the talk about the Western bloc of nations in this connection is misleading and irrelevant. We and the Russians have an equal need that Europe be organized in a stable and progressive way. We face equal risks of friction, quarreling, and even war, in the event that we continue to pursue the policy of aggravated competition for political dominance in every area which comes up for discussion.

The emergence and development of strong European Regional Councils within the United Nations, both for political and for economic problems, should threaten the security of neither West nor East. The Czechs and the Poles could participate in such activities without becoming anti-Soviet pawns, or ceasing to be friendly with their great neighbor. Such plans for a European regional grouping, subject always to the authority of the Security Council, should expressly exclude the possibility that Europe could be a cohesive military threat in either direction. The independence of Europe must be guaranteed by the agreement and self-interest of nations. Competitive intervention in Europe from East and West is far too dangerous to be continued.

The organization of European Regional Councils would not of itself solve the tensions which prevail between the countries of Eastern and Western Europe. Europe will continue to be under pressure during the period of its adjustment to the new status of the Soviet Union. If, however, the formation of a European Union would not solve such problems, it should provide a procedure for their peaceful solution. In politics, as in law, procedure is often the key to results. Dealing with European problems on a European basis should minimize the number of issues which would require direct Soviet-American adjudication and agreement. In the councils of a European Federation, many of the most trying quarrels of diplomacy would have a changed aspect, and others would disappear.

Without a strong Germany, a European Union in loose federation would be an organization which could stabilize and harmonize the relations of East and West. In fact, enduring good relations between us and the Soviet are hard to imagine on any other basis. Unstable shifts in this or that country from the Russian orbit or the Western orbit would create friction, and insecurity, on a dangerous scale. The policy of European unity is not an alternative to the policy of close association with the Soviet Union. On the contrary it is the only course which will permit a concert of action between the Soviet and the United States to take place on a stable and assured basis.

The war-time Allies cannot solve the political problems of central and eastern Europe independently. They are common problems and must be settled together. Germany is not our ally but our enemy, and will remain our potential enemy during the next two generations. We can hope for the reeducation of the Germans, and their reintegration into the community of Europe. But we cannot base our foreign policy on the assumption that such a miracle has already taken place. The problem of Europe is the central issue of world politics, and the problem of Germany is the central core of the European problem. Until it is affirmatively and progressively settled, the relations between the Soviets and the West will be suspicious and uneasy. Mutual suspicion can lead to the break-down of unity, and a competitive quest for security through unilateral action rather than allied negotiation. In that process the Germans would have another chance to bid for world power by promising each ally in turn its support against the others. Thus once more bad diplomacy could lose the peace.

UNIFICATION WITH AN ALTERNATIVE [3]

For a year and a half now, each of the occupation armies has been busy creating in its own zone a new little state in the image of its maker. This process of fragmentation was somewhat checked last autumn when the British and American zones were merged. (Merger may be too strong a term for the establishment of German-staffed agencies to administer the finances, exports and imports, industry, communications, and agriculture of the two zones.) But the merger emphasized the deep split between the Russian and the Western zones. The Russians, if they choose, can block unification indefinitely. A good many Americans have wondered why the United States does not give up and accept the split of Germany.

The United States has not given up, and the reasons are compelling—as usual, more compelling than the State Department has found occasion to suggest. For one thing, the destruction of a modern state is not something to decide on before breakfast— the United States invested a third of a million lives in its own effort to remain one country. Were Germany split, Germans would not soon, if ever, give up the idea of reunion. The result might be, as Dr. Kurt Schumacher, leader of the Social Democrats in the British and United States zones, warned last October, the creation of "a center of unrest and disorder for all Europe."

Politics are also involved. From Paris last summer Mr. Molotov told the Germans that Russia would oppose any dismemberment of Germany. The Russian-sponsored Socialist-Unity party has taken the cue and has become a vigorous spokesman for a

[3] From article by John Kenneth Galbraith, member of the Board of Editors, *Fortune*; formerly with the State Department. *Fortune*. 35:126-7+. January 1947. Copyright Time Inc. Reprinted by permission.

single Germany. The other parties are also strong advocates of unification. Were the United States to accept a split of Germany, it would lose the friendship of all the present political parties in Germany and leave Russia the leading sponsor of what Germans, next to food, want most.

To give up on the unification of Germany would also mean withdrawal from Berlin, which is deep in the Soviet zone, and the experience there during the past year does not justify such a retreat. Although the Allied Control Council has passed its basic disagreements on reparations and unification to the Council of Foreign Ministers, work has continued on a wide range of lesser questions. General Clay's patient and brilliant bargaining has earned him not only the profound respect (though not necessarily the deep affection) of his Russian, French, and British colleagues but also has won such liberal measures as four-power inspection of disarmament in all Germany, exchange of oil, rubber dyestuffs, and other basic commodities between the Russian and American zones, and city-wide and genuinely free elections in Berlin—to pick only three examples at random. These day-to-day negotiations, conducted without pyrotechnics, provide a hope that business can be done in the future.

Finally the economics of a divided Germany are alarming. All important land connections between eastern and western Europe pass through Germany; Germany traded with both East and West. To split Germany would be to destroy one of the main bridges between eastern and western Europe and to confirm in economics American acceptance of two Europes. What would be left of Germany in the West would have a permanent food deficit that could be covered only by large exports of manufactured goods, based in turn on large imports of raw materials. Thus, in the near future, Germany would be a new claimant on scarce food and raw-materials supplies and, in the near distance, a rather frantic competitor in world markets. The United States should not, if it can avoid it, take responsibility for forcing a change. . . .

To wait any longer for unification would be intolerable if it delayed progress toward the next objective: economic recovery in western Germany. . . . Fortunately German recovery does not depend on unification, and unification will not become urgent for economic reasons until Eastern and Western Germany are in the happy position of having something more to trade.

At the Potsdam conference the United States delegation was still undecided about Germany's frontiers. President Truman and Mr. Byrnes leaned to putting the Ruhr and Rhineland under an international control and giving the Saar to France. Their political advisers argued that the Germans so divorced from their homeland would agitate forever for reunion. The economists on the delegation argued that without Ruhr exports the rest of Germany would be a permanent relief client of its former enemies. No decision was reached by the conference; United States policy remained undecided for many months. On Germany's frontiers the American performance has been sloppy.

At Stuttgart Mr. Byrnes wound up the unfinished business in the West: he declared that the Ruhr and Rhineland should stay in Germany and the Saar should go to France. The decision on the Ruhr and Rhineland accords with both the desires of the people and the requirements of the Germany economy. France objects, partly because of her ancient fear of a strong Germany, and partly because, with England out of the world coal market, French industry is grimly dependent on Ruhr coal. France could, however, be given an unconditional guarantee of a share in Ruhr coal. Some special surveillance of the Ruhr industries, even in addition to that provided in the disarmament treaty, might elide some of her fears about her security.

The Saar decision is more debatable though not so important. The Saar has fewer than a million people, compared with 11 million in the Rhineland and Ruhr, and before the war mined only 14 million tons of coal a year, or about one tenth as much as the Ruhr. The Saar's industry is also integrated with that of France; the Saar blast furnaces use Lorraine ore and the Lorraine steel mills get their coke from the Saar. A good many Saarlanders, including the leaders of both the Christian Socialist and Social Democratic parties in the area (but not the Communists), think life would be happier were the Saar a part of France, at least for a few years. However, the Saar was separated from Germany once before and it did not stick.

The great misfortune is in the East. There the Oder traces a line south from Stettin on the Baltic to within a couple of hours' easy motoring distance from Berlin and then curves off to the east. Beyond the bend the western Neisse River leads off south to the Czech frontier. East of the Oder-Neisse line are Pomerania, a large chunk of Brandenburg, and all of Lower Silesia—all agricultural regions—and the coal and steel province of Upper Silesia. These provinces before the war produced about one fourth of Germany's food, and about one fourth of it was shipped to other parts of Germany. Still farther east, beyond the old Polish corridor, is East Prussia, also an agricultural province, and the peacetime home of Germany's warmakers since the days of the Teutonic knights.

At Potsdam the northern half of East Prussia was given to Russia and the southern half was allotted provisionally to Poland. The euthanasia of this nest of landed troublemakers is accepted by the United States. Prior to Potsdam the Poles had taken possession of the provinces west of the corridor and east of the Oder-Neisse line. Stalin argued that the Oder-Neisse should become the new eastern boundary of Germany. The United States and the United Kingdom objected and, in a final compromise, the Poles were allowed to stay in possession and the final decision was postponed until the peace conference.

This unhappy deal was followed by many months of diplomatic neglect: the Poles evicted the German population and in a referendum approved incorporating the area into Poland. Not until Mr. Byrnes's speech at Stuttgart were they formally reminded that their claim to these provinces was unsanctioned. By the Yalta agreement, which fixed Poland's eastern frontier on the Curzon Line, Poland was to get some German territory. In addition to East Prussia, Upper Silesia, which has a mixed population of Poles and Germans and industries that would complement Poland's agriculture, would have been a logical award. Carving off the agricultural provinces—especially of Lower Silesia, Pomerania, and Brandenburg—was thoroughly unjustified. Poland does not need any more farmland and there have been many reports during the past year that, from her decimated population, she has been unable to find settlers for the new territory.

In making peace there is no chance whatever of removing all causes of future grievance—Hitler showed, in fact, that a German demagogue will as readily use an imaginary grievance as a real one. Real grievances, however, win the support of men of good conscience in other countries. Although the United States will undoubtedly urge a revision of the Oder-Neisse line, its chances at this late hour are not very bright. Despite rumors that Russia might agree to a new frontier, her statements have all been to the contrary.

ONE OR MORE GERMANIES: THE ECONOMICS OF PARTITION [4]

Any discussion of the future of Germany may begin with two premises which, at this date, will meet with almost universal acceptance. One is that the German nation must not be permitted to rebuild the military power which has just been destroyed at so staggering a cost. The second is that it would be unwise, inhumane, and probably impossible to achieve this end by attempting to deindustrialize Germany. It is of course evident that the industrial activity which we consider essential to the life of millions of Germans and to the economic health of Europe is also the stuff of which a war machine is made, and it is in seeking a way out of this dilemma that we separate into two camps. In one are to be found those who advocate restoring as much as possible of the former economic and political unity of Germany, believing that a program of inspection could be relied on to keep German militarism in hand. In the other camp are those who, not convinced that the American and British publics can be trusted to maintain forty years of vigilance against Germany, would restrain Germany from reuniting.

For the present at least, Germany is very effectively partitioned along the line of the iron curtain. Nevertheless, a long-term policy, looking forward to an ultimate withdrawal of all occupation forces from Germany and the reunion of the Western and the Russian zones, should not overlook, as a feasible and

[4] From article by Charles A. Knudson, University of Illinois. *International Journal.* 3, no. 1:56-66. Winter 1947-1948.

efficacious act of partition, the severance of Rhineland-Westphalia from the German state.

It should be pointed out at once that this is not the same thing as the internationalization of the Ruhr. Rhineland-Westphalia is a well-integrated and well-defined economic province, which in 10 per cent of the 1937 area of Germany had 20 per cent of the entire German population, and the same proportion of the people engaged in industry. It produces three fourths or more of the Reich's output of coal, three fourths of the pig iron and steel, and 30 per cent of the lignite (*Braunkohl*). The part of Rhineland-Westphalia commonly known as the Ruhr is the relatively small district, some fifteen miles wide and forty miles long, between the Ruhr and the Lippe rivers, which has the principal coal-field and the greatest concentration of heavy industry. About one fourth of the region's population of twelve million is concentrated here.

The plan for internationalizing the Ruhr does not contemplate keeping the area out of the German state, but rather installing there an international authority exercising a super-sovereignty at a point of the German economy where preparations for war might be difficult to conceal. Such an arrangement might be tried, *faute de mieux,* but seems to the writer far less desirable than the unequivocal separation from the Reich of the whole economic region of which the Ruhr is a part.

The question at once arises as to who would annex the region, or, if it were to be set up as an independent state, who would occupy it to prevent reunion with the rest of Germany. No one of Rhineland-Westphalia's western neighbors—France, Belgium and Luxembourg, the Netherlands—would be willing to undertake such a responsibility alone, but united in some sort of a federal union for this and other purposes, they might be. With cultural autonomy, the largest possible measure of self-government, and the expectation of an eventual place of equality in the union, Rhineland-Westphalia might not find separation from the Fatherland too difficult to bear. It is the purpose of these pages to outline briefly the reasons for believing that such separation would not injure the economy either of Rhineland-Westphalia or of the rest of Germany.

It is popular at the moment to assert the contrary. Mr. Herbert Hoover has said that "there can be no separation or different regime of the Ruhr or Rhineland from the New Germany: that is the heart of her industrial economy." Mr. James P. Warburg, who writes extensively on Germany, has phrased in this manner his objection to the Polish annexations in the East and the French project for internationalizing the Ruhr: "It would create a rump Germany which, minus breadbasket and coal, would be either a plague center or a permanent charity patient living mostly on the American taxpayer." And Mr. Molotov said, in a session of the Conference of Foreign Ministers on July 10, 1946, that "Germany cannot live without the Ruhr."

Views such as these rest upon certain concepts of domestic and international trade, and certain postulates as to the probable effects on trade of new political boundaries. If the political severance of Rhineland-Westphalia were to mean the end of customary trade relations with other regions of Germany, if it were true that territories had to be under the same political sovereignty to trade with each other, if it were true that European nations enjoy a very high degree of economic self-sufficiency and have largely self-contained economic systems, then Messrs. Hoover, Warburg, and Molotov would be talking sound economics, in their metaphoric way. But if these postulates are not true, then the statements quoted are inaccurate, fallacious, and most thoroughly misleading.

It is a convenience, of course, to think of nations as economic units, and it is quite common to think of them as the most natural ones. A single national government, a single currency and tariff system, a single statistical organization, all provide a classification of obvious usefulness. But one need only turn the pages of any statistical handbook to see Europe not as a collection of fenced-in economies, but as a community of nations which, at least in times of peace and relative normalcy, trade extensively and profitably with one another. Indeed, no one of these nations, particularly among the highly industrialized ones, could keep its present population alive or maintain its customary standards of living without carrying on most if not all of its usual foreign trade.

And within the several national frameworks we should perceive the existence of well-defined regional groupings, and patterns of inter-regional trade which are likely to be maintained even when political boundaries change. It is true of course that political boundaries mean tariff lines, and that tariffs, by intent and in effect, constitute partial obstacles to trade. But it would be the grossest error to assume that, as between European nations, tariffs stand in the way of the great currents of commodity exchange which have resulted from the modern world's specialization and division of labor. So when Mr. Molotov says that Germany cannot live without the Ruhr, his statement is beside the point, since it is not proposed to restrict peaceful trade between Rhineland-Westphalia and the rest of Germany. All that partition would seek to accomplish would be to keep the Ruhr's industrial plant from being used to build another war machine to serve the aggressive designs of Germany or of any other nation.

Before going on with a discussion conceived in terms of Germany's economic regions, we should enumerate them. Erwin Scheu distinguishes nine, R. E. Dickinson ten, the difference being that the latter makes a separate region of Schleswig-Holstein. Dickinson's list is as follows: 1. The Baltic Provinces (East Prussia, Pomerania, Mecklenburg); 2. Berlin and Brandenburg; 3. Silesia; 4. Central Germany (State and Province of Saxony, Thuringia, Anhalt); 5. Schleswig-Holstein and Hamburg; 6. Lower Saxony (Hanover, Oldenburg, Brunswick, Bremen); 7. Rhineland-Westphalia; 8. The Rhine-Main Region (Hesse, Hesse-Nassau, Rhenish Palatinate); 9. Baden and Württemberg; 10. Bavaria. To Poland have now gone, for better or for worse, Silesia, East Prussia, a third of Brandenburg and two thirds of Pomerania. The remainder of regions 1 and 2, together with *Mitteldeutschland*, "the economic epitome and heartland of Germany" (Dickinson), constitute the Russian zone of occupation. France has a zone made up of contiguous parts of regions 7, 8, and 9. Britain holds the rest of regions 5, 6, and 7; the United States the remainder of regions 8, 9, and 10. Of these ten regions, Rhineland-Westphalia and Central Germany are industrial areas of the first rank, the Rhine-Main Region and

Berlin rank next, and there are scattered industrial centers elsewhere.

To say that Rhineland-Westphalia is the heart of the German economy is meaningful in the sense that the region is the principal source of certain commodities which are extensively bought by other regions of Germany, above all coal and steel. But this organic metaphor overlooks two other equally prominent features of the region's economy. One is that there is a high degree of integration within the province: many industries require no market outside Rhineland-Westphalia. The other is that the region's trade with foreign nations is very extensive and more vital in some respects than trade with other parts of Germany. Rhineland-Westphalia is a heavy importer of food, of iron ore (from Sweden and France), of pyrites (from Spain and Norway), of phosphate fertilizers, petroleum, wool, and cotton. In return, the region has coal to sell abroad, iron, steel, ironware, and machinery. . . .

The food situation is the feature of German economic geography which has received most widespread popular attention in the past year or two, unfortunately in a vastly over-simplified and highly inaccurate presentation which we may call the breadbasket myth. It is usually stated in about these terms: Eastern Germany is more fertile and productive than Western Germany, and has food surpluses which the Poles and the Russians are now turning away from their normal market in Western Germany, as a result of which this latter region is in desperate straits and requires huge imports of food from abroad.

This much is true: Eastern Germany, as a whole, had agricultural surpluses in normal times, and a part of these were marketed in Western Germany. But it is not true that Eastern Germany is more fertile and productive than Western Germany. It is not true that Western Germany depended principally on Eastern Germany to make up its food deficits. And it is certain that in the past two years the food surpluses of the East have been so sharply reduced that they are not worth taking into account.

The distribution of more fertile and not-so-fertile farm land shows no favoritism as between East and West. In efficiency of cultivation, the East (except *Mitteldeutschland*) has always lagged behind the West. . . . It was not superior productivity which made Eastern Germany a food surplus area, while Western Germany had a food deficit, but rather the lower proportion of total population to total area. And in any event, what was left of the Eastern surpluses after supplying the deficit areas of Berlin and the State of Saxony was only a fraction of what was needed in the West. Germany as a whole has been a food deficit area for three quarters of a century, and heavy imports for the benefit of the West have long been the rule. . . . That the amount of food Western Germany at present needs to import from abroad is ususually large is due less to the loss of access to the East than to the general decline in agricultural yields, which must now be even more pronounced in Germany than it was towards the end and just after the first world war. The East never was Germany's bread-basket, and today could serve as such less than ever, in the great upheaval following the Polish annexations.

The breakbasket myth has lost ground in the past year, and the attention of the public, as well as that of the occupation authorities, has very properly turned more to the problem of production, agricultural and industrial. A British-American decision has recently given the Germans in the combined zone at least permission to produce more in the factories than did an earlier schedule agreed on by the Big Four powers. This step may be of some help, psychologically, at this point, and is to be applauded. But our approbation cannot be extended to the reason generally given for encouraging Western German industry. We are told that it is because the iron curtain cuts off access to Eastern Germany's food surpluses that more goods must be produced for export, to pay for the increased imports required. There has crept in here one of the fallacies of economic nationalism which bedevils much of our thinking about Germany and the German future. To say that German industry must be stimulated to pay for the importation of food not now available on the domestic market is to imply that, if the food were available at home, industry would not have to be so stimulated. As a matter of fact, the need for increased production would exist even if Germany were being administered as a single economic unit, and even if there were sizeable food surpluses in the East. Goods have to be paid for; they are not given away either within a national economy or across international boundaries. If a worker in Frankfort or Essen is to buy food, it must be with the fruit of his labor, whether the food is grown on a farm ten miles away, or in Mecklenburg in the Russian zone, in East Prussia, in Hungary, in the United States, or in the Argentine. If he has no buying power, the whole land may run with milk and honey and he will still go hungry, as so many Americans did in the early thirties, when there was more food than we knew what to do with.

Economic nationalism has a language all its own to describe the phenomena of international trade, not in terms of pure and simple economics, but with reference rather to the goals of national power and self-sufficiency. To take an example, the return of Alsace-Lorraine to France in 1918 removed from the German Reich a territory which had yielded 21 of the 28 million metric tons of iron ore mined in Germany in 1913. Using the language of economic nationalism, one would say that Germany "lost" three quarters of her iron ore, and was henceforth obliged to import vastly larger quantities of that commodity from abroad, to pay for which there had to be a corresponding increase in exports. In terms of nonnationalistic economics, however, Germany didn't lose anything at all. Both before and after the reunion of Lorraine to France, Germans who wanted the iron ore had to buy and pay for it. The chief difference was on paper, the exchanges between the iron-producing region and the complementary coal-producing region (in the Ruhr) now being entered under the heading of exports and imports, instead of under that of domestic sales and purchases.

Deeply imbued as she was with economic nationalism, Germany naturally felt impoverished by the loss of territories, and alleged that this would cause real economic hardship. The Armistice terms had returned Alsace-Lorraine to France; the Treaty of Versailles called for the cession to Poland of the territories in the East having a predominantly Polish population. These were two of President Wilson's Fourteen Points. The

German reaction to them is stated in a note of May 13, 1919, deriving from the German Economic Commission charged with studying the effect of the proposed conditions of peace on the situation of the German people, and was addressed by Herr Brockdorff-Rantzau to M. Clemenceau. Taking note of the loss of German merchant tonnage, of the required deliveries of coal, of the cession of territories rich in iron ore and zinc, and the prospect of giving up the two food surplus provinces of Posen and West Prussia, the note made the following predictions.

If the Conditions of Peace are put into force, it simply means that many millions in Germany will perish. . . . No aid, important and of long duration as it might be, could bring a halt to this wholesale death. The peace would demand of Germany a greater human sacrifice than the war devoured in four years and a half. . . . Those who sign the Treaty will pass a sentence of death upon many millions of German men, women, and children.

The reply of the Allies took up one by one the contentions of the German note. We shall quote two passages from it.

Great stress is laid upon the proposal that on the Eastern side Germany shall be deprived of the regions specially devoted to the production of wheat and potatoes. This is true. But the Note fails altogether to observe that there is nothing in the Peace Treaty to prevent either the continued production of these commodities in the areas in question, or their importation into Germany. On the contrary, the free admission of the products of the Eastern districts is provided for during a period of three years.

To complete the story, it should be pointed out that the Germans, if they had their share of hard times, did not die by the millions, as Brockdorff-Rantzau predicted. And as to the food surpluses of the ceded provinces, it was Germany which moved to stop their importation, about 1925.

Another section of the Allied reply may be recalled for its applicability, *mutatis mutandis,* to the present proposal for the severance of Rhineland-Westphalia.

Stress is also laid upon the hardships alleged to be inflicted upon Germany by the necessity of importing in future iron ores and zinc. It is not understood why Germany should be supposed to suffer from conditions to which other countries contentedly submit. It would appear to be a fundamental fallacy that the political control of a country is essential in order to procure a reasonable share of its products. Such a proposal finds no foundation in economic law or in history. . . .

There is not the slightest reason to believe that a population is destined to be permanently disabled because it will be called upon in future to trade across its frontiers instead of producing what it requires from within. A country can both become and can continue to be a great manufacturing country without producing the raw materials of its main industries. Such is the case, for example, with Great Britain, which imports at least one half of her food supplies and great preponderance of her raw materials from abroad. There is no reason whatever why Germany under the new conditions should not build up for herself a position both of stability and prosperity in the European world.

For those who accept the clichés of economic nationalism, and have difficulty in imagining prosperity except in proportion to national self-sufficiency, a Germany without Rhineland-Westphalia must seem handicapped. To others, the handicap would seem only to affect the nation's war potential, and not its ability to achieve a robust prosperity.

Every economic region within a nation is as real an economic unit as the nation itself. It produces what it can produce profitably, first for local consumption and then for export from the region in exchange for commodities which cannot be produced locally in sufficient quantity or at a competitive price. The population of any region adjusts itself to the region's developed productive capacity, so that in normal times every region is self-supporting. The test of this is simple. Do the inhabitants of a given area earn their living, or do they not? For example, to take a political subdivision of Germany at random, do the seven million inhabitants of Bavaria normally earn their livelihood, or are so many of them usually unemployed that the gainfully employed population of the state cannot support them, and must call for contributions from other parts of Germany? If Bavaria normally keeps its population alive without receiving more from national charitable funds than it contributes to them, then Bavaria is a self-supporting economic unit.

When we ask this same question concerning all Germany less Rhineland-Westphalia, it must certainly be answered that the area is normally self-supporting. Either that, or it lives in part on the charity of Rhineland-Westphalia, a hypothesis at once contrary to fact and fundamentally absurd. Those who say

that Germany without this region would be reduced to beggary
seem to overlook the varied and widely distributed natural resources of Germany, and to forget that four fifths of German
industry, as measured by the number of industrial workers, is
after all located elsewhere than in Rhineland-Westphalia. The
smaller Germany, they say, would lack coal. The answer to
this is that it lacks coal now. Germans outside Rhineland-
Westphalia who want Ruhr coal have to import it from that
region, buying and paying for it just as do purchasers who live
in Switzerland, Italy, France, Belgium, or the Netherlands. These
nations are not normally charity patients because they require
more coal than they produce within their own boundaries.

The Germans will of course try, in an effort to retain their
unity and their territory of 1937 (as next best to that of 1943, or
1913), to persuade their conquerors of hardships which partition
would impose. We may expect them to put forward again and
again the sophistries of economic nationalism. What is disquiet-
ing and disheartening is the popularity of this brummagem
economics on our side: too many Britons and Americans return
from visits to occupied Germany talking like Brockdorff-Rantzau,
and one looks vainly in high places for someone to answer with
the economic good sense of the Allied experts who drafted
Clemenceau's reply. . . .

That Eastern and Western Germany will continue to be
separated politically is certainly for the best, considering the
difficulty we have in cooperating with the Russians. More trade
with their zone would be helpful, but we should not form an
exaggerated idea of this East-West trade: new orientations and
developments could compensate for it. We would do well to
stress production, and to make up with renewed effort for our
long failure to accord proper facilities for the trade of Western
Germany with the other nations of Western Europe, around
the great half-circle from Sweden to Switzerland and Italy.
These nations, with the United States, Britain, of course, Brazil,
Argentina, and India, used to account for half of Germany's
foreign trade, and for the smaller of them trade with Germany
was an almost vital part of the national economy.

Next, in anticipation of the time when Eastern and Western Germany may again be joined together, we should decide now that Rhineland-Westphalia shall not be part of a reunited Germany, and begin to build the region's new régime. With freedom to trade with Germany assured, under supervision, no German on either side of the new boundary would need to suffer economic hardship or disadvantage. The somewhat smaller Germany would still be equal in natural and industrial resources to any Western European nation, and superior to most. Germans would suffer in their national pride, to the extent that it is based on size and total power, but we must not be asked to take too much account of this, as it is precisely our task, and our grave responsibility, to see that so destructive a power is not again set free.

REPORT ON BIG FOUR PARLEY [5]

The general issue [at the Council of Foreign Ministers in London] was simple. It was whether or not Germany was to continue divided or whether the Allies could agree to recreate a unified Germany. Unless this could be achieved, all other questions relating to Germany would remain academic.

What, then, were the particular obstacles to the achievement of German economic and political unity?

The United States delegation considered that there were certain fundamental decisions which the four occupying powers should take if German unity was to be achieved. These were:

1. The elimination of the artificial zonal barriers to permit free movement of persons, ideas and goods throughout the whole territory of Germany.

2. The relinquishment by the occupying powers of ownership of properties in Germany seized under the guise of reparations without four-power agreement.

3. A currency reform involving the introduction of new and sound currency for all Germany.

[5] From address by George C. Marshall, Secretary of State, December 19, 1947. *New York Times*. p. 4. December 20, 1947. Reprinted by permission.

4. A definite determination of the economic burdens which Germany would be called upon to bear in the future, that is, the costs of occupation, repayment of sums advanced by the occupying powers and reparations.

5. An over-all export-import plan for all of Germany.

When these basic measures had been put into effect by the occupying powers, then the establishment under proper safe-guards of a provisional government for all Germany should be undertaken.

Reparations soon emerged as a key issue. In the Eastern zone of Germany the Soviet Union has been taking reparations from current production and has also, under, the guise of repara-tion, seized vast holdings and formed them into a gigantic trust embracing a substantial part of the industry of that zone. This has resulted in a type of monopolistic strangle-hold over the economic and political life of Eastern Germany which makes that region little more than a dependent province of the Soviet Union.

A very strong reason, in my opinion, for our failure to agree at London was the Soviet determination not to relax in any way its hold on Eastern Germany. Acceptance of their claims for reparations from current production from the Western zones would extend that strangle-hold over the future economic life of all Germany.

The Soviet position was nowhere more clearly indicated than by Mr. Molotov's categoric refusal to furnish the Council of Foreign Ministers with information concerning the reparations already taken from the Eastern zone or indeed any information at all concerning the situation there until full agreements had been reached. In effect, we were to tell them what has occurred in the Western zones, which we had already done, and they tell us nothing.

That refusal to provide information absolutely essential for decisions as to the organization of German unity would by itself have made any agreement impossible.

A remarkable illustration of the Soviet position in this matter was their carping criticism of the economic procedure in our zones, which we freely publish for the world to read, while virtually in the same breath blandly refusing to provide any data at all concerning their zone. . . .

No real ground was lost or gained at the meeting, except that the outlines of the problems and the obstacles are much clearer. We cannot look forward to a unified Germany at this time. We must do the best we can in the area where our influence can be felt.

All must recognize that the difficulties to be overcome are immense. The problems concerned with the treaty settlements for Italy and the satellite countries were simple by comparison since none of those countries were divided into zones of occupation and all of them had an existing form of government. Germany by contrast is subdivided into four pieces—four zones. No trace of national government remains.

There is another, and I think even more fundamental, reason for the frustration we have encountered in our endeavor to reach a realistic agreement for a peace settlement. In the war struggle, Europe was in a large measure shattered. As a result, a political vacuum was created and until this vacuum has been filled by the restoration of a healthy European community, it does not appear possible that paper agreements can assure a lasting peace. Agreements between sovereign states are generally the reflection, and not the cause of genuine settlements.

It is for this very reason, I think, that we encountered such complete opposition to almost every proposal the Western powers agreed upon. The Soviet Union has recognized the situation in its frank declaration of hostility and opposition to the European Recovery Program. The success of such a program would necessarily mean the establishment of a balance in which the sixteen Western nations who have bound their hopes and efforts together would be rehabilitated, strong in forms of government which guarantee true freedom, opportunity to the individual and protection against the terror of governmental tyranny.

The issue is really clear-cut and I fear there can be no settlement until the coming months demonstrate whether or not the civilization of Western Europe will prove vigorous enough to rise above the destructive effects of the war and restore a healthy society. Officials of the Soviet Union and leaders of the Communist parties openly predict that this restoration will not take place. We, on the other hand, are confident in the rehabilitation of Western European civilization with its freedoms.

EXCERPTS

Russia recognized the crucial character of the German question long before we did. Though it was she who had insisted most upon the quadripartite occupation of Germany and who had also refused to cooperate in achieving the economic unity of the German country which was to make this partition economically feasible, Molotov has since promised the ultimate political unity of the nation, a gesture used by Communist propaganda to hide the real situation. No one close to the situation seriously believes that Russia intends to let go of her part of Germany. Why should she? She has an excellent plan for conquering the whole of Germany ideologically from the vantage point of the part she dominates by occupation. She has a better chance of doing that in a divided Germany than in a united one. As a divided Germany sinks into economic misery, Russia hopes to conquer her ideologically by attributing this misery to capitalistic exploitation.—*Reinhold Niebuhr, Professor of Applied Christianity, Union Theological Seminary. Life. O. 21, '46. p. 67. Copyright, Time Inc.*

The central and almost the most serious problem which glares upon the Europe of today is the future of Germany. Without a solution of this problem, there can be no united Europe. Except in the framework and against the background of a united Europe, this problem is incapable of solution. In a continent of divided national states, Germany and her hard-working people will not find the means or scope to deploy their energies. Economic suffocation will inevitably turn their thoughts to revolt and revenge. Germany will once again become a menace to her neighbors and to the whole world; and the fruits of victory and liberation will once more be cast away.

On the wider stage of a United Europe, German industry and German genius would be able to find constructive and peaceful outlets. Instead of being a center of poverty and danger, the German people would be enabled to bring back prosperity in no small measure, not only to themselves, but to the whole continent.

Germany today lies prostrate, famishing among ruins. Obviously no initiative can be expected from her. It is for France and Britain to take the lead. Together they must, in a friendly manner, bring the German people back into the European circle. No one can say, and we need not attempt to forecast, the future constitution of Germany. Various individual German states are at present being re-created. These are the old states and principalities of the Germany of former days to which the culture of the world owed so much. Without prejudice to any future question of German federation, these individual states might well be invited to take their place in the Council of Europe. Thus in looking back to happier days we should hope to mark the end of that long trail of hatred and retaliation which has already led us, victors and vanquished alike, all into the pit of squalor, slaughter and ruin.

The prime duty and opportunity of bringing about this essential reunion belongs to us and to our French friends across the Channel. . . . It is true that this task of reconciliation requires on the part of France, which has suffered so cruelly, an act of faith, sublime in character; but it is by this act of faith and by this act of faith alone that France will regain her historic position in the leadership of Europe.—*Winston Churchill, former Prime Minister of Great Britain. Speech, May 14, 1947, before United Europe Movement. London.*

Anglo-American-French unity on Germany would put the issue of a unified Germany squarely up to Moscow. In general, world events have produced a crisis in Soviet foreign affairs. Diplomatically and politically, Stalin had things his way during the war and for a year after V-E Day. Now conditions are very different. These new circumstances confront Russia's rulers with the most fateful decision of their careers. Shall they be reconciled to a Western diplomatic victory in Germany and China, and elsewhere, which frustrates their further expansion and may involve the ultimate surrender of earlier gains? Shall they acquiesce in the unification of Germany and China, the two major nations where the East-West antagonism is being fought out? Or shall they enter a fierce political battle with the West, hold what they have in Germany and other places, and trust that sooner or later Russia will be able to resume her forward march as the result of an American business slump, which the Russians frequently discuss with great hope, or of a cooling of Anglo-American relations, which has been a Communist expectation since 1919, or of a windfall in the form of an election victory by some appeaser in some Western country, or of an upsurge of Communist sentiment in Greece, France, anywhere?

It is Moscow's dilemma. The gyrations of Soviet foreign policy, the way Moscow blows hot one day and cold the next, the way Molotov smiles one morning and frowns the next, are evidence that the Soviets cannot make up their minds which line to adopt: with the West, or against the West? The answer, Moscow knows, must be in deeds, not words. Words no longer convince. The Soviet Government agreed to German economic unity by signing the Potsdam agreement in August 1945. Then it frustrated that unity. The questions now are: Will the Russians again promise to unify Germany? Will they keep their promise this time? What do they want us to pay them for the promise which they may or may not keep?

If Stalin decides to go with the West, Berlin will feel it first and Germany will be unified according to the American plan. If Stalin rules against world cooperation, Berlin will feel that too, and Germany will split apart. It is in Berlin that the Bolsheviks must soon show, by their actions, whether they will collaborate or separate.—*Louis Fischer, writer and lecturer; author of various works on Russia. Plain Talk. Ja. '47. p. 8-9.*

One of the main issues which must be solved is the postwar problem of Germany. There are today two schools of thought concerning the future of this country: controlled centralization and controlled disintegration. It is the conviction of this writer that the restoration of a central government of

Germany in which Prussia is included would be a great mistake. Fortunately the plan of establishing a number of autonomous states as existed before Bismarck's unification and prussianization of Germany has recently gained momentum. The closing together of these autonomous states in a loose confederation and Zollverein must be considered as a favorable solution provided that the Prussian Brandenburg, that cradle of German militarism and aggression, would not be included. For, if we want to be fair to humanity Prussia must be broken inexorably. Since such a German confederation would comprise only one sixth of the 350 million Europeans, a federal government of Europe with its federal military organization could very easily stop any revival of German aggression.

Thus the United States of Europe would be able to secure the peace within her borders, while the United Nations Security Organization would safeguard her integrity. Such a solution of the German-European problem has so far found no official consideration. And yet, the question whether Germany shall remain divided into four military zones, or whether a German confederation of the demilitarized autonomous states shall become a member of the European federation, will be decisive for the maintenance of peace in Germany, Europe and the world. When we remember how long it took in this country to reconcile the North and the South after the Civil War we may realize how long it will take before the psychological effects of this war are overcome. There are barriers of sufferings which cannot be easily forgotten! The opposition of the tortured and oppressed Europeans will certainly make postwar collaboration with the Germans difficult. But for the sake of Europe, cooperation with all European peoples is an economic necessity. For the sake of Europe, therefore, the newly created German confederation must after a period of transition be accepted into the family of the European Commonwealth of Nations with equal rights and equal duties.

It would be Germany's great chance of revenge if the Anglo-Saxons and the Soviets would not agree on a common plan for the solution of the German-European problem. It would mean that both parties would insist on keeping the dividing line of

Europe which may become the silver line of the revival of German power and nationalism. This line agreed upon at Yalta
was established solely as a strategic limit where the Allied
armies advancing from the East and West should meet. Today
it is still cutting across the bleeding European body, and her
wounds cannot heal unless it is abandoned by the Big Four in
mutual understanding and collaboration.—*Leopold C. Klausner,
formerly Director General of the Pan American Union. World
Affairs Interpreter. Summer '46. p. 143-5.*

If in the postwar period America and Britain had adhered
to all the principles—let us say, for example, the democratic
principles—of the Yalta and Potsdam conferences on the German question, which made possible and fruitful the collaboration
of the great Allies against Hitlerite Germany, with the aim of
liquidating the remnants of fascism, then collaboration between
the Soviet Union, the United States and Britain would also today
produce good results.

But the United States and Britain have departed from these
democratic principles and have violated the decisions jointly
taken. This can be said with regard to such radical questions
as the democratization and demilitarization of Germany, and the
payment of reparations to countries which suffered from German
occupation.

As a result of postwar Anglo-American policy the British
and American zones of occupation of Germany were united into
a jointly administered bizonal territory—which has been given
the name of "Bizonia" in the press—so that an Anglo-American
policy could be unilaterally carried out there independently of
the Control Council, in which representatives of all four occupying powers participate.

Our representatives in Germany are today virtually concerned
only with the Soviet zone. A situation has arisen which cannot
but·produce alarm among the German people also, since, as the
result of the Anglo-American policy, there exists the joint zone
and other zones, but there is no Germany, no single German
state.

The Soviet Union considers it necessary that the decisions of the Yalta and Potsdam conferences on the German question, decisions which provided for the restoration of Germany as a single, democratic state, should be put into effect. Moreover, in the Soviet Union it is entirely understood that the joint zone is not Germany and that the German people has a right to the existence of its own state, which, it goes without saying, must be a democratic state and must not create the threat of new aggression for other peace-loving states.

At the present time there exists the Anglo-American plan—by giving some alms to calm the population of the Anglo-American zone of Germany—for basing themselves here on the former capitalists who were recently the Hitlerite support, and for utilizing with their aid the joint zone with its Ruhr industrial basin as a threat against those countries which do not display slavish submissiveness with regard to the Anglo-American plans for domination in Europe.

The Soviet Union, in common with other democratic states, stands for peace and international collaboration on democratic principles. Under present conditions, this demands the uniting of all forces of the anti-imperialist and democratic camp in Europe and beyond the boundaries of Europe, so that an insurmountable barrier shall be created against imperialism, which is becoming more active, and against its new policy of aggression.

The rallying of democratic forces and courageous struggle against imperialism in its new plans for war adventures will unite the peoples into a powerful army, the equal of which cannot be possessed by imperialism, which denies the democratic rights of the people, infringing on the sovereignty of the nations and basing its plans on threats and adventures.

What can the policy of imperialism offer people? Nothing but strengthening of oppression, the rebirth of the vestiges of hated fascism and imperialistic adventures.—*Viacheslav M. Molotov, Foreign Minister of the Soviet Union. Address, November* 6, 1947. *Forum. Ja. '48. p.* 37-8.

Only in recent months, . . . a policy seems to have been emerging. . . . This policy seems to view the German problem as an aspect of a much broader problem, a problem which we may call indeed the basic one of United States and world policy of the postwar time. This problem is that of finding a way which renders it possible for two such fundamentally different powers as the United States and the U.S.S.R. peacefully to live together in one world. By this one problem every other problem of international relations is now being overshadowed. . . . It would be unrealistic to be afraid of any new aggression on the part of Germany alone. In a world dominated by the United States and the U.S.S.R. a lone wolf Germany would not have a shadow of a chance, and the people who know that best are the Germans themselves. The only chances Germany would have in any future war would be as an ally of either the United States or U.S.S.R. Since we are neither thinking of aggression nor even of disturbing the delicate balance of power which is now emerging between the two giants, we have no intention of wooing Germany as an ally. But we must also see to it that Germany neither becomes somebody else's ally nor that the German space becomes a battle ground for competing interests. Faced with the alternative of a partition of Germany into an eastern and western half, or into a whole group of independent or semi-independent states on the one hand, and the preservation or, better, reestablishment of Germany as a unified country, the responsible makers of our foreign policy seem to have come to the conclusion that only the latter solution is more conducive to peace. Nothing would be more disturbing than a political void in central Europe. One Balkan has been enough. United States policy, as it has been formulated by ex-Secretary of State Byrnes, seems thus to be aiming at the reestablishment of a unified Germany, which, in order not to constitute a threat to the world, must be able to maintain for its population a decent standard of living and must also be demilitarized, completely neutral, and therefore, thoroughly democratic. The new Germany is to constitute a larger Switzerland, which can fulfill its function in the world only if it becomes as democratic in spirit as Switzerland has been. This whole policy is thus based upon the assumption that Germany can be democratic. But after all, the majority of the population of Switzerland is as German as that of the Reich.

The lines on which United States military government has been working in recent months are in accordance with such a policy. In this respect we have to note first the efforts of the military governor to induce the Control Council to implement those provisions of the Potsdam declaration which provide for the establishment of central German agencies in the fields of economic administration and to remove the boundaries between the several zones of occupation. That the former efforts have not yet succeeded at all, and the latter to a very limited extent only, has not been due to any lack of vigor on the part of the United States element in the Allied control authority, but solely to the opposition encountered on the part of the French and, perhaps, also the Soviet. However, American initiative has brought about at least the economic unification of the zones of occupation of the United States and of the United Kingdom and the invitation to join in this unification is still being held open to the other two occupation powers. It has been consistently the United States which has maintained the principle that Germany ought to be preserved and, therefore, administered as a unit. What little constructive legislation has so far been adopted by the Control Council, has overwhelmingly originated with American delegates, who have also consistently been striving for the maintenance of uniformity of legislation in all those branches of the law in which lack of uniformity would impede economic unity. For the same reasons, United States Military Government, when it began to reestablish German self-government, has refrained from creating any central German administration upon a zonal basis, the existence of which might later stand in the way of central government of the whole country.—*Max Rheinstein, University of Chicago Law School; for eighteen months member of Military Government in Germany. Congressional Record. Mr. 31, '47. p. A 1441.*

During and immediately after the war, there were many suggestions that the peace settlement require separation of the Ruhr from Germany. In the United States, Secretary of the Treasury Morgenthau proposed that the Ruhr-Rhineland area be made an international zone under control of the United Nations.

In Europe, French Foreign Minister Bidault said the Ruhr "must be treated as a political entity independent of Germany and placed under a regime of internationalization both political and economic."

Almost from the start objections were raised to the plan for a separate Ruhr state. In the first place it seemed obvious that the loss of this vital area would encourage irredentist action for revision of the settlement. Secondly, political separation of the Ruhr would make a self-supporting Germany almost impossible, since the exports of Ruhr products are needed to finance necessary imports. The United States Foreign Economic Administration pointed out, furthermore, that "though the truncated area might lack the economic means to support a major war, its resources might permit military aggression on a scale sufficient to recover the detached area and other bordering territory."

French proposals for detachment of the Ruhr were rejected outright by the U.S.S.R., although within France they had received Communist party support. Foreign Minister Molotov stated the Russian position, July 10, 1946: "Without the Ruhr Germany cannot exist as an independent and viable state." He proposed that "the Ruhr should be placed under an interallied control of four countries with the object of preventing a revival of war industries in Germany."

The United States also rejected the French separate-state proposal. At Stuttgart, September 5, 1946, Secretary of State Byrnes said: "The United States will favor such control over the whole of Germany, including the Ruhr and Rhineland, as may be necessary for security purposes. But it will not favor any controls that would subject the Ruhr and the Rhineland to the political domination or manipulation of outside powers."

Great Britain expressed warm sympathy with the special interests of France in future control of the Ruhr but rejected the proposal for a separate Ruhr state. Foreign Minister Bevin proposed internationalization of Ruhr industry as an alternative.

In an effort to come to an agreement with the French, the British outlined proposals in May 1946 for making the Ruhr a distinct province within a loosely federated Germany, but with its economy entirely under the control of Britain, France, the

United States, the Soviet Union, Belgium, the Netherlands and Luxembourg.

One of the British suggestions was that ownership of the Ruhr mines and industries be placed in an international consortium of these seven countries, the profits from such industries to be returned to the German people. A second suggestion was to place the ownership in a kind of public corporation that could be German and operate under the jurisdiction of a German provincial administration, but with the Allies retaining complete control of production. In making these suggestions, the British agreed that if the control system should be stalemated by German resistance, the Allies would put the region under military occupation—as the French had done in 1923—and would detach it completely from Germany if necessary.

The French submitted a plan for the internationalization of Ruhr industry in February 1947 which they believed would insure effective control even though the Ruhr were not made a separate state as the French government still desired. It provided that mines and factories would be transferred "as a joint possession" to the nations united in the struggle against Germany. An "International Administration of the Coal Mines of the Ruhr" and an "International Administration of the Blast Furnaces and Steel Mills of the Ruhr" would be established with administrative boards representative of all affiliated countries and Germany, the general managers and district chiefs to be of Allied nationality. Net profits would be remitted to the territorial authorities, except when withheld to enforce German compliance with Allied regulations. Mechanical and chemical industries, whose management would not be internationalized, were to be affiliated in compulsory trade associations, with Allied commissioners in each organization given the necessary powers to regulate the activities of the affiliated concerns.

A commissioner for the Ruhr would be designated by the United Nations to provide the liaison between the territorial and the Allied administrations. He would have the power to withhold profits and to call on Allied security forces stationed in or near the Ruhr to enforce Allied authority.—*F. L. Van Schaick. "Rehabilitation of the Ruhr." Editorial Research Reports. F. 18, '48. p. 118-20.*

A year after the drafting of the Potsdam Agreement Germany is farther removed from political and economic unity than it was at the time of the Potsdam Conference. The Eastern half is moving more and more in the direction of a one-party dictatorship reinforced by a state-controlled economy; the Western half is drifting along in the vacuum of a purposeless freedom which has been unable to solve either political or economic problems.

Can the gap between East and West still be closed? The obstacles which block the way to unification are by now tremendous. In fact, with the creation of the Socialist Unity party in the Soviet zone they have become almost insurmountable. It is difficult to see how the Russians could consent to the revival of an independent Social Democratic party after forcing a single workers' party on Eastern Germany. Yet if the Western powers are to remain faithful to their political principles, they will have to insist on the restoration of political freedom as a preliminary to Germany's unification.

Another difficulty results from the disagreement of the Big Three as to the organization of the future Germany. A large and influential group in the West has long favored the federalization of the country as the best assurance against the re-emergence of Germany as an aggressive power. The latest plan of Washington and London calls for the creation of a loose union of eleven or twelve virtually autonomous states. The Russians, on the other hand, have always favored a strongly centralized government as best able to cope with unruly elements, provided, of course, that that government met their specifications. Plans to federalize Germany have therefore been promptly denounced by Moscow as merely paving the way for a new fascism.

This, as should not be overlooked, is also good politics. For by demanding the centralized unification of Germany, Russia is making herself the spokesman of Germany's foremost wish. At the recent conference of Foreign Ministers at Paris, M. Molotov skillfully drove home this point when he insisted that the Soviet Union would never give its consent to the federalization or dismemberment of Germany without German approval. If Secretary of State Byrnes challenged this statement, it was not recorded in the press. The impression was thus created, not only in Germany, but even in this country, that only the Western powers could be held responsible for the breakup of Germany into an Eastern and a Western half.

Thus deep-rooted differences block the way to a joint settlement of the German problem. The situation is aggravated by the bitter distrust separating East and West. This distrust feeds of course on what it witnesses in the other camp. Russian high-handedness and Western negligence have given rise to ever deepening suspicions concerning the other side's intentions. More than any other single factor this distrust has prevented the reaching of a workable agreement. As a result, Russia, as was shown, has been concerned primarily with preventing Germany from being used by potential enemies. In positive terms this has now come to mean evidently the integration of Eastern Germany, politically and economically, into the Russian security zone of Eastern Europe.

The time to check this trend is running out. Unless it can be done without delay, the reunification of Germany may no longer be realizable. In that case Western Germany would have to become closely associated with Western Europe. The success of such a rapprochement would of course depend on its willingness to accept the latter's political and ideological outlook —something which it can be expected to do only if the West supports Western Germany's democratic elements much more actively and helps it to achieve that social and political security without which no change of attitude is likely.

The east-west partition of Germany would mean the liquidation of the German state in a more fundamental way than may ever have been envisaged. It would eliminate the last potential buffer zone between Russia and the West in Europe. It would require far-reaching political and economic adjustments. Above all, it would immediately give birth to a nationalist movement in Germany dedicated to the reunification of the country. For the permanent division would run counter to the hopes of every German. No party, from the Communists to the Liberal Democrats, has failed to demand in its program the preservation of a united Germany. Even the German press, which has scrupulously avoided questioning Allied policy, has insisted on the restoration of German unity. Needless to say, therefore, any movement opposing the permanent partition of Germany would enjoy nation-wide support. The danger of such a movement would lie not in its physical strength, which would be small unless it got outside help, but in the fact that its success would depend on its ability to upset the existing state of affairs. War, in fact, would seem the most promising, if not the only way of reunifying Germany. The German nationalists would therefore see their main task in increasing the friction between the western powers and Soviet Russia. They would play up existing difficulties and create others. They would try to revive dormant suspicions and stir up new ones. In short, they would do whatever they could to make cooperation between East and West ever more difficult. Considering the existing tension, this danger should not be taken lightly.

It would be a fatal mistake, therefore, to look upon the halving of Germany as an easy way out. It might solve some problems, but it would create others hardly less serious. For this reason it is difficult to see how it could contribute to Russia's security needs more satisfactorily than a joint solution of the German problem. This realization may induce the Russians to change their ways before the break between their zone and the Western zone becomes irreparable. At the same time it is clear that Western policy too is due for some thorough overhauling in order to insure better cooperation between East and West.— *Andreas Dorpalen, writer and lecturer on international affairs; Visiting Professor, Department of History and Government, St. Lawrence University. Virginia Quarterly Review. O. '46. p. 595-7.*

BIBLIOGRAPHY

An asterisk (*) preceding a reference indicates that the article or a part of it has been reprinted in this book.

BOOKS, PAMPHLETS AND DOCUMENTS

Allen, Edward J. and others. Shall we rebuild Europe with German labor? (Journeys behiond the news, no. 23) p. 152-9. mim. Social Science Foundation of the University of Denver. Denver, Colo. Ja. 31, '45.

Allen, James S. World monopoly and peace. 288p. International Publishers. New York. '46.

Anderson, Mosa. Germany and Europe's future. (Peace aims pamphlet 35) 16p. Universal Distributors. 38 Union Square. New York 3. '46.

Bach, Julian, Jr. America's Germany; an account of the occupation. 310p. Random House. New York. '46.

Baker, Gretta. Germany is winning the war. 8p. mim. Society for the Prevention of World War III. 515 Madison Ave. New York 22. '47.

Barraclough, G. Origins of modern Germany. 481p. Basil Blackwell. Oxford. '47.
Germany yesterday, to-day and to-morrow. p. 456-66.

Barth, Karl. Only way; how can the Germans be cured? 122p. Philosophical Library. New York. '47.

Basch, Antonin. Price for peace; the new Europe and world markets. 209p. Columbia University Press. New York. '45.

Berge, Wendell. Cartels; challenge to a free world. 266p. Public Affairs Press. Washington, D.C. '44.

Brailsford, H. N. Our settlement with Germany. 176p. Penguin Books. New York. '44.

Brandt, Karl. Germany is our problem. (Human events pam. no. 2) 18p. Human Events Inc. 608 S. Dearborn St. Chicago 5. Ja. '46.

Brandt, Karl. Is there still a chance for Germany? America's responsibility. (Human affairs pamphlet no. 30) 46p. Henry Regnery Co. Hinsdale, Ill. My. '48.

Brecht, Arnold. Federalism and regionalism in Germany; the division of Prussia. (Institute of world affairs. Monograph series) 202p. Oxford University Press. New York. '45.
Bibliography, p. 191-2.

British Information Services. Britain and European reconstruction. 34p. (Reference Division. I.D.700) 34p. The Services. 30 Rockefeller Plaza. New York 20. F. '47.

Brockway, A. Fenner. German diary. 148p. Victor Gollancz. London. '46.

Brown, Lewis H. Report on Germany. 247p. Farrar, Straus & Co. New York. '47.

Butler, Harold. Peace or power. 269p. Faber and Faber. London. '47.
    German reckoning. p. 87-112.

*Byrnes, James F. Address at Stuttgart, Germany, September 6, 1946. 6p. mim. Department of State. Washington, D.C. '46.
    Same. Department of State Bulletin. 15:496-501. S. 15, '46; Vital Speeches of the Day. 12:706-9. S. 15, '46; International Conciliation. 424:469-80. O. '46; Current History. n.s. 11:403-10. N. '46.

Byrnes, James F. Speaking frankly. 324p. Harper & Bros. New York. '47.

Carr, E. H. International relations between the two world wars (1919-1939). 303p. Macmillan & Co. London. '47.

Chamberlain, Lawrence H. and Snyder, Richard C., eds. American foreign policy. p. 581-612. Rinehart & Co. New York. '48.

Chamberlin, William H. European cockpit. 330p. Macmillan Co. New York. '47.

Crofts, Alfred. Germany in the modern world. (Journeys behind the news. v. 10, no. 16) 98-103p. mim. Social Science Foundation of the University of Denver. University Park. Denver 10, Colo. Ja. 5, '48.

Dallin, David J. Big three; the United States, Britain, Russia. 292p. Yale University Press. New Haven. '45.
    Between Germany and Russia, p. 105-32.

Dean, Vera Micheles. Russia: menace or promise. 158p. Henry Holt & Co. New York. '47.
    Bibliography, p. 157-8. Pages 5-90 also published as Headline series, no. 58. Foreign Policy Association. 22 E. 38th St. New York 16. Jl.-Ag. '46.

Dickinson, Robert E. Regions of Germany. 175p. Kegan, Paul, Trench, Trubner & Co. London. '45.

Doberer, Kurt K. United States of Germany. 167p. Lindsay Drummond. London. '44.
    Bibliography, p. 163-7.

Duggan, Stephen. German problem. (Pamphlet series no. 10) 22p. Institute of International Education. New York. '44.

Ebenstein, William. German record; a political portrait. 334p. Farrar & Rinehart. New York. '45.

Elliston, Herbert. Germany: most explosive situation in the world. 16p. Washington Post. Washington, D.C.
    Reprint from September 22, 1946 issue.

Engelmann, Susan C. German education and re-education. 147p. International Universities Press. New York. '45.

Ergang, Robert. Europe in our time; 1914 to the present. 710p. D. C. Heath & Co. Boston. '48.
    Bibliography: Germany, p. 697.

Fischer, Louis. Great challenge. 346p. Duell, Sloan and Pearce. New York. '46.

Foundation for Foreign Affairs. Field report on the French zone in Germany. (Foundation information pamphlet no. 1) 26p. The Foundation. 1136 18th St. Washington 6, D.C. '46.

Friedrich, Carl J. and Associates. American experiences in military government in World War II. 436p. Rinehart & Co. New York. '48.
Germany, p. 197-295.

Fuller, C. Dale. Political trends in Europe: is Germany becoming democratic? (Journeys behind the news, no. 27) 9p. mim. Social Science Foundation of the University of Denver. Denver, Colo. Mr. 9, '46.

Gates, Caleb F. Future policies in Germany. (Journeys behind the news, no. 54) 379-83p. mim. Social Science Foundation of the University of Denver. Denver, Colo. S. 16, '46.

Ginsberg, David. Future of German reparations. (Planning pamphlets nos. 57-58) 79p. National Planning Association. 800 21st St. Washington 6, D.C. Mr. '47.

Glickman, David L. Big 4 in Germany; the treatment of Germany as an economic unit. (Planning pamphlets nos. 54-55) 76p. National Planning Association. 800 21st St. Washington 6, D.C. F. '47.

Gollancz, Victor. In darkest Germany. 252p. Henry Regnery Co. Hinsdale, Ill. '47.

Great Britain. House of Commons. Parliamentary Debates. 437, no. 105:1726-837. My. 15, '47. Foreign affairs. Ernest Bevin and others.

Great Britain. House of Commons. Parliamentary debates. 446, no. 47: 385-411. Ja. 22, '48. Address to Commons. Ernest Bevin.
Same with title Organization of the postwar world. Vital Speeches of the Day. 14:226-34. F. 1, '48; Excerpts. United States News & World Report. 24: 68-70. F. 6, '48.

Grossman, Vladimir. Pan-Germanic web: remaking Europe. 179p. Macmillan Co. Toronto. '44.

Hauser, Heinrich. German talks back. 215p. Henry Holt & Co. New York. '45.

Hermens, Ferdinand A. Potsdam or peace; the choice before us. (Human events pamphlet no. 13) 30p. Human Events Associates. 608 S. Dearborn St. Chicago 5. '46.

Hill, Henry H. Teacher education in Germany. In American Association of Teachers Colleges. Twenty-sixth yearbook, 1947. p. 66-7. The Association. C. W. Hunt, Sec.-Treas. State Teachers College. Oneonta, N.Y. '47.

Hill, Russell. Struggle for Germany. 260p. Harper and Bros. N.Y. '47.

Hilldring, John H. and others. Germany and the occupation. (Our foreign policy. Program 66) 19p. National Broadcasting Co. 30 Rockefeller Plaza. New York 20. My. 18, '46.

Hiller, Kurt, ed. After nazism—democracy? 204p. Lindsay Drummond. London. '45.

Holborn, Hajo. American military government; its organization and policies. 243p. Infantry Journal Press. Washington, D.C. '47.

Hutton, Bud and Rooney, Andy. Conqueror's peace; a report to the American stockholders. 92p. Doubleday & Co. Garden City, N.Y. '47.

Ingrim, Robert. After Hitler Stalin? 255p. Bruce Publishing Co. Milwaukee. '46.

Jerome, V. J. Treatment of defeated Germany. 107p. New Century Publishers. New York. '45.

Joesten, Joachim. German press in 1947. (New Germany reports no. 1) 20p. mim. The Author. 86-22 Grand Ave. Elmhurst, L.I. New York. S. '47.

Joesten, Joachim. Germany: what now? 331p. Ziff-Davis Publishing Co. Chicago. '48.

Kaufmann, F. Wilhelm. Germany—the pivot. 4p. mim. Publicity Bureau. Oberlin College. Oberlin, O. My. 29, '46.

Kinney, Mrs. Charles B. Shall we collect reparations from Germany? (Journeys behind the news, no. 22) p. 145-51. mim. Social Science Foundation of the University of Denver. Denver, Colo. Ja. 24, '45.

Knappen, Marshall. And call it peace. 213p. University of Chicago Press. Chicago. '47.

Kurtz, John W. What are we doing in Germany? 4p. mim. Publicity Bureau. Oberlin College. Oberlin, O. Mr. 20, '46.

Lemkin, Raphael. Axis rule in occupied Europe; laws of occupation, analysis of government, proposals for redress. 674p. Carnegie Endowment for International Peace. Division of International Law. 700 Jackson Place. Washington 6, D.C. '44.

Lippmann, Walter. Cold war: a study in U. S. foreign policy. 62p. Harper and Bros. New York. '47.

Ludwig, Emil. Moral conquest of Germany. 183p. Doubleday, Doran & Co. Garden City, N.Y. '45.
     Condensed. Reader's Digest. 46:115-22. Je. '45.

Marshall, George C. Address, Chicago, November 18, 1947. 7p. mim. U. S. Department of State. Washington, D.C.
     Same. Commercial and Financial Chronicle. 166:2053+. N. 20, '47; Congressional Record. 93:(daily)A4551-3. N. 20, '47; Department of State Bulletin. 17:1024-8. N. 30, '47; New York Times. p. 8. N. 19, '47; Vital Speeches of the Day. 14:98-101. D. 1, '47; World Report. 3:32-5. D. 2, '47.

Michaltscheff, Theodor. Germany: democracy in peril. 8p. War Resisters League. 5 Beekman St. New York 7. '45.

Midwest Institute of International Relations. Proceedings, June 1-8, 1946. 104p. mim. [Sponsored by American Friends Service Committee and Drake University]. American Friends Service Committee. 918 Locust Ave. Des Moines 9, Iowa. '46.
Partial contents: Krueger, M. C. Economic factors in the German occupation. p. 81-5; Hall, Martin. Can Germany live with Europe? p. 90-5; Hall, Martin. German youth—promise or threat? p. 95-9.

Minshall, Thomas H. Future Germany. 216p. W. W. Norton & Co. New York. '43.

Molotov, V. M. Molotov on the future of Germany. 24p. Universal Distributors. 38 Union Square. New York 3. '46.

Morgan, John H. Assize of arms; the disarmament of Germany and her rearmament (1919-1939). 357p. Oxford University Press. New York. '46.

Morgenthau, Henry, Jr. Germany is our problem. 239p. Harper & Bros. New York. '45.

Nelson, Harold I. Soviet policy abroad. (Behind the headlines. Vol. 7, no. 3) 25p. Canadian Institute of International Affairs. 230 Bloor St. W. Toronto 5. '47.

Noth, Ernst E., pseud. (Paul Krantz). Bridges over the Rhine. tr. by R. Reil and H. Corbett. 317p. Henry Holt & Co. New York. '47.

*Padover, Saul K. Failure of the re-education of Germany. *In* Pennsylvania. University. School of Education. Education in transition; thirty-fourth annual schoolmen's week proceedings; March 18-22, 1947. p. 21-31. The University. Philadelphia. '47.

Palyi, Melchior. Creeping paralysis of Europe. (Human events pamphlet no. 25) Henry Regnery Co. Hinsdale, Ill. D. '47.

Petersen, Howard C. and Fisher, Sterling. Situation in Germany. (Program 123) 4p. Our Foreign Policy. Box 30, Station J. New York 27. Je. 21, '47.

Phelps, Edith M., ed. Partition of Germany. *In* University debaters' annual, 1944-1945. p. 9-48. H. W. Wilson Co. New York. '45. Bibliography, p. 40-8.

Pollock, James K., ed. Change and crisis in European government. 253p. Rinehart & Co. New York. '47.

Pollock, James K. What shall be done with Germany? 62p. Carleton College. Northfield, Minn. '44.

Pollock, James K. and Meisel, J. H., eds. Germany under occupation; illustrative materials and documents. 306p. George Wahr Pub. Co. Ann Arbor, Mich. '47.

Preus, Ernest G. Merchants of death. (Win the peace pamphlet no. 4) 80p. Universal Distributors. 38 Union Square. New York 3. '45.

Price, Hoyt and Schorske, Carl E. Problem of Germany. (Studies in American foreign relations, no. 5) 161p. Council on Foreign Relations. 58 E. 68th St. New York 21. '47.

Ratchford, B. U. and Ross, William D. Berlin reparations assignment; round one of the German peace settlement. 259p. University of North Carolina Press. Chapel Hill. '47.

Robinson, H. Lukin. On terms of peace with Germany. (Behind the headlines. Vol. 5, no. 5) 25p. Canadian Institute of International Affairs. 230 Bloor St. W. Toronto. Je. '45.

Rodnick, David. Postwar Germans; an anthropologist's account. 233p. Yale University Press. New Haven. '48.

Röpke, Wilhelm. Solution of the German problem. tr. by E. W. Dickes. 282p. G. P. Putnam's Sons. New York. '47.

Roucek, Joseph S., ed. Governments and politics abroad. 585p. Funk & Wagnalls Co. New York. '47.
  Germany, p. 150-92; Bibliography, p. 191-2.

Sayers, Michael and Kahn, Albert E. Plot against the peace; a warning to the nation! 258p. Dial Press. New York. '45.

Scheele, Godfrey. Weimar republic. 360p. Faber & Faber. London. '46.

Schultz, Sigrid. Germany will try it again. 238p. Reynal and Hitchcock. New York. '44.

Schwarzschild, Leopold. World in a trance; from Versailles to Pearl Harbor. 445p. L. B. Fischer Publishing Corp. New York. '42.

Simons, Hans. Europe and world peace. *In* Midwest Institute of International Relations. Proceedings. May 31-June 7, 1947. p. 110-18. mim. [Sponsored by American Friends Service Committee and Drake University]. American Friends Service Committee. 918 Locust Ave. Des Moines 9, Iowa. '47.

Society for the Prevention of World War III. Don Edwards' bill of rights; radio script. 7p. mim. The Society. 515 Madison Ave. New York 22. '48.

Sokolovsky, V. D. Demilitarisation and democratisation of Germany; statement before Control Council in Berlin, November 21, 1947. 19p. Universal Distributors. 38 Union Square. New York 3. '47.

Summers, Robert E., comp. Economic aid to Europe: the Marshall plan. (Reference Shelf. Vol. 20, no. 2) 271p. The H. W. Wilson Co. New York. Mr. '48.

10 eventful years; a record of events of the years preceding, including and following World War II, 1937 through 1946. Vol. 2, p. 465-76. Germany. Encyclopaedia Britannica. Chicago. '47.

Thorp, Willard and others. Germany's coal; key to the Marshall plan. (NBC University of the Air. Program 131) 4p. Our Foreign Policy. Box 30, Station J. New York 27. Ag. 16, '47.

United Europe Movement. United Europe; speeches, May 14, 1947. Archbishop of Canterbury and others. 24p. The Movement. St. Stephens House. Westminster. London. '47.
  Winston Churchill. p. 4-13; *Same.* Current History. n.s. 13:104-5. Ag. '47; Vital Speeches of the Day. 13:553-4. Jl. 1, '47; World Report. 2:35-8. Je. 3, '47.

United States. Department of State. American policy in occupied areas. (Publication 2794) 31p. Supt. of Docs. Washington 25, D.C.
Articles reprinted from Department of State Bulletin, July 14, 1946, August 18, 1946, February 9, 1947 and March 9, 1947, with added new material.

*United States. Department of State. Occupation of Germany; policy and progress, 1945-46. (United States of America publication 2783; European series 23) 241p. Supt. of Docs. Washington 25, D.C. Ag. '47.

United States. Department of State. Report of the United States Education Mission to Germany. (Publication 2664; European series 16) 50p. Supt. of Docs. Washington 25, D.C. '46.

United States. Department of State. United States economic policy toward Germany. (Publication 2630; European series 15) 149p. Supt. of Docs. Washington 25, D.C. '46.

Van Valkenburg, Samuel. Peace atlas of Europe. 179p. Duell, Sloan and Pearce. New York. '46.

Verrina, pseud. German mentality. 344p. George Allen & Unwin. London. '46.

Walker, Jerry. World empire; communism's great challenge. 72p. Cosmos Publishing Co. New York. '48.
Germany—key to world peace, p. 55-9.

Warburg, James P. Deadlock over Germany. (Behind the headlines. Vol. 8, no. 2) 28p. Canadian Institute of International Affairs. 230 Bloor St. W. Toronto 5. Ap. 15, '48.

Warburg, James P. Germany—bridge or battleground. 386p. Harcourt, Brace & Co. New York. '47.

Warburg, James P. Germany, nation or no-man's-land. (Headline series no. 60) 63p. Foreign Policy Association. 22 E. 38th St. New York 16. N.-D. '46.

Warburg, James P. Put yourself in Marshall's place. 93p. Simon and Schuster. New York. '48.

Weber, August. New Germany in a new Europe. tr. by M. Firth. 207p. Lindsay Drummond. London. '45.

Weymouth, Anthony, pseud., ed. Germany: disease and treatment; based on the memoranda of the Post-War Policy Group. 132p. Hutchinson & Co. London; New York. '45.

White, William L. Report on the Germans. 260p. Harcourt, Brace & Co. New York. '47.

Whyte, Anne. Future of Germany; with extracts from the texts of the main international agreements affecting the final settlement for Germany. (Tract series no. 262) 26p. Fabian Publications. 11 Dartmouth St. London S.W. 1. F. '47.

Wolfers, Arnold. United States policy toward Germany. (Memorandum no. 20) 29p. mim. Yale Institute of International Studies. New Haven, Conn. F. 21, '47.

Zbinden, Hans. Whither Germany? 90p. Henry Regnery Co. Hinsdale, Ill. '48.

Ziemer, Gregor. German youth still challenges one world. *In* National Congress of Parents and Teachers. Proceedings. Vol. 50, p. 36-9. My. 20-22, 1946. The Congress. Chicago. '47.

Zink, Harold. American military government in Germany. 272p. Macmillan Co. New York. '47.

PERIODICALS

*Academy of Political Science. Proceedings. 21:522-32. Ja. '46. Reparations problems. Isador Lubin.

Academy of Political Science. Proceedings. 21:540-51. Ja. '46. American occupation policies in Germany. J. J. McCloy.

Academy of Political Science. Proceedings. 22:439-50. Ja. '48. American economic policy relating to Germany and western Europe. L. H. Brown.

Adult Education (London). 20:17-24. S. '47. Education for democracy in Germany. K. R. Stadler.

Adult Education (London). 20:54-60. D. '47. Volksbildung in the Russian zone of Germany. K. R. Stadler.

Adult Education Bulletin. 12:37-43. D. '47. Adult education in the U. S. zone of Germany. R. C. Deming.

America. 76:429-33. Ja. 18, '47. Education mission to Germany. F. N. Pitt.

American Affairs. 8:70-1. Ja. '46. Colmer Committee on Russia and Germany.

American Association of University Women. Journal. 40:70-7. Ja. '47. Re-education of the German people. H. C. White.

American Economic Review. 36:642-9. My. '46. Future of the German economy. C. B. Hoover.

American Federationist. 54:4-6. F. '47. What about Germany? W. C. Doherty and Israel Feinberg.

American Journal of International Law. 40:sup. 21-31. Ja. '46. Arrangements for control of Germany by Allied representatives, September 20, 1945; text of agreement between the governments of the United Kingdom, the United States of America, and the Union of Soviet Socialist Republics, and the provisional government of the French Republic on certain additional requirements to be imposed on Germany.

American Journal of International Law. 40:303-31. Ap. '46. Transfer of civilian manpower from occupied territory. J. H. E. Fried.

American Journal of International Law. 40:803-11. O. '46. American military government courts in Germany. E. E. Nobleman.

American Journal of International Law. 40:sup. 117-34. O. '46. United States, France, United Kingdom, Netherlands, Belgium, Yugoslavia, Luxembourg; final act and annex of the Paris Conference on Reparation, January 14, 1946.

American Journal of International Law. 41:650-9. Jl. '47. Quadripartite military government organization and operations in Germany. E. E. Nobleman.

*American Journal of International Law. 41:807-27. O. '47. Denazification law and procedure. Elmer Plischke.

American Magazine. 140:46-71+. Jl. '45. Can the Kaiser's boys save Germany? J. W. Gerard.

American Magazine. 140:20-1+. N. '45. German business, still a menace. E. D. Thomas.

American Magazine. 142:23+. N. '46. 360,000 P.W.'s; the hope of Germany. R. L. Kunzig.

American Magazine. 144:50-1+. S. '47. Revenge is expensive. C. S. Strike.

American Mercury. 59:180-5. Ag. '44. German plans for the next war. H. C. Wolfe.

American Mercury. 61:753-7. D. '45. German problem. H. S. Commager.

American Mercury. 62:726-33. Je. '46. Our educational failure in Germany. Gregor Ziemer.
  Excerpts. Education Digest. 12:16. S. '46.

American Mercury. 63:654-60. D. '46. Reparations and World war III. E. W. Pauley.
  Reply. American Mercury. 64:378. Mr. '47. B. I. Hovde.

American Perspective. 1:80-96. My. '47. French zone revisited.

American Perspective. 1:181-210. S. '47. Agrarian reform: a test of allied occupation policy.

American Perspective. 1:211-35. S. '47. Polish-German frontier: Polish claims and diplomatic history.

American Political Science Review. 39:464-73. Je. '45. Role of the public in a new Germany. J. K. Pollock.

American Political Science Review. 40:749-59. Ag. '46. New political parties of Germany. R. G. Neumann.

American Political Science Review. 40:1097-112. D. '46. Political scientist looks at military government in the European theater of operations. Harold Zink.

*American Political Science Review. 41:1188-93. D. '47. Is a peace treaty with Germany legally possible and politically desirable? Hans Kelsen.

American Scholar. 13, no. 3:309-21. [Jl.] '44. Germany can be re-educated. Joseph Katz.

American Scholar. 15, no. 2:180-8. [Ap.] '46. Rededication of German scholarship; tr. by M. Zuckerkandl. Karl Jaspers.

American Scholar. 16, no. 1:46-56. [Ja.] '47. Germany: test tube of peace. R. N. Berkes.

American Sociological Review. 11:67-78. F. '46. Sociological principles and occupied Germany. Clifford Kirkpatrick.

American Teacher. 31:15-17. F. '47. United States Mission reports on education in Germany. William Benton.

Annals of the American Academy. 240:1-6. Jl. '45. New tools for peaceful settlement. Sarah Wambaugh.

*Annals of the American Academy. 246:125-9. Jl. '46, Postwar treatment of Germany. Henry Morgenthau, Jr.

Annals of the American Academy. 246:130-42. Jl. '46. Economics of fear. M. J. Bonn.

Annals of the American Academy. 255:77-83. Ja. '48. What is our purpose in Germany? J. H. Hilldring.

Army Quarterly (London). 54:117-23. Ap. '47. Legacy of the Nazi regime. F. E. Isaac.

Atlantic Monthly. 173:78-85. My. '44. What is German? Thomas Mann.

Atlantic Monthly. 176:43-6. Ag. '45. Germany's third try. Lord Vansittart.

Atlantic Monthly. 176:45-9. N. '45. Can the Nazis learn? Nora Waln.

Bankers', Insurance Managers' and Agents' Magazine. 163:214-18. Mr. '47. Nationalisation and the unity of Germany. M. J. Bonn.

Banking. 40:40+. N. '47. What to do about Germany. M. S. Szymczak.

Business Week. p. 113-14+. Je. 23, '45. Ruhr: farm or factory?

Business Week. p. 19-22. Ja. 5, '46. Weak Germany? drastic FEA proposals for deindustrialization.

Business Week. p. 112. My. 11, '46. U.S.S.R. and Germany in 1950; shifting seats of power.

Business Week. p. 116. Je. 29, '46. Our stake in a unified Germany.

Business Week. p. 112. Mr. 8, '47. German reparations muddle.

Business Week. p. 105-6+. My. 17, '47. German exports start to roll.

Business Week. p. 15-16. Jl. 26, '47. Doing business in two worlds: Marshall plan.

Business Week. p. 101-2+. S. 6, '47. Ruhr industry: a challenge.

Business Week. p. 69. Ja. 3, '48. West German merger due.

Business Week. p. 106. F. 7, '48. Bizonia lowers trade bars; Joint Export Import Agency.

Business Week. p. 109-10. Mr. 6, '48. Russia milks its German zone.

Canadian Forum. 27:79-80. Jl. '47. Germany's aims. Kurt Schumacker.

Canadian Forum. 27:104-6. Ag. '47. Germany and Europe. R. T. McKenzie.

Catholic World. 163:11-19. Ap. '46. From behind the iron curtain. T. C. Petersen.

Catholic World. 163:107-14. My. '46. What they are doing to Germany. Erik von Kuehnelt-Leddihn.

Catholic World. 165:107-15. My. '47. From Potsdam to Moscow. F. A. Hermens.

Catholic World. 166:299-306. Ja. '48. Vicisti, Schicklgruber? Nazism, defeated, triumphs? Eugene Bagger.

Central European Observer. 23:357-8. N. 8, '46. Where does Germany stand politically? A. J. Fisher.

Central European Observer. 24:91-2. Ap. 3, '47. German trade in Europe.

Chemical Age (London). 57:559-60. O. 25, '47. Scale of reparations announced.

Chemical Engineering. 55:98-102. Ja. '48. Fabulous I. G. Farben disintegrates. J. J. Christie.

Christian Century. 63:589-91. My. 8, '46. What do we want in Germany? Dorothy Thompson.

Christian Century. 65:108-10. Ja. 28, '48. Russian Germany, a dissenting report. Jerome Davis.
    Reply. Christian Century. 65:177-8, 211. F. 11-18. '48. John Friedmann; Helmut Kuhn.

Christian Science Monitor. 39:5. N. 1, '47. Official secrecy fails to hide deterioration in Soviet zone.

Christian Science Monitor Magazine. p. 3. Mr. 1, '47. Is Soviet winning Germans? J. E. Williams.

Collier's. 116:12-14+. N. 10, '45. Golden octopus; Farbenindustrie. Paul Winkler.

Collier's. 117:12-13+. F. 9, '46. Failure in Germany. Drew Middleton.

Collier's. 119:18-19+. Mr. 8, '47. Moscow: pay-off on peace. Samuel Lubell.

Collier's. 120:16-17+. N. 1, '47. Let's get Germany off our back! condensation of report to President Truman. L. H. Brown.

Collier's. 120:8, 11+. N. 8, '47. Germany's underground wants war. Sigrid Schultz.

Collier's. 120:26+. N. 15, '47. Germany, Russia and the U.S.A. Sigrid Schultz.

Commentary. 2:227-32. S. '46. Germany is no more; life among the ruins. Alfred Doeblin.

*Commentary. 3:517-25. Je. '47. Re-educating the Germans. F. L. Neumann.
    Discussion. Commentary. 4:286-8. S. '47.

Commerce Magazine. 44:15-16+. Ap. '47. German exports revived slowly. Alexander Boeker.

Commerce Magazine. 44:24-6+. S. '47. Can Germany be revived—or should it? J. S. Knowlson.

*Commercial and Financial Chronicle. 164:478+. Jl. 25, '46. Inside Russian occupied Germany. Karl Brandt.
Same. Vital Speeches of the Day. 12:688-92. S. 1, '46; *Separate.* 10p. Commercial and Financial Chronicle.

Commercial and Financial Chronicle. 164:1267+. S. 5, '46. Progress on implementing Potsdam economic provisions; interview with Brigadier General William H. Draper, Jr. H. M. Bratter.

Commercial and Financial Chronicle. 164:1645+. O. 3, '46. German economic situation. H. M. Bratter.

Commercial and Financial Chronicle. 165:283+. Ja. 16, '47. Economic progress in Germany. W. H. Draper, Jr.

Commercial and Financial Chronicle. 165:646+. Ja. 30, '47. Republican plan for Europe; address, January 17, 1947. J. F. Dulles.
Same with title Europe must federate or perish. Vital Speeches of the Day. 13:234-6. F. 1, '47.

Commercial and Financial Chronicle. 165:1117+. F. 27, '47. German economy in state of pernicious anaemia. Wilhelm Röpke.

Commercial and Financial Chronicle. 165:2731+. My. 22, '47. German situation. M. S. Szymczak.

Commercial and Financial Chronicle. 165:3242-3. Je. 19, '47. Our interest in German foreign trade; address, June 13, 1947. M. S. Szymczak.
Same. Congressional Record. 93:(daily)A3085. Je. 17, '47.

Commercial and Financial Chronicle. 166:713+. Ag. 21, '47. Chaos to allied German controls and reparations. M. J. Bonn.

Commercial and Financial Chronicle. 166:714+. Ag. 21, '47. Revived Germany essential to Marshall plan; summary of report. L. H. Brown.

Commercial and Financial Chronicle. 166:809+. Ag. 28, '47. Germany revisited. J. S. Knowlson.

Commercial and Financial Chronicle. 166:1413+. O. 9, '47. What to do about Germany. L. H. Brown.

Commercial and Financial Chronicle. 166:2045+. N. 20, '47. Are we doing our own job in Europe? Burnett Walker.

Commercial and Financial Chronicle. 166:2370+. D. 11, '47. Prosperous Germany is essential! J. Goudriaan.

Commercial and Financial Chronicle. 167:106+. Ja. 8, '48. Germany's sorry outlook. J. Van Galen.

Commonweal. 47:561-3. Mr. 19, '48. Silesian Ruhr. H. C. Sutton.

Congressional Record. 93:(daily) A671-2. F. 20, '47. Statement of Steuben Society of America.

Congressional Record. 93:(daily) A1280-3. Mr. 24, '47. Report on economic mission to Germany and Austria. Herbert Hoover.

Congressional Record. 93:(daily) A1390-1. Mr. 27, '47. Future political structure of Germany. Dorothy Thompson.

Congressional Record. 93:(daily) 2936. Mr. 31, '47. Administration and control of Germany; resolution adopted by National Conference on the German Problem, March 6, 1947.

Congressional Record. 93:(daily) A1440-3. Mr. 31, '47. Military government in Germany. Max Rheinstein.
Condensed. University of Chicago Magazine. 39:5-8. Ap. '47.

Congressional Record. 93:(daily) 4395-6. Ap. 30, '47. Destruction of fertilizer plants in Germany; letter from Secretary of War. R. P. Patterson.

Congressional Record. 93:(daily) A2823-4. Je. 5, '47. Occupation troops in Germany. Julius Klein.

Congressional Record. 93:(daily) A3233-4. Je. 21, '47. Nazi revival in many lands seen—a survey lists German officials. Mallory Browne.

Congressional Record. 93:(daily) 9157-61. Jl. 15, '47. Our policy toward Germany. G. G. Sadowski.
Also separate with title Rebuilding Germany for World war III? 4p. The Author. House Office Bldg. Washington, D.C.

Congressional Record. 93:(daily) 10120-2. Jl. 24, '47. German coal and European recovery. J. A. Blatnik.
Also separate. 4p. The Author. House Office Bldg. Washington, D.C.

Congressional Record. 93:(daily) A4045-6. Jl. 24, '47. Too strong Germany? T. L. Stokes.

Congressional Record. 93:(daily) 10346-53. Jl. 25, '47. Can we afford to follow Herbert Hoover's advice again? G. G. Sadowski.
Also separate. 8p. The Author. House Office Bldg. Washington, D.C.

Congressional Record. 93:(daily) A4125-6. Jl. 26, '47. How to get reparations out of Germany.

Congressional Record. 93:(daily) A4325-7. Ag. 15, '47. German cartel conspirators aided by Great Britain and some of our own financiers and industrialists. A. J. Sabath.

Congressional Record. 93:(daily) 11431-5. D. 11, '47. On the road to peace. J. H. Folger.

Congressional Record. 93:(daily) A5165-6. D. 17, '47. Why's and wherefore's of the Marshall plan. N. M. Mason.

Congressional Record. 93:(daily) 11721-2. D. 18, '47. Dismantling and removal of plants in Germany. J. O. Eastland.

Congressional Record. 94:(daily) A813. F. 12, '48. Dismantling of German factories.

Congressional Record. 94:(daily) A978. F. 19, '48. Germany and the Marshall plan. C. M. Gilpin.

Congressional Record. 94:(daily) A1046-7. F. 23, '48. Conditions in Germany.

Congressional Record. 94:(daily) A1336-9. Mr. 2, '48. Germany's share in the Marshall plan. Jean Pajus.
Reprint from Central European Observer (London). F. 6, '48.

Congressional Record. 94:(daily) A1382. Mr. 3, '48. Ruhr and European unity. J. K. Javits.

Congressional Record. 94:(daily) A1916. Mr. 23, '48. Our military government in Germany. G. A. Dondero.

Congressional Record. 94: (daily) 3646-50. Mr. 25, '48. Monopolists, cartelists and international bankers. G. G. Sadowski.
  Also separate to p. 3649, *with title* Did we fight to restore Germany's power? 7p. The Author. House of Representatives. Washington, D.C.
Congressional Record. 94: (daily) A2234. Ap. 6, '48. Elbe frontier; retraining the German mind. Sumner Welles.
Congressional Record. 94: (daily) A2246-7. Ap. 6, '48. Conditions in Germany; Judge J. J. Moriarty plan.
Congressional Record. 94: (daily) A2320-1. Ap. 12, '48. Two German governments. Walter Lippmann.
Congressional Record. 94: (daily) A2323-5. Ap. 12, '48. Hunger in Bizonia; facts submitted by the American Association for a Democratic Germany.
Congressional Record. 94: (daily) A3967-9. Je. 11, '48. Shameful failure of our new deal and military policies in Germany. O. K. Armstrong.
Contemporary Review. 168:17-22. Jl. '45. Peace and the Ruhr. H. Powys Greenwood.
Contemporary Review. 168·70-5. Ag. '45. Re-education of Germany. H. N. Brailsford.
Contemporary Review. 169:10-14. Ja. '46. Germany after twelve years. Veit Valentin.
Contemporary Review. 169:214-20. Ap. '46. Problem of German industry. Edgar Stern-Rubarth.
Contemporary Review. 169:302-6. My. '46. Re-educating the Nazi child. D. A. Wickham.
Contemporary Review. 170:148-52. S. '46. Germany and allied unity. Tibor Mende.
Contemporary Review. 171:139-45. Mr. '47. French plan for Germany. Geoffrey Fraser and W. W. Crotch.
Contemporary Review. 172:275-80. N. '47. German snapshots. Norman Bentwich; Vera Daniel.
Current History. n.s. 9:81-7. Ag. '45. Germany's gains through reparations. Alzada Comstock.
Current History. n.s. 9:104-11. Ag. '45. German press, yesterday and tomorrow. F. E. Hirsch.
Current History. n.s. 9:193-8. S. '45. German reparations: the Potsdam plan. Alzada Comstock.
Current History. n.s. 9:199-206. S. '45. Reparations, gain or loss? F. E. Hirsch.
Current History. n.s. 9:240-50. S. '45. Big three report on the Potsdam conference.
Current History. n.s. 9:284-93. O. '45. Outlook in Europe; Potsdam conference and Europe's future. S. B. Fay.
Current History. n.s. 11:101-8. Ag. '46. Rebuilding Germany's schools. G. T. Trial and M. K. Goldsmith.
Current History. n.s. 11:459-68. D. '46. Soviet Union: cordon sanitaire. F. L. Schuman.

Current History. n.s. 11:500-6. D. '46. Germany: self-government. S. B. Fay.

Current History. n.s. 12:69-73. Ja. '47. Anglo-American statement on German zones merger. J. F. Byrnes and E. Bevin.

Current History. n.s. 12:205-11. Mr. '47. German balance sheet. F. E. Hirsch.

Current History. n.s. 12:321-8. Ap. '47. Europe's expellees. S. B. Fay.

Current History. n.s. 12:477-82. My. '47. France plans for peace. E. J. Knapton.

Current History. n.s. 12:508-19. My. '47. Yalta, Potsdam and Teheran agreements; texts.

Current History. n.s. 12:573-9. Je. '47. Post-war German parties. Claire Nix.

Current History. n.s. 13:149-52. S. '47. Germany after two lost wars; the deeper problems of reconstruction. F. E. Hirsch.

Current History. n.s. 13:166-72. S. '47. Military control directive for Germany, July 15, 1947; text.

Current History. n.s. 13:204-9. O. '47. What future for Germany? F. E. Hirsch.

Current History. n.s. 13:232-4. O. '47. German level of industry revision; plan released August 29, 1947; text.

Current History. n.s. 14:44-6. Ja. '48. Address to Foreign Ministers' Council, November 26, 1947. V. M. Molotov.

Department of State Bulletin. 13:885-92. D. 2, '45. Relations between the American forces of occupation and the German people; report to the President. Byron Price.

Department of State Bulletin. 14:114-26. Ja. 27, '46. Reparation from Germany; final act and annex of the Paris conference on reparation. *Same.* International Conciliation. 420:215-38. Ap. '46.

Department of State Bulletin. 15:764-71. O. 27, '46. Report of the Education Mission to Germany.

Department of State Bulletin. 15:1102-4. D. 15, '46. Economic integration of U.S. and U.K. zones in Germany; with memorandum of agreement.

*Department of State Bulletin. 16:223-33. F. 9, '47. Beginnings of self-government in the American zone of Germany. V. H. Cassidy.

Department of State Bulletin. 16:294-8. F. 16, '47. United States policy on German youth activities.

Department of State Bulletin. 16:443-7. Mr. 9, '47. Decartelization law for United States zone in Germany.

*Department of State Bulletin. 16:913-18. My. 11, '47. American policy concerning German monopolies. Isaiah Frank.

Department of State Bulletin. 17:186-93. Jl. 27, '47. Text of directive to commander-in-chief of U.S. forces of occupation, regarding the military government of Germany, July 11, 1947.

Department of State Bulletin. 17:530-1. S. 14, '47. Soviet objections to industrial plan for Ruhr refuted.

Department of State Bulletin. 17:1262-7. D. 28, '47. Anglo-American agreement regarding Germany; with text of agreement.

Dublin Review. 219:9-20. Jl. '46. Towards the solution of the German problem. Karl Reimann.

Economic Council Letter. No. 178:1-4. N. 1, '47. Time for this folly to stop! M. K. Hart.

Economist (London). 150:527-32. Ap. 6, '46. German crisis.
Also separate. National Peace Council. Peace aims pamphlet 37. 20p. Universal Distributors. 38 Union Square. New York 3. '46.

Economist (London). 152:91-2. Ja. 18, '47. German unity in question.

Economist (London). 152:131-2. Ja. 25, '47. Plans for Europe.

Economist (London). 152:228-9. F. 8, '47. Smaller powers and Germany.

Economist (London). 152:441-2. Mr. 29, '47. German constitution.

Economist (London). 152:588-9. Ap. 19, '47. British zone as partner.

Economist (London). 153:22-3, 68-70. Jl. 5-12, '47. French in Germany.

Economist (London). 153:179-81. Ag. 2, '47. Battle for western Germany.

Economist (London). 153:389-90. S. 6, '47. Away from Potsdam.

Economist (London). 153:631. O. 18, '47. D-day for dismantling.

Economist (London). 153:678-9. O. 25, '47. Will Germans resist dismantling?

Economist (London). 153:707-8. N. 1, '47. New deal for Germany.

Economist (London). 153:945-6. D. 13, '47. Germany; the real issue.

Economist (London). 153:987-8. D. 20, '47. What next for Germany?

Economist (London). 154:121-2. Ja. 24, '48. Power for Frankfurt.

Economist (London). 154:139-41. Ja 24, '48. German economy in 1947.

Editorial Research Reports. 1, no. 21:403-18. Je. 2, '45. Labor reparations. B. W. Patch.

Editorial Research Reports. 2, no. 17:717-38. O. 23, '46. Future of Germany. B. W. Patch.

Editorial Research Reports. 1, no. 20:381-98. My. 21, '47. Federation of Europe. B. W. Patch.

Editorial Research Reports. 1, no. 7:109-22. F. 18, '48. Rehabilitation of the Ruhr. F. L. Van Schaick.

Education. 66:9-17. S. '45. Re-education of Germans. Thomas Woody.

Education. 68:7-10, 201-4. S., D. '47. Present educational problems of Germany. Edmund Venzlaff.

Education Digest. 13:1-3. S. '47. Education in Germany today. L. W. Prakken.

Education Digest. 13:1-6. O. '47. American educational policy in Germany. L. W. Prakken.

Educational Forum. 13:218-25. Ja. '48. Remaking the Germans. W. W. Brickman.

Educational Leadership. 4:516-19. My. '47. Let's face the facts—and act! B. M. Bowen.

Educational Record. 28:33-44. Ja. '47. Youth activities in Germany. P. M. Limbert.

Engineer (London). 184:221. S. 5, '47. Level of German industry; revised plan for the British and American zones.
Excerpts. Foreign Commerce Weekly. 28:18. S. 27, '47.

Facts on File; Weekly World News Digest. 516 5th Ave. New York 18.
See current issues and cumulative indexes.

Federal Reserve Bulletin. 33:681-8. Je. '47. Our stake in German economic recovery; address before Economic Club of Detroit, May 19, 1947. M. S. Szymczak.
Same. Vital Speeches of the Day. 13:700-4. S. 1, '47.

Foreign Affairs. 23:567-81. Jl. '45. Treatment of Germany. Jacob Viner.

Foreign Affairs. 24:337-40. Ja. '46. Fuel crisis in Europe. Karl Brandt.

Foreign Affairs. 24:571-8. Jl. '46. Agreement on Germany: key to world peace. Georges Bidault.

Foreign Affairs. 24:579-90. Jl. '46. Has our policy in Germany failed? E. S. Mason.

Foreign Affairs. 25:421-32. Ap. '47. Alternatives for Germany. A. W. Dulles.

Foreign Affairs. 25:537-49. Jl. '47. Europe revisited. H. F. Armstrong.

Foreign Affairs. 26:24-35. O. '47. Can France again be a great power? André Géraud.

Foreign Affairs. 26:325-34. Ja. '48. France and the economic recovery of Europe. André Philip.

Foreign Policy Bulletin. 26:2-3. Ja. 10, '47. Unification alone will not solve German economic problem. W. N. Hadsel.

Foreign Policy Bulletin. 26:1-2. Mr. 28, '47. What kind of settlement for Germany? V. M. Dean.

Foreign Policy Bulletin. 27:2. Ap. 16, '48. German unity key issue in Berlin crisis. W. N. Hadsel.

Foreign Policy Reports. 21:222-31. N. 1, '45. Allied military rule in Germany. W. N. Hadsel.

Foreign Policy Reports. 21:283-95. Ja. 15, '46. U.S. policy in Europe. V. M. Dean.

Foreign Policy Reports. 22:158-68. S. 15, '46. Ruhr: object of allied rivalries. W. N. Hadsel.

Foreign Policy Reports. 23:198-212. N. 1, '47. American policy toward Germany. J. K. Pollock; E. S. Mason.

Fortnightly. 163(n.s. 157):381-8. Je. '45. Slav and German. Ernst Klein.

Fortnightly. 164(n.s. 158):154-60. S. '45. Potsdam, Russia and Central Europe. Lewis Einstein.

Fortnightly. 165(n.s. 159):365-72. Je. '46. Reparations and politics. R. P. Schwarz.

Fortnightly. 165(n.s. 159):401-7. Je. '46. Germany in Europe. Stephen Spender.

Fortnightly. 167(n.s. 161):233-9, 320-9. Ap.-My. '47. Military government of Germany. W. Friedmann.

Fortnightly. 168(n.s. 162):332-7. N. '47. German reparations. Tibor Mende.

Fortnightly. 169(n.s. 163):19-23. Ja. '48. Russian zone of Germany.

Fortune. 34:164-7+. O. '46. Return of the west. W. S. Schlamm.

Fortune. 34:128-39+. D. '46. Ruhr.

*Fortune. 35:126-7+. Ja. '47. Is there a German policy? J. K. Galbraith.
   Same abridged with title U.S. policy. Life. 22:98+. F. 10, '47.

Fortune. 35:78-83+. F. '47. In Russia's Europe. Hal Lehrman and Gilbert Burck.

Fortune. 35:2-3. Mr. '47. European unity: dream and hard reality.

Fortune. 36:82-3+. Jl. '47. Der papierkrieg: the war of paper work.

Forum. 104:114-19. O. '45. Re-education of Germany: an American experiment. F. H. Cramer.

Forum. 104:215-21. N. '45. Peace-making in 1919 and 1945; why the Council of Foreign Ministers failed. S. B. Fay.

Forum. 105:385-90. Ja. '46. German destruction or regeneration? F. E. Hirsch.

Forum. 105:396-402. Ja. '46. Our responsibility for German universities. S. B. Fay.

Forum. 105:488-92. F. '46. Potsdam policies; what Europe needs is more production. F. A. Hermens.

Forum. 105:792-6. My. '46. Agricultural dilemma in Germany; the conflicts of Potsdam must be resolved. Alexander Boeker.

Forum. 106:7-14. Jl. '46. Germany: east or west? Wolfgang von Eckardt.

Forum. 106:140-1. Ag. '46. Can Germany wait? Sumner Welles.

Forum. 106:252-6. S. '46. Germany; what are the merits of the Molotov plan for a centralized Germany?

Forum. 108:85-90. Ag. '47. Two years after Potsdam. F. E. Hirsch.

*Forum. 108:164-5+. S. '47. Forum: is our occupation policy in Germany a failure? Yes! F. H. Cramer; No! D. G. White.

*Forum. 108:257-64. N. '47. Denazification or renazification? F. A. Hermens.

Forum. 109:35-44. Ja. '48. Marshall vs. Molotov; excerpts from speech of November 6, 1947. V. M. Molotov; and from speech of November 18, 1947. G. C. Marshall.

Free World. 12:52-4. S. '46. Divide and conquer, German style. W. H. Hale.

Freedom & Union. 1:12-13. D. '46. Federal union and the Germans. Alexander Boeker.

Freedom & Union. 2:13-15. Ap. '47. Federalism: Germany's lost key. Wilhelm Röpke.

Freedom & Union. 3:12-15. Mr. '48. U.S. job in Germany. Barry Bingham.

Geographical Review. 36:194-221. Ap. '46. Ruhr coal-mining district. C. D. Harris.

Harper's Magazine. 191:385-90. N. '45. Military occupation can't succeed, by a member of the RAF.

Harper's Magazine. 191:515-23. D. '45. Our failure in Germany. W. H. Hale.

Harper's Magazine. 195:97-106. Ag. '47. Negotiating with the Russians. J. B. Reston.

Harper's Magazine. 196:173-9. F. '48. What is happening in Germany? P. W. Bidwell.

Harper's Magazine. 196:180-8. F. '48. Battle for German youth. F. M. Hechinger.

Harvard Educational Review. 16:79-84. Mr. '46. German university re-opens. Frederic Lilge.

Harvard Educational Review. 16:255-72. O. '46. Year in Berlin education. C. W. Meister.

Illustrated London News. 211:686. D. 20, '47. Prospect before Germany. Cyril Falls.

*Index. 27, no. 3:47-60. [S.] '47. Germany: its prewar economic importance and plans for reconstruction.

Information Service (Federal Council of the Churches of Christ in America). 26:1-8. F. 15, '47. Political reconstruction in Europe.

Institute of International Education News Bulletin. 23:19-23. D. '47. Development of U.S. student program with Germany and Austria. Ruth Hubbard.

Institute of World Affairs. Proceedings. 21, no. 2:48-52. D. '45. German attitude as a factor in maintaining the peace in Europe. D. H. Webster.

Institute of World Affairs. Proceedings. 21, no. 2:172-6. D. '45. Germany and the peace. H. N. Gilbert.

Institute of World Affairs. Proceedings. 22:21-8. Je. '46. Political heritage of the war. Ralph Lutz.
   Same. World Affairs Interpreter. 17:160-70. Jl. '46.

Institute of World Affairs. Proceedings. 23:43-5. D. '46. United States policy and Germany; round table.

*Institute of World Affairs. Proceedings. 23:141-9. D. '46. United States policy in the re-education of Germany. W. M. Landeen.
  Same. World Affairs Interpreter. 18:148-60. Jl. '47.

International Affairs. 23:30-41. Ja. '47. Quadripartite rule in Berlin; an interim record of the first year of the Allied control authority. Anne Whyte.

International Affairs. 24:30-62. Ja. '48. Education in occupied Germany: a field study. Helen Liddell.

International Conciliation. 427:3-33. Ja. '47. Japan and Germany: problems in reeducation. G. F. Zook.

International Conciliation. 436:784-881. D. '47. European recovery program; summary of reports. M. J. Fox and A. Winslow.

*International Journal. 3:56-66. Winter '47-'48. One or more Germanies: the economics of partition. C. A. Knudson.

Iron Age. 160:202+. O. 16, '47. New level of German industry pushes top steel production up.

*Journal of Central European Affairs. 6:227-40. O. '46. American denazification program in Germany. Harold Zink.

Journal of Central European Affairs. 6:337-50. Ja. '47. Peacemaking in perspective. F. W. Pick.

Journal of Central European Affairs. 7:81-4. Ap. '47. Secretary Marshall on Germany's eastern frontiers.

Journal of Central European Affairs. 7:162-96. Jl. '47. Peacemaking in perspective. F. W. Pick.

Journal of Education (London). 79:388+. Jl. '47. German youth to-day; impressions of a recent visit. J. G. Lang.

Journal of Higher Education. 19:13-20. Ja. '48. Higher education in Germany. R. J. Havighurst.

Journal of Modern History. 18:251-60. S. '46. Allies and Germany's future. Carl Landauer.

Journal of Modern History. 19:239-53. S. '47. United States economic policy toward Germany; review of recent literature. Carl Landauer.

Journal of Politics. 8:329-49. Ag. '46. American military government organization in Germany. Harold Zink.

Ladies' Home Journal. 65:73+. Mr. '48. Time of peril; excerpts from On active service. H. L. Stimson and M. Bundy.

Life. 21:65-8+. O. 21, '46. Fight for Germany. Reinhold Niebuhr.
  Same abridged. Time. 48:31. O. 21, '46; Reader's Digest. 50:69-72. Ja. '47.

Life. 23:40. N. 17, '47. Molotov plan.

Life. 23:44. D. 15, '47. New policy for Germany.

London Quarterly of World Affairs. 12:203-10. O. '46. Germany: democracy or autocracy? W. W. Schuetz.

Michigan Educational Journal. 25:9+. S. '47. Light burns low in the schools of Germany. L. W. Prakken.
  Same. Ohio School. 25:261+. S. '47; Minnesota Journal of Education. 28:211-12. Ja. '48.

Modern Review. 1:179-89. My. '47. Germany and the future of Europe. G. N. Shuster.

Modern Review. 1:422-30. Ag. '47. Problems of German re-education. Clara Menck.

Modern Review. 1:431-7. Ag. '47. German cartels today. George Lobbenberg.

Monthly Labor Review. 62:895-903. Je. '46. Future levels of German industrial employment. J. A. Flexner.

Monthly Labor Review. 65:459-60. O. '47. United States labor policy in Germany.

Nation. 161:6-7. Jl. 7, '45. Can Germany fight again? I. F. Stone.

Nation. 161:276-9, 331-3, 362-4, 397-9, 682-4. S. 22, O. 6-20, D. 22, '45. Military government in Germany. S. K. Padover.

Nation. 161:433-4. O. 27, '45. Morgenthau's plan for Germany. Leon Henderson.

Nation. 162:93-5. Ja. 26, '46. Wanted: a plan for Germany. V. M. Dean.

Nation. 163:8-10. Jl. 6, '46. Future of the Ruhr and Rhineland. Fritz Sternberg.

Nation. 164:9-11. Ja. 4, '47. Will Russia stay in Germany? Joel Carmichael.

Nation. 164:146-50. F. 8, '47. Cancer spot of Europe; diagnosis of the German problem. Fritz Sternberg.

Nation. 164:299-300. Mr. 15, '47. German cartels and AMG. George Lobbenberg.

Nation. 164:333-4. Mr. 22, '47. Russia and reparations. Keith Hutchison.

Nation. 165:88-9. Jl. 26, '47. What plan for Germany? Freda Kirchwey.

Nation. 165:142-3. Ag. 9, '45. Who's a Nazi in Bavaria? M. S. Davis.

Nation. 165:185. Ag. 23, '47. Self-portrait of Germany. J. Alvarez del Vayo.

Nation. 165:586. N. 29, '47. Does this make sense? Keith Hutchison.

National City Bank. p. 104-7. S. '46. Germany; the first year since Potsdam.

National Review (London). 126:382-8. My. '46. Germany—is our occupation really necessary? Justin Richardson.

National Review (London). 128:125-37. F. '47. Can Germany be re-educated? John Stonborough.

National Review (London). 128:203-13. Mr. '47. Quadripartite control in Germany. C. P. Harvey.

National Review (London). 129:382-92, 490-3. N.-D. '47. Displaced persons [in the British zone]. Alec Dickson.

Nation's Business. 33:28-30+. Jl. '45. Germany, problem prisoner of the world. F. B. Wolf.

Nation's Business. 33:21-2+. O. '45. World's greatest treasure hunt. E. W. Hullinger.

Nation's Business. 35:44-6+. Mr. '47. Germany is our peace frontier. J. L. Reynolds.

Nation's Schools. 40:47. S. '47. Key to the German question. Emil Ludwig.

New Europe. 4:17-19. O. '44. Trouble is with the German people. M. Van Blankenstein.

New Republic. 112:584-5. Ap. 30, '45. Russia's plans for Germany. R. A. Davies.

New Republic. 112:638-9. My. 7, '45. Shall German labor rebuild Europe? A. Yugow.

New Republic. 113:62-8. Jl. 16, '45. Germans have no rights; with editorial comment. Heinz Eulau.

New Republic. 113:215-17. Ag. 20, '45. Population transfers. Heinz Eulau.

New Republic. 113:457-60, 493-5, 522-4, 889-91. O. 8-22, D. 31, '45. Germany's economic future. Heinz Eulau.
Titles are: Should Germany be industrialized?; Germany cannot be agricultural; German industry and Europe's trade; Reparations for peace.

New Republic. 114:897-8. Je. 24, '46. Rule or ruin in Germany. Alan Barth.

New Republic. 116:27-30. Mr. 10, '47. How strong is Germany? Olag Hoeffding.

*New Republic. 116:30-2. Mr. 10, '47. Strength through indifference. Robert Wohlforth.

*New Republic. 117:13-19. O. 6, '47. Germany's cartels are at it again. J. S. Martin.

New Statesman and Nation. 31:334, 374-5, 411. My. 11, 25, Je. 8, '46. Education in Germany. Heinrich Fraenkel.

New Statesman and Nation. 32:92, 114. Ag. 10-17, '46. Report on Germany. J. P. Warburg.

New Statesman and Nation. 33:66. Ja. 25, '47. Economic consequences of fusion. Maurice Edelman.

New Statesman and Nation. 33:410-11. Je. 7, '47. Germany after Moscow. Ashley Bramall.

New Statesman and Nation. 34:43. Jl. 19, '47. East and West.

New York Herald Tribune. N. 23, '47. Consequences of dismantling German war plants. Dorothy Thompson and others.

New York Times. p. 10. Je. 6, '45. Texts of the four major Allies' statements on the control of Germany.

New York Times. p. 12. Mr. 23, '47. Proposals by Marshall and Molotov; texts of statements to Council of Foreign Ministers, Moscow, 1947. March 22, 1947.

New York Times. p. 3E. N. 30, '47. Why the others shun Molotov's democracy. E. L. James.

New York Times. p. 7. D. 7, '47. Molotov asks end of bi-zonal plan. Drew Middleton; Texts of Soviet proposals on Germany.

New York Times. p. 10E. D. 7, '47. Unifying Germany; restoration urged of sovereign republic to achieve peace. Friedrich Stampfer.

New York Times. p. 6. D. 9, '47. Molotov statement in Big Four and his economic proposals on Germany.

New York Times. p. 3. D. 11, '47. Marshall statement on reparations. G. C. Marshall.

New York Times. p. 3E. D. 14, '47. Partition of Germany is seen in London. Drew Middleton.

New York Times. p. 8. D. 15, '47. Text of reply to Soviet charges concerning United States activities in Germany. G. C. Marshall.

New York Times. p. 3+. D. 16, '47. Statements at closing session of Big Four; London, December 15, 1947. G. C. Marshall; V. M. Molotov.

*New York Times. p. 4. D. 20, '47. Radio report on Big 4 parley; broadcast, Washington, December 19, 1947. G. C. Marshall. Same. World Report. 3:38-9. D. 30, '47.

New York Times. p. 7E. Ja. 18, '48. New battle of Berlin looms among the Big Four; Russia's veiled demands that others get out disturb German capital. Delbert Clark.

New York Times. p. 16. Ja. 23, '48. Excerpts from foreign policy speech in Commons. Ernest Bevin.

New York Times. p. 14. Ja. 29, '48. French protest on plan for bi-zonal administration; text.

New York Times. p. 4E. F. 1, '48. New problems arise with shift in Germany; adjustments needed with transfer of rule from army to civilians. Delbert Clark.

New York Times. p. 4E. F. 8, '48. Anti-occupation spirit developing in Germany; attack on U.S. denazification laws raises many questions of policy. Delbert Clark.

New York Times. p. 4. F. 9, '48. Marshall letter on German plants. G. C. Marshall.

New York Times. p. 26. F. 18, '48. Military government steps back, but not out. A. O'H. McCormick.

New York Times. p. 12. F. 21, '48. Clash between policy and the job at hand in the Ruhr. A. O'H. McCormick.

New York Times. p. 12. F. 21, '48. German reparations; continuation of program advocated as aiding output of western Europe; with editorial comment. J. C. C. Edelstein.

New York Times. p. 4E. F. 29, '48. Six nations plan Germany's future. H. L. Matthews.

New York Times. p. 8E. Mr. 1, '48. German reparations. Christopher Emmet.

New York Times. p. 8E. Mr. 7, '48. German reparations; political objections stated to dismantling of plants. Christopher Emmet.

New York Times. p. 1+. Mr. 13, '48. Clay orders halt in decartelizing Germany's trusts. Delbert Clark.

New York Times. p. 4E. Mr. 14, '48. Formula for the Ruhr is difficult to apply; internationalization, if carried out, promises great benefits to Europe. Delbert Clark.

New York Times. p. 8E. Mr. 14, '48. German recovery; line of defense against Soviet expansion. W. R. Mathews.

New York Times. p. 5E. Mr. 28, '48. Dispute in Berlin has wide meaning. Delbert Clark.

New York Times. p. 22. Ap. 2, '48. German reparations; least wasteful place to use idle machinery felt to be Germany. H. C. Furstenwalde.

New York Times. p. 3E. Ap. 4, '48. With time against them, Russians press hard; Berlin move. Raymond Daniell.

New York Times. p. 5. Ap. 5, '48. United States and Russian notes on Soviet-imposed control of Berlin traffic.

New York Times. p. 12. Ap. 10, '48. German self-government; editorial.

New York Times. p. 5E. Ap. 11, '48. Split-up of Germany moves rapidly nearer. Delbert Clark.

New York Times. p. 12. Ap. 20, '48. French limit fusion in Germany to trade but oppose statehood. Lansing Warren.

New York Times. p. 14. Je. 8, '48. Text of communique on the six-power London conference on western Germany.

New York Times Magazine. p. 10+. Jl. 27, '47. Danger of a neonazism. H. R. Trevor-Roper.

New York Times Magazine. p. 5-7+. Ag. 3, '47. Like a vast queue, waiting for hope. Lester Markel.

*New York Times Magazine. p. 14+. D. 7, '47. How much in plant shall Germany pay? A. Z. Carr.

New York Times Magazine. p. 8-9+. Je. 6, '48. Germany: a formula. A. W. Dulles; A warning. E. V. Rostow.

Newsweek. 25:120. Je. 11, '45. Future of German industry. Raymond Moley.

Newsweek. 26:46+. O. 8, '45. Rhine Ruhrland? Russian opposition to the internationalization of the Rhineland and the Ruhr.

Newsweek. 27:52. My. 20, '46. Master of the Ruhr. H. F. Kern.

Newsweek. 28:46-7. Jl. 15, '46. Riddle of the Ruhr: a Big Four showdown approaches. J. P. O'Donnell.

Newsweek. 28:39. Jl. 22, '46. Two viewpoints on the fate of Germany. V. M. Molotoff; J. F. Byrnes.

Newsweek. 28:40+. S. 16, '46. American way for Germany.

Newsweek. 28:36+. S. 23, '46. Russia, reparations, and the Reich.

Newsweek. 29:40-1. F. 24, '47. Trojan horse in Berlin? Stalin's trouble-shooter prepares.

Newsweek. 29:68. Je. 16, '47. America's stake in the Reich.

Newsweek. 30:34. Jl. 14, '47. Soviet suitor and his propaganda machine.

Newsweek. 30:35. Jl. 14, '47. Glimpses of tyranny behind the Russian zone's curtain. James O'Donnell.

Newsweek. 30:33. Jl. 21, '47. Two worlds, two Reichs. Edward Weintal.

Newsweek. 30:45-6. Ag. 4, '47. Riddle of the Ruhr.

Newsweek. 30:85+. Ag. 11, '47. Learning British; Wilton Park school, England.

Newsweek. 30:22. Ag. 18, '47. Background of a squabble E. K. Lindley.

Newsweek. 30:50-2. O. 27, '47. Business man's report; unify Germany, feed it; condensation of report. L. H. Brown.

Newsweek. 31:71. F. 23, '48. Inconsistencies of European aid; dismantling of German industrial plants. Henry Hazlitt.

Nineteenth Century. 138:192-205. N. '45. Orderly and humane; forcible eviction of millions from their homelands. F. A. Voigt.

Nineteenth Century. 138:270-4; 139:90-6. D. '45, F. '46. Mass expulsions. R. H. M. Worsley.

Nineteenth Century. 141:115-24. Mr. '47. Russia and the German state. F. A. Voigt.

Nineteenth Century. 143:142-6. Mr. '48. Germany's information services. C. B. Birdwood.

Paint, Oil and Chemical Review. 110:18-20+. D. 25, '47. Russia and world peace. E. M. Dirksen.
  Address, Atlantic City, November 13, 1947.

Plain Talk. 1:3-9. Ja. '47. On the island of Berlin. Louis Fischer.
  Condensed. Reader's Digest. 50:71-5. F. '47.

Plain Talk. 1:19-24. Je. '47. Workable plan for Germany. Wilhelm Roepke.

Plain Talk. 1:5-8. D. '47. Soviet pattern for Germany. Alexander Boeker.

Planning; a broadsheet issued by P E P (Political and Economic Planning). 14, no. 277:209-28. Ja. 23, '48. Local government in Bizonia.
  Reprinted by the New Republic. 40 E. 49th St. New York.

*Planning. No. 256:1-23. O. 4, '46. Europe and the Ruhr.

Political Affairs. 26:204-15. Mr. '47. German problem and big three unity. Joseph Clark.

Political Quarterly. 16:277-87. O.-D. '45. Local government in occupied Germany. W. A. Robson.

Political Quarterly. 18:323-30. O. '47. Berlin and the Russian zone. Heinrich Fraenkel.

Political Science Quarterly. 61:535-6. D. '46. Political reeducation of the Germans: the emergence of parties and politics in Werttemberg-Baden, May 1945-June 1946. Moses Moskowitz.

Political Science Quarterly. 62:321-53. S. '47. On depression and war: Nazi phase. Arthur Schweitzer.

Prevent World War III. No. 17:10-12. O.-N. '46. Germany in defeat; excerpt from Assize of Arms. J. H. Morgan.

Bi-monthly bulletin published by the Society for the Prevention of World War III, Inc. 515 Madison Ave. New York 22.

Prevent World War III. No. 22:1-4. O.-N. '47. Germany first; failure of our German policy.

Prevent World War III. No. 22:10-13 O.-N. '47. Why do the Nazis remain in charge?

Prevent World War III. No. 24:34-6. Mr.-Ap. '48. Hitler still lives on in German hearts; excerpts from Bridges over the Rhine, by E. E. Noth.

Progressive. 12:9-10. Mr. '48. Last laugh is Hitler's. Alexander Boeker.

Public Administration Review. 6, no. 1:1-9. Winter '46. American control organization in Germany. H. J. Heneman.

Public Opinion Quarterly. 11:179-88. Summer '47. German opinion and American isolationism. F. W. Williams.

Quarterly Journal of Economics. 60:1-55. N. '45. Problems of European reconstruction. Nehemiah Robinson.

Quarterly Review. 285:152-67. Ja. '47. Germany approaches the cross-roads. Jonathan Blow.

Quarterly Review. 285:208-22. Ap. '47. Building democracy in Germany. Harold Ingrams.

Reader's Digest. 46:115-22. Je. '45. Moral conquest of Germany. Emil Ludwig.

Reader's Digest. 48:87-92. F. '46. We are bungling the job in Germany. Frederic Sondern, Jr.

Reader's Digest. 52:109-14. F. '48. It's time to do something about Germany. O. K. Armstrong.

Same. Congressional Record. 94:(daily) A1033-5. F. 20, '48.

Reader's Digest. 52:130-6. Je. '48. Idiocy of our de-nazification policy. L. P. Lochner.

Review of Politics. 8:354-80. Jl. '46. Germany today. Clara Menck.

Review of Politics. 9:153-72. Ap. '47. Denazifying the Reich. Elmer Plischke.

Review of Politics. 9:173-82. Ap. '47. France faces Germany. Maurice de Gandillac.

Review of Politics. 9:284-96. Jl. '47. American occupation policies in Germany. Harold Zink.

Review of Politics. 9:322-30. Jl. '47. Western frontiers of Russia. Robert Strausz-Hupe.

Reviewing Stand. Northwestern University on the Air. 5, no. 25:1-12. N. 25, '45. What shall be our policy in Germany? Howard Becker and others.
Bibliography, p. 11-12.

Reviewing Stand. Northwestern University on the Air. 10, no. 3:1-12. Ja. 25, '48. Behind the iron curtain. Stanislaw Mikolajczyk and others.
Bibliography, p. 11-12.

Rotarian. 66:18-20. Je. '45. Disarmament of Germany. O. G. Villard.

Rotarian. 69:14-17. Jl. '46. France, the Ruhr, and the Rhineland. Andre Ganem.

Rotarian. 70:24-5. F. '47. What is ahead for Germany's youth? F. M. Dunbaugh.

Round Table (London). 36:20-5. D. '45. Germany under allied control; an economic study of the Potsdam plan.

Round Table (London). 36:307-12. S. '46. Hollow continent; peace-making without Germany.

Round Table (London). 37:35-41. D. '46. Four out of hand; plight of Germany under control.

Round Table (London). 38:425-31. D. '47. Plight of the conquered; economic background of the London conference.

Saturday Evening Post. 217:18-19+. Ap. 14, '45. How will we govern our slice of Germany? Demaree Bess.

Saturday Evening Post. 218:14-15+. D. 8, '45. Untold tragedy of Potsdam. Samuel Lubell.

Saturday Evening Post. 218:9-10+. Ja. 26, '46. How we botched the German occupation. Demaree Bess.

Saturday Evening Post. 218:18-19+. Je. 22, '46. Unhappy land. Robert Fuoss.

Saturday Evening Post. 219:18-19+. O. 26, '46. Starving playground of power politics. E. O. Hauser.

Saturday Evening Post. 219:20-1+. N. 16, '46. Can Germany ever feed its people? Karl Brandt.

Saturday Evening Post. 219:24-5+. Ap. 12, '47. Are the Russians brewing another German deal? Werner Knop.

Saturday Evening Post. 219:23+. Je. 14, '47. True meaning of the iron curtain. E. O. Hauser.

Saturday Evening Post. 220:15-16+. Mr. 6, '48. Faint blueprint for peace. Martin Sommers.

Saturday Evening Post. 220:12. Mr. 13, '48. Looting with consent; barter centers, United States army in Germany. Martin Sommers.

Saturday Review of Literature. 28:7-9+. Je. 23, '45. Plan for the future of Germany: decentralization offers some basis for independence. F. A. Hayek.

Saturday Review of Literature. 28:11. O. 6, '45. Germany is our problem, by Henry Morgenthau, Jr.; review. Hans Kohn.

School and Society. 61:337-40. My. 26, '45. Germany in the postwar world. N. P. Mead.

School and Society. 66:481-4. D. 27, '47. University in Germany today. D. P. Cottrell.

School and Society. 66:511-19. D. 27, '47. Educational literature review; education under totalitarianism and reconstruction. W. W. Brickman.

School and Society. 67:198. Mr. 13, '48. Adult education in Germany; opinion survey.

School Life. 29:3-6. Jl. '47. Teachers and children in German schools. Bess Goodykoontz.

School Life. 30:10-24. O. '47. Some problems basic to the rebuilding of public education in Germany; symposium. Bess Goodykoontz and others.

Science News Letter. 48:228. O. 13, '45. Curb German production; Engineering Council's recommendations.

Senior Scholastic. 50:15. Ap. 14, '47. Germany's future: big question for the Big Four.

Senior Scholastic. 51:10-11. Ja. 5, '48. Big Four split, 3-1.

Social Action. 13, no. 2:7-37. F. '47. Problems of German reconstruction. C. E. Carpenter.

Social Education. 8:312-16. N. '44. Germany's tomorrow. Max Wolff.

Social Education. 9:255-8. D. '45. German problem can be simple. René Albrecht-Carrié.

Social Education. 11:340-2. D. '47. Redirection of German education. B. W. Phillips.

Social Research. 13:135-82. Je. '46. Economic problem of Germany. Alvin Johnson and Ernest Hamburger.
    Also separate. (Occasional papers) 135-82p. Institute of World Affairs. New York.

Social Research. 14:59-74. Mr. '47. Denazification; a letter from a German anti-Nazi lawyer to his friend, an American scholar; tr. by B. Salz; with a foreword by Alvin Johnson.
    Reply. Social Research. 14:365-9. S. '47. Karl Loewenstein.

Social Research. 14:304-20. S. '47. Experiment in political education. H. W. Ehrmann.

*Social Studies. 38:207-17. My. '47. American military government after two wars. W. A. Russ, Jr.

South Atlantic Quarterly. 45:286-96. Jl. '46. German reparations. Walter Sulzbach.

South Atlantic Quarterly. 46:1-11. Ja. '47. No German policy is possible; the denazification policy in the American zone. Joel Carmichael.

South Atlantic Quarterly. 46:12-26. Ja. '47. Parties and classes in postwar Germany. Hans Meyerhoff.

South Atlantic Quarterly. 46:167-81. Ap. '47. What is happening in the German universities. W. P. Cumming.

Southern Economic Journal. 113:247-56. Ja. '47. Revival of free labor organizations in the United States occupation zone in Germany, a preview. Samuel Liss.

Soviet Russia Today. 16:7-9+. D. '47. Devil and Jimmy Byrnes. Frederick L. Schuman.

Spectator (London). 176:629. Je. 21, '46. Partition of Germany. M. J. Bonn.

Spectator (London). 177:255. S. 13, '46. Hope for Germany; the Stuttgart speech.

Spectator (London). 179:771. D. 19, '47. Russia and Germany; a Russian historian's reply to the B.B.C. Evgeny Tarle.
Discussion. Spectator. 179:802. D. 26, '47.

Survey Graphic. 34:190-4+. My. '45. Europe and the Mediterranean. C. M. Dean.

Teachers College Record. 47:345-53. Mr. '46. Re-education of the Germans. W. F. Russell.
Same condensed. Educational Digest. 12:16. S. '46.

*Teachers College Record. 49:10-18. O. '47. Democracy in Germany, if. . . . L. T. Hopkins.

This Month. p. 54-62. O. '46. Russia's colonial empire in Europe. Lawrence Matthews.
Also separate. 9p. This Month. 247 Park Ave. New York 17.

This Month. p. 25-34. N. '46. Inside Soviet Germany. Boris Shub.

Time. 48:34. D. 16, '46. As the Ruhr goes; U. S.-British zonal economic merger.

Times Educational Supplement (London). 1682:389. Jl. 26, '47. American zone; army helps German youth.

Town Meeting (Bulletin of America's Town Meeting of the Air). 11, no. 36:1-24. Ja. 3, '46. What must we do to denazify the German people? E. C. Lindeman and others.

Town Meeting (Bulletin of America's Town Meeting of the Air). 12, no. 14:1-24. Ag. 1, '46. How can Germany be united? H. V. Kaltenborn and others.

Town Meeting (Bulletin of America's Town Meeting of the Air). 12, no. 28:1-24. N. 7, '46. How can we make a lasting peace with Germany. H. V. Kaltenborn and others.

Town Meeting (Bulletin of America's Town Meeting of the Air). 12, no. 45:1-24. Mr. 6, '47. What should be our program for Europe at the Moscow conference? Dorothy Thompson and others.

Town Meeting (Bulletin of America's Town Meeting of the Air). 13, no. 1:1-23. My. 1, '47. What should we do about Germany now? Louis Lochner and others.

Town Meeting (Bulletin of America's Town Meeting of the Air). 13, no. 30:1-23. N. 18, '47. What future for Germany? J. P. Warburg and others.
Partial text. New York Herald Tribune. p. 24, N. 19, '47.

United Nations World. 1:32-7. Mr. '47. Rise and fall of the Morgenthau plan. Fred White.

United States News. 20:26-7. My. 3, '46. American drive for quick peace: a stable Europe as our objective.

United States News. 20:15-16. My. 31, '46. Cost of peace to United States: $2,000,000,000-a-year burden.

United States News. 21:24. S. 13, '46. Line for U. S. action in Germany: Mr. Byrnes' answer to Russian segregation of Eastern zone.

United States News. 22:19-20. Mr. 14, '47. Struggle over German peace.

United States News. 22:13-14. Mr. 21, '47. U. S. subsidy to Soviet Russia? fear that our aid to Reich will become reparations to Moscow.

United States News. 22:19-20. Ap. 4, '47. Dilemma in revival of Reich.

United States News. 22:58+. Ap. 25, '47. Secretary Marshall's strategy in his meeting with Premier Stalin.

United States News. 23:19-21. Ag. 1, '47. Why Russia keeps Europe split.

United States News. 23:16-17. O. 24, '47. Our next steps in cold war; plans for Reich revival, more propaganda.

United States News. 23:36-7. O. 24, '47. Hypothetical war; logical conclusion of U. S. policy is proposal that force be used to coerce Russia into compliance with Allies' terms of peace settlement. David Lawrence.

United States News. 23:16-17. O. 31, '47. Lagging peace; rise of tension with Soviet as told in memoirs of Mr. Byrnes.

United States News. 23:16-17. N. 28, '47. Our next steps in cold war.

United States News & World Report. 24:68-71. Ja. 16, '48. How Russia fights the Marshall plan; Communist program to combat U. S. aid abroad; from speech delivered September 1947. Andrei Zhdanov.

United States News & World Report. 24:16. Ja. 23, '48. Resisting Soviet push in Berlin.

United States News & World Report. 24:19-21. Ja. 30, '48. Building up the Soviet bloc; Molotov plans.

United States News & World Report. 24:20-1. F. 13, '48. Steps toward a united Europe.

United States News & World Report. 24:25. F. 20, '48. Rising German sales to America.

United States News & World Report. 24:26-7. F. 20, '48. Strategy in war of documents.

United States News & World Report. 24:30. Ap. 9, '48. Soviet squeeze in Berlin as test of U. S. firmness.

University of Chicago Round Table. 376:1-15. Je. 3, '45. Moral regeneration of Germany. Max Lerner and others.

University of Chicago Round Table. 436:1-18. Jl. 28, '46. Are we re-educating the Germans and the Japanese? Ernest Colwell and others.

University of Chicago Round Table. 459:1-20. Ja. 5, '47. Are we re-educating for democracy in Germany? Earl McGrath and others.

University of Chicago Round Table. 470:1-20. Mr. 23, '47. Moscow conference and the future of Europe. Hans Morgenthau and others.

University of Chicago Round Table. 516:1-30. F. 8, '48. What should America do now in Bizonia? W. H. Draper and others; Special supplement on Report on Germany. R. J. Havighurst.

USSR Information Bulletin. 8:145-8. Mr. 17, '48. Note of the Soviet government on the London conference.

Virginia Quarterly Review. 22, no. 4:581-97. [O.] '46. Split occupation of Germany. Andreas Dorpalen.

*Virginia Quarterly Review. 23, no. 1:18-33. [Ja.] '47. Partition of Germany and the unity of Europe. E. V. Rostow.

Virginia Quarterly Review. 24, no. 1:29-42. [Ja.] '48. Dilemma in Germany. C. E. Schorske.

Vital Speeches of the Day. 11:657-61. Ag. 15, '45. What to do with Germany? Karl Brandt.

Vital Speeches of the Day. 11:667-72. Ag. 15, '45. Potsdam declaration; report on the tripartite conference of Berlin.
  Same. Current History. n.s. 9:240-50. S. '45; Same with list of delegations. International Conciliation. 413:539-57. S. '45.

Vital Speeches of the Day. 12:620-2. Ag. 1, '46. Soviet policy in Germany; delivered July 10, 1946. V. M. Molotov.

Vital Speeches of the Day. 13:354-7. Ap. 1, '47. Reparations, antidote for war. E. W. Pauley.

Vital Speeches of the Day. 13:398-9. Ap. 15, '47. United States wants one Germany; delivered March 31, 1947. G. C. Marshall.

Vital Speeches of the Day. 13:402-3. Ap. 15, '47. German-Polish frontier; delivered April 9, 1947. G. C. Marshall.

Vital Speeches of the Day. 13:418-23. My. 1, '47. Patient sinks while doctors deliberate; report on Moscow conference, April 28, 1947. G. C. Marshall.
  Same. World Report. 2:41-5. My. 13, '47; Current History. n.s. 12: 585-92. Je. '47.

Vital Speeches of the Day. 13:450-3. My. 15, '47. We cannot let ourselves be stymied; report on Moscow conference. J. F. Dulles.
  Same. International Conciliation. 432:449-59. Je. '47; World Report. 2: 45-7. My. 13, '47.

Vital Speeches of the Day. 14:45-7. N. 1, '47. Can we afford to let western Europe drift? L. H. Brown.

World Affairs (London). n.s. 1:253-61. Jl. '47. Interregnum in Germany. W. W. Schuetz.

World Affairs (London). n.s. 1:409-18. O. '47. With the Americans in Germany. A. G. Bettany.

World Affairs Interpreter. 17:189-95. Jl. '46. Denazification and re-education in Germany. R. N. Berkes.

World Report. 1:26-7. Ag. 8, '46. Making Germany pay.

World Report. 1:10-11. N. 12, '46. Top issues of German treaty are unification and reparations.

World Report. 1:10-11. D. 17, '46. U. S., Britain launch program to save Germany from collapse; economic merger of occupation zones.

World Report. 2:7. Ja. 14, '47. Freeing little Nazis aids German recovery.

World Report. 2:22-3. Ja. 14, '47. France, Soviet may compromise on Germany to get reparations.

World Report. 2:22-3. Ja. 28, '47. German cartels may survive as segments of old combines.

World Report. 2:17. F. 11, '47. Shortages bar quick solution of food problem in Germany.

World Report. 2:12-13. F. 18, '47. Russia fails in bid to replace Germany in chemical industry.

World Report. 2:26-7. F. 18, '47. European federation; union of continental countries depends on Big Four's solution of German problem.

World Report. 2:12-13. F. 25, '47. Is nazism reviving in defeated Germany?

World Report. 2:28-9. Mr. 4, '47. Britain, U. S. prepare to move German freight via lowlands.

World Report. 2:7. Mr. 11, '47. Germany to be asked to repay relief cost; Britain, U. S. want reimbursement given priority over reparations.

World Report. 2:44-7. Ap. 1, '47. Statements to Council of Foreign Ministers, Moscow, March 14, 17 and 18, 1947. G. C. Marshall.

World Report. 2:46-7. Ap. 1, '47. Views of allies on reparations.

World Report. 2:5-6. Ap. 22, '47. German occupation prolonged by disagreements at Moscow.

World Report. 2:18-19. Ap. 22, '47. Communists use food shortages to stir up trouble in the Ruhr.

World Report. 2:14-15. Ap. 29, '47. Poland races to make Silesia powerhouse of her new state.

World Report. 2:22-3. Ap. 29, '47. Communist state takes shape in Russia's zone of Germany.

World Report. 2:7-8. My. 13, '47. Anglo-U. S. differences delay recovery of western Germany.

World Report. 2:8. My. 20, '47. U. S. considers reviving German merchant fleet.

World Report. 2:20-1. My. 27, '47. Communism seeping into west Germany.

World Report. 2:10-11. Je. 3, '47. Black market stalls German recovery.

World Report. 2:12-13. Je. 10, '47. Germans to help manage own economy; new council in U. S.-British zone.

World Report. 2:20-1. Je. 10, '47. Governing western Germany: 1,000,000-man job.

World Report. 2:36-7. Je. 17, '47. Bi-zonal reorganization for Germany; text of agreement made public by U. S. War Department June 6, 1947.

World Report. 3:17. Jl. 1, '47. U. S. moves to check communism in Germany.

World Report. 3:8-9. Jl. 8, '47. How Marshall plan will aid Germany.

World Report. 3:8-9. Jl. 22, '47. Test of U. S., Soviet methods in revival of Germany.

World Report. 3:16. Jl. 22, '47. French change in mark as pattern for Germany.

World Report. 3:8-11. Jl. 29, '47. Western allies' 3-way split over Ruhr.

World Report. 3:10-11. Jl. 29, '47. Coming economic lag in Soviet Germany.

World Report. 3:33-7. Jl. 29, '47. Revised basis for U. S. rule in Germany; directive to Military Governor, July 11, 1947.

World Report. 3:8-9. Ag. 5, '47. U. S. scheme to double Ruhr coal output.

World Report. 3:8-9. S. 2, '47. Business cure to raise output of coal in Ruhr.

World Report. 3:8-9. S. 9, '47. Anglo-American failure in Germany.

World Report. 3:33-5. S. 9, '47. Level of industry plan for Germany; text of joint State and War departments' announcement of Revised Level of Industry Plan for American and British zones in Germay, August 28, 1947.

World Report. 3:36-9. S. 23, '47. Program to raise output of Ruhr coal; recommendations advanc.. as result of Anglo-American talks on production.

World Report. 3:19. O. 21, '47. Failure of America to train German youth.

World Report. 3:22-3. O. 28, '47. Issues in building up Germany and Japan.

World Report. 3:15-17. N. 18, '47. Why Germany is failing as producer.

World Report. 3:29-39. N. 18, '47. Report of Harriman Committee on European Recovery and U. S. aid; summary of findings presented to President.

World Report. 3:10-11. N. 25, '47. Speed-up in stripping Nazi plants.

World Report. 3:5-7. D. 2, '47. Economic slump in Soviet Germany.

World Report. 3:14-15. D. 9, '47. Germans' efforts to revive cartels

World Report. 3:36-9. D. 9, '47. Soviet-U. S. clash at Big Four meeting; statements at Council of Foreign Ministers, London, November
26, 1947. V. M. Molotov; G. C. Mashall; and statement by
Secretary Marshall November 27, 1947.
First two also in Current History. n.s. 14:29-43, 44-6. Ja. '48.

World Report. 3:20-1. D. 16, '47. Where reparations go; shipments
of equipment from U. S. zone of Germany.

World Report. 3:33-5. D. 16, '47. Molotov's stand at Big 4 meeting;
text of statement at London, December 8, 1947.

World Report. 3:5-6. D. 23, '47. New phase of U. S.-Soviet cold
war.

World Report. 3:34-5. D. 23, '47. Marshall's view of deadlock at
London; statements, London, December 15, 1947. G. C. Marshall.

World Report. 3:36-7. D. 23, '47. Molotov's defense of Soviet stand;
partial text of statement, London, December 15, 1947. V. M.
Molotov.

World Report. 3:10-11. D. 30, '47. Increase in Europe's East-West
trade.

World Report. 3:18-19. D. 30, '47. Loss of American assets in Soviet
sphere.

World Report. 4:5-6. Ja. 6, '48. New costs in western Germany.

World Report. 4:7. Ja. 6, '48. French price for merger of occupation
zones.

World Today (London). 3:424-31. O. '47. Germany revisited; some
impressions after two years.

World Today (London). 4:25-40. Ja. '48. Feeding of western Germany.

Yale Review. n.s. 34, no. 4:577-86. [Je.] '45. Rehabilitation of
Europe. Alvin Johnson.

Yale Review. n.s. 36, no. 1:38-45. [S.] '46. Two sides of the German
problem. Alvin Johnson.

Yale Review. n.s. 37, no. 3:385-99. [Mr.] '48. Germany and European economic recovery. C. B. Hoover.

SPEECH AND DEBATING

Anthology of Public Speeches. Mabel Platz, comp. 895p. 1940. $3.75.
Selections from speeches representing all cultures from Pericles and Cicero to Chiang Kai-shek and Neville Chamberlain.

Competitive Debate: Rules and Strategy. By G. M. Musgrave. 128p. 1945. $1.25.

Extempore Speaking: A Handbook for the Student, the Coach, and the Judge. D. L. Holley. 115p. 1947. $1.50.

Discussion Methods: Explained and Illustrated. By J. V. Garland and C. F. Phillips (Reference Shelf. Vol. XII, No. 2) 2d ed. rev. 378p. 1940. $1.25.

High School Forensics: An Integrated Program. By A. E. Melzer. 153p. 1940. 90c.

Oral Interpretation of Literature in American Colleges and Universities. By M. M. Robb. 242p. 1941. $2.75.

Representative American Speeches. By A. C. Baird, comp. Published annually in The Reference Shelf. Eight volumes now available. Prices vary.
Each volume contains representative speeches by eminent men and women on public occasions during the year. Each speech is prefaced by a short sketch of the speaker and the occasion.

Selected Readings in Rhetoric and Public Speaking. By Lester Thonssen, comp. 324p. 1942. $3.